PATANJALI

YOGA SUTRAS

The Heart of Yoga

GURUDEV
SRI SRI RAVI SHANKAR

Sri Sri Publications Trust, India.

Patañjali Yoga Sūtras
Gurudev Sri Sri Ravi Shankar

1st Edition 2022

Published by:

Sri Sri Publications Trust
The Art of Living International Centre, Gate No-7,
21st Km, Kanakapura Road,
Udaypura, Bangalore – 560082
Email: info@srisripublications.com
Website: www.artofliving.store
Toll Free 1800-258-8888

ISBN: 9789391598068

Layout by: Sri Sri Publications Trust

Printed in India by:

Contents

VIBHŪTI PĀDA

KAIVALYA PĀDA

KEY TO TRANSLITERATION

Vowels

अ a आ ā इ i ई ī उ u ऊ ū ऋ ṛ ॠ ṝ

ए ē ऐ ai ओ औ au

ḥ *(visarga)*

Consonants

Gutturals:	क् k	ख् kh	ग् g	घ् gh	ङ् ṅ
Palatals:	च् c	छ् ch	ज् j	झ् jh	ञ् ñ
Cerebrals:	ट् ṭ	ठ् ṭh	ड् ḍ	ढ् ḍh	ण् ṇ
Dentals:	त् t	थ् th	द् d	ध् dh	न् n
Labials:	प् p	फ् ph	ब् b	भ् bh	म् m
Semivocals:	य् y	र् r	ल् l	व् v	
Sibilants:	श् ś	ष् ṣ	स् s		
Aspirate:	ह् h				

ॐ नमः प्रणवार्थाय शुद्धज्ञानैकमूर्तये ।
निर्मलाय प्रशान्ताय दक्षिणामूर्तये नमः ॥

om namaḥ praṇavārthāya śuddhajñānaikamūrtayē
nirmalāya praśāntāya dakṣiṇāmūrtayē namaḥ

Salutations to the embodiment of Praṇava (Om),
the personification of the Pure, Non-Dual Knowledge,
the Stainless and Tranquil; Salutations to Śrī Dakṣinamurti

Introduction

yogena cittasya padena vācām malam

śarīrasya ca vaidyakena |

yo'pākarot tam pravaram munīnām patañjalim

prāñjalirānato'smi ||

योगेन चित्तस्य पदेन वाचां मलं शरीरस्य च वैद्यकेन ।

योऽपाकरोत् तं प्रवरं मुनीनां पतञ्जलिं प्राञ्जलिरानतोऽस्मि ॥

I offer salutations with folded hands to the noblest in the lineage of sages, Maharṣi Patanjali, who removed impurity from the mind through yoga, from speech through grammar and from the body through the science of medicine.

yogena cittasya padena vācām

Maharṣi Patañjali has given us three things. The first is yoga, through the Yoga Sūtra. He says, "Through yoga we get rid of the impurities in the mind, in the *cittā*, in the consciousness."

He is also a proponent of grammar and phonetics. Our happiness and misery depend on how and what we speak. If we are imperfect in our speech, we cannot be successful in life. Maharṣi Patañjali is also a proponent of right speech. Through his sūtras he talks about the expression of life through speech and how speech can be refined.

malam śarīrasya ca vaidyakena

He tells you how you can remove impurities from your system through āyurveda. Yoga, speech and āyurveda—the contribution of Maharṣi Patañjali to these three fields is immense.

We bow to the great sage who has given us these instruments to purify our body, speech and mind.

Yoga Sūtra forms one of the most important scriptures of the Vaidika literature, Vaidika lore. *Vedas* are the main body of which the *Vedānga* (limbs) and the *Upānga* (subordinate limbs) are attributed to many scriptures. *Śikṣā* (phonetics), *Chandas* (rhyme and meter), *Vyākaraṇa* (grammar), *Nirukta* (use of words), *Kalpa* (vaidika rituals) and *jyotiṣa* (astrology) are the limbs (vedānga). *Ṣaḍa Darśana* or the six philosophies are the subordinate limbs (upānga).

Yoga Sūtra is one of the subordinate limbs, the others being *Nyāya, Vaiśeṣika, Sānkhya, Purva Mimāmsā* and *Vedānta* or *Uttara Mimāmsā*.

Nyāya is the first of the six. Nyāya is logic or reason. The *Nyāya Śāstra* examines the means of knowing; whether your knowledge, your perception and the means of acquiring the knowledge are correct. All these parameters are measured by Nyāya.

Vaiśeṣika is the science of all material objects in this universe. What is matter? What is an atom? How is the mind also a part of these?

Sānkhya, the third darśana, talks about consciousness and matter. This is analysis. Analyzing the creation as the inert and the conscious (*jada* and *cetana*), nature and consciousness, the manifest and the unmanifest (*Prakṛti* and *Puruṣa*).

The fourth philosophy, the one that we are going to embark on is the Yoga Sūtra by Maharṣi Patañjali. Maharṣi Patañjali was a scientist to the core and gave us formulas on different aspects of our consciousness.

Yoga does not mean just *āsanas*. Āsanas, too, are a part of it but today when we think 'yoga', we only think about its āsana aspect. Āsanas are actually a very minuscule part of yoga. The major portion is about the Self, about the consciousness. It is a highly intellectual exercise and you have to be really sharp and alert to pick up the finer points. That is why I call yoga 'The Science of Consciousness'.

Samādhi Pāda

The Discipline of Yoga

atha yoga-anuśāsanam || 1 ||

अथ योगानुशासनम् ॥ १ ॥

Now, the discipline of yoga.

When you say 'Now', it means that you must have prepared yourself prior to this. For yoga to happen, you must have a certain standard of understanding, certain knowledge. Only then can you say, "Now let's embark on yoga."

Atha (now) is a very auspicious word. What happens when you snap your fingers and say, 'Now'? You suddenly become alert. Your mind is right here. When you say 'Now', the presence of mind is created right away. For a student to learn something, first of all, a presence of mind is needed and that moment is very auspicious.

Before beginning or learning anything, the ancient people performed the *mangalācharana* (an auspicious step), which brings the mind to the present moment—Now! It also implies that you are prepared; ready to learn, and have the inclination to walk on this path. When you have the right teacher, at the right time, then you can say, "Now, let us begin."

Anuśāsanam—let us now talk about the discipline of yoga.

Śāsana means to rule; the rules that society or somebody else imposes on you.

Ānuśāsana means self-discipline. Yoga is not an imposition but a discipline that you take on willingly; rules that you impose on yourself.

Now, why is yoga called a discipline?

When does the need for discipline arise?

When you are thirsty, you want to drink water. You do not feel that it is a rule to drink water when you are thirsty. When you are hungry you eat, you don't feel that you need to have discipline for eating when you are hungry. You don't need discipline to enjoy nature. No discipline is necessary for enjoyment. A child never says that it has the discipline to run to its mother when s/he sees her.

When is discipline relevant? When something is not enjoyable. Discipline arises when something is not very charming to begin with, but you know that it would ultimately result in something good and enjoyable.

A diabetic exercises discipline when it comes to eating sugar. Someone with cholesterol has to be disciplined about not consuming too much fat. This is because though fats may be tasty, unpleasant complications may arise later.

When you are in joy, or at peace, or truly happy, then you are already in the Self. No discipline is needed there. But when it is not so and the mind wags its tail, discipline is essential to calm it down so that it can come back to the Self. The fruit of this process is eventually bliss and happiness.

There are three types of happiness—*sāttvika, tāmasika* and *rājasika*.

Sāttvika happiness is not so enjoyable to begin with, but it eventually leads to joy. That happiness which is felt after a certain discipline is sāttvika. Discipline is necessary to enjoy this authentic, sāttvika happiness. The purpose of discipline is to attain joy, not to torture oneself unnecessarily.

Rājasika happiness appears very enjoyable in the beginning but ends up in misery and suffering. It is caused by following the wrong discipline. It may also arise from a lack of discipline.

Sometimes people impose a discipline on themselves which does not give them or anybody else any joy at any time. This is tāmasika happiness. Tāmasika happiness is not happiness at all; it is just misery from the beginning to the end.

That is why Maharṣi Patañjali began with 'Now', when things are not clear and when your heart is not in the right place.

Yoga anuśāsanam—nobody has imposed the discipline of yoga on you. It is self-imposed. What are the rules that you have imposed on yourself? When you wake up in the morning, you brush your teeth. You do it before going to bed too. This is your discipline. But this has been imposed on you from childhood. When you were a child, your mother or father imposed it on you. Once it became a habit and you understood that it was good for you, it was no longer their rule. It became 'your' rule. Keeping yourself clean and observing hygiene, exercising, meditating, being kind, considerate, and not being rude—all these rules that you have imposed on yourself are your discipline.

What does this discipline of yoga do? It is the discipline to unite yourself; unite all the loose ends of your existence.

The Modulations of the Mind

yogaḥ-citta-vṛtti-nirodhaḥ || 2 ||

योगश्चित्तवृत्तिनिरोधः ॥ २ ॥

Yoga is restraining the modulations of consciousness.

yogaścitta-vṛtti-nirodhaḥ

Yoga is having a say over the modulations or *vṛttis* (tendencies) of the mind.

tadā draṣṭuḥ svarūpe-avasthānam || 3 ||

तदा द्रष्टुः स्वरूपेऽवस्थानम् ॥ ३ ॥

Then (when the modulations of consciousness are restrained) the seer abides in the nature of the seer.

What happens when you have a say over the modulations of the mind? You get established in the seer. The nature of the seer is different from that of the scenery. When you are caught in the modulations of the mind, you are lost in the scenery. But in yoga, what do you do? You bring your attention back to yourself, back from the scenery to the seer. When you have a say over the modulations of the mind, you repose in the nature of the seer, in the nature of the Self. Otherwise, what has been happening?

vṛtti-sarūpyam itaratra || 4 ||

वृत्तिसारूप्यम् इतरत्र ॥ ४ ॥

At other times (other than when Yoga happens), (the seer) identifies with the modulations of the mind.

When you are not in the Self, your mind is engrossed in the modulations. It is engaged in the outside world all the time. Your eyes are open and you are caught up in all that you see. Similarly, you are caught up in all that you smell, hear, touch and taste. When you are awake, you are constantly engaged in the activities of the senses, and when you go back to the sleep and dream states, you are completely shut off. Even in the sleep and dream states, the same memories come up. So, you are never calm and quiet. When you unite all the loose ends of your existence, your perception is not turned outside; 'you' become the object of your perception.

When simple people or children watch a movie, they become totally involved in it. At that time, nothing else exists but the movie. When you have a backache or pain in your legs, it seems more intense if you are idle. But when you are engaged in watching a movie, then you do not feel the pain. You do not feel your body at all; you are not even aware that you are sitting. That is the intense interest the movie has kindled in you. Your consciousness has assumed the form of that movie, of that vṛtti.

Once people were watching a movie in a village. They saw that the hero was being tortured by the villain. The audience actually rushed towards the screen with sticks and stones to hit the villain.

Our consciousness assumes the form of the vṛtti.

The purpose of yoga is to bring integrity in you and complete you, make you whole. You are looking at this book. Now become aware of your eyes which are looking at the book. Become aware of the mind that is looking through those eyes. Now, for a moment, close your eyes. Just squeeze them. Feel your eyes and take your attention from the eyes to the mind, that is all over your head. Now, become aware of your whole body, your heart and the very core of your existence—the 'I' that is you. Rest and relax there, right there. You realize that you are not interested in seeing, smelling, hearing, tasting, feeling or touching anything. Retrieve your mind from all the five senses to the core of your existence.

draṣṭuḥ svarūpe'vasthānam

Abiding in the nature of the seer is yoga. Whenever you experience joy, ecstasy, bliss, or happiness in life, knowingly or unknowingly, you are abiding in the nature of the seer. At other times, you are involved in the different activities of your mind.

vṛtti sārūpyamitaratra

You assume the form of the modulation in the mind. What are the activities in the mind?

vṛttayaḥ pañcatayyaḥ kliṣṭā akliṣṭāḥ || 5 ||

वृत्तयः पञ्चतय्यः क्लिष्टा अक्लिष्टाः ॥ ५ ॥

These modulations are of five types, which could express themselves as problematic or non-problematic.

There are certain vṛttis that cause trouble or difficulties and there are others that do not. These are the five modulations of the mind. What are they?

pramāṇa-viparyaya-vikalpa-nidrā-smṛtayaḥ || 6 ||

प्रमाणविपर्ययविकल्पनिद्रास्मृतयः ॥ ६ ॥

Wanting proof, incorrect understanding, delusion, sleep and dwelling in the memory (are the five types of modulations).

There are five modulations of the mind in which the seer is lost. What are the modulations?

Pramāṇa—proof. The mind wants proof for everything. It seeks proof of your perception; your understanding of an object.

Viparyaya—wrong perception; a perception which is different from reality.

Vikalpa—imagination, delusion; that which you have imagined does not exist at all.

Nidrā—sleep.

Smṛti—memory.

pratyakṣa-anumāna-agamāḥ pramāṇāni || 7 ||

प्रत्यक्षानुमानागमाः प्रमाणानि ॥ ७ ॥

Proof is sought in three ways—through experiential, inferred or reliable sources.

In the waking state of consciousness, we want proof for everything.

Pratyakṣa—the first kind of proof is a direct experience. Our mind constantly wants some obvious, solid experiential proof.

Anumāna—the second kind is an inference, a guess. When there is smoke you infer that there was a fire. You have not seen the fire, but the smoke indicates that there must have been a fire.

Āgama—the third kind is the proof that is found in the scriptures. When you find a bottle labeled 'Poison', you will not say, "No, I don't believe it! I want to test it first." You can't taste it. You can't say, "I want proof, I want to personally experience it." How can you experience poison? You have to accept what is written on the bottle as proof of the truth.

Materia Medica tells us about combinations of herbs that are good to treat diseases. Since all of this is written in the materia medica, we accept it as proof.

You cannot acquire all the knowledge which has been accumulated over centuries in the scriptures in one lifetime. You read about a war in a history book, you can't say, "No! I don't believe in the book. I want to see whether the World War really happened. How do I know? I was not there then." You were not there but you have to believe the documentation that is available. This is āgama. Pratyakṣa, anumāna, and āgama—these three types of perception or understanding of proof verify whether what you know is correct or not.

Yoga happens when you drop this tendency. Then alone can you abide in the Self. Retrieving from this activity of the mind—of wanting proof—is being released from that tendency and going back to the Self. You may need proof of whether you are in Switzerland or not through your senses. But you do not need proof to know whether you are 'here' or not through your senses. This is a very subtle point! You could be taken to Austria or even somewhere in Canada. You will see similar snowy mountains and lakes there. You may think that you are in Switzerland but you are not. Your senses may fool you. But the feeling of 'I am' and 'I exist' is beyond proof.

Abiding in the Self does not need proof. Truth cannot be understood through proof. Anything that can be proved can also be disproved. Truth is beyond proof or disproof. God is beyond proof. You can neither prove nor disprove God.

Proof is connected with logic and logic is very limited in its purview. It is the same with enlightenment and with love. Love cannot be proved or disproved. Someone's actions or behaviour is not proof of love. Many movie actors and actresses exhibit a lot of love and romance in their movies without actually experiencing real love or romance. One can act the emotion of love very well without feeling it or living it.

Proof is one of the main things that you are stuck with in this world; you want proof for everything. This is not in the realm of the seer. The seer is beyond proof.

viparyayo mithyā-jñānam atadrūpa-pratiṣṭham || 8 ||

विपर्ययो मिथ्याज्ञानम् अतद्रूपप्रतिष्ठम् ॥ ८ ॥

Incorrect understanding is when there is a gap between perception and reality.

Viparyaya is wrong understanding. You are stuck in your mind due to a wrong perception.

viparyayo mithyā jñānam atadrūpa pratiṣṭham

Things are not the way you think they are. You perceive things wrongly. Most of the time you impose your own views, ideas, and feelings on others. You think that this is how things are but they are not actually so.

You may have an inferiority complex, and thereby consider someone's behaviour to be very arrogant. Actually they are not arrogant, and you are not being ill-treated by them. But you feel that you are being ill-treated. You feel that you have not been respected. It is because you do not respect yourself enough that you think that others do not respect you. This tendency of your mind is viparyaya.

A good friend of yours suddenly starts being rude to you, and you wonder what has happened to them.

You wonder what it is that you have done to cause this. You do not understand that they are imagining things about you in their minds. It is not because they are bad or any such thing. It is this activity of the citta, of the mind, that is predominant at that time.

Suddenly, people may feel that they are not being loved.

Many parents have this problem with their children. They get so perplexed! They do not know what to do and how to prove their love to their children.

Proof is of no importance once viparyaya dominates. Pramāṇa does not survive, and logic fails because the mind is now more active in the second modulation, the second vṛtti—viparyaya. Correct knowledge appears briefly somewhere in the mind but returns to the background again and wrong information—viparyaya—sticks on.

śabda-jñāna-anupātī vastu-śūnyo vikalpaḥ || 9 ||

शब्दज्ञानानुपाती वस्तुशून्यो विकल्पः ॥ ९ ॥

Where there are no objects corresponding to words and ideas in the mind, it is called imagination.

Vikalpa is a total delusion of the mind. It is not wrong knowledge that the mind is stuck in but in total imagination. Two of the very common examples that have been given by the masters of yore are 'The lotus flower in the sky' and 'The horns of a rabbit'. Rabbits do not have horns. A horn is true, a rabbit is true, but when you say a rabbit has horns—this is vikalpa. A flower is true, the sky is true, but if you think the flower is in the sky, it is a delusion.

Vikalpa could be of two types. One could be just a joyful and pleasurable fantasy, and the other could be a baseless fear. Even fear is a vikalpa. You may be apprehensive about what will happen if you die the next day. You imagine that you've met with an accident and have become disabled. These are all just thoughts that have no basis. Baseless fears in the mind or fantasies are called vikalpa.

abhāva-pratyaya-alambanā vṛttiḥ-nidrā || 10 ||

अभावप्रत्ययालम्बना वृत्तिर्निद्रा ॥ १० ॥

Sleep is when the mind embraces emptiness.

No one else has ever defined sleep in such a beautiful manner! When the mind has no content, it gets into a state called sleep.

abhāva pratyaya ālambanā vṛttir nidrā

Sleep is that modulation of the mind in which it takes recourse to a content-less state.

anubhūta-viṣaya-asampramoṣaḥ smṛtiḥ || 11 ||

अनुभूतविषयासंप्रमोषः स्मृतिः ॥ ११ ॥

Memory is the inability to let go of past experiences.

Smṛti means those experiences that your mind could not let go of. Every morning you brush your teeth, you have breakfast, but that doesn't remain in your mind as a memory. Do you remember what breakfast you had the day before yesterday? One week ago? Last month? Can you tell me what clothes you wore on December 31st or on November 30th? Do you remember? No! Because these details are not important. These acts were neither pleasurable nor painful, so they didn't make an impact on the consciousness. When you are unable to let go of some experience that you have had, it remains as a memory.

Pleasant experiences create cravings and unpleasant experiences create fear and trauma in the mind. This is what memory is all about.

When you are awake, are you in any of these four modulations (pramāṇa, viparyaya, vikalpa, smṛti)? Then, that is not meditation. That is not yoga.

Are you looking for some proof? Are you debating with yourself? Are you hanging on to wrong knowledge or concepts about things? You do not know how things are because the whole world is fluid. There is nothing fixed here—neither people's minds nor their thoughts. Go one step further, and you can say that anything can change any time, in any manner. The whole world is a field of all possibilities. But your mind fixes things, people, ideas, places, everything into definite items, quantities. It quantifies them, "This is how it is," with the use of:

i) proof

ii) wrong information

iii) vikalpa, fantasies or fears

iv) by dwelling in the past experiences

These four modulations and sleep, the fifth modulation, are the five different vṛttis of the mind.

These five vṛttis are not bad. It is not that they should not be there.

yogaścitta vṛtti nirodhaḥ

These vṛttis are *kliṣṭa akliṣṭa*—some are difficult, some are not. Some are painful and some are not. If you do not get sleep, it is painful. If you sleep too much, even then, it is painful. Isn't it? If you forget everything and can't remember anything, it is painful. At the same time if you cannot forget anything, that too is painful.

Similarly, proof can be painful and it can be without pain also. Perhaps, that is why there is a proverb in English, 'Ignorance is bliss!' You do not know something, and you are blissful but when you get the proof, the truth can be hard-hitting and painful. However, the truth need not always be painful.

viparyayo mithyā jñānam

When you are ignorant, you remain in your own little world and it may be comforting for a while but wrong understanding is really painful eventually.

Vikalpa (imagination) can be pleasurable. You imagine that you have become an angel with wings and are flying around in the sky. But if you imagine that everybody is against you and out to get you, it is very painful. Your imagination could be painful or without pain.

These five vṛttis are indispensable but if they are not in your control then you can never come back to the Self. So, to understand the nature of the seer, we must have a say over these five modulations of the mind.

Now, how to do this? How will you get over the overpowering nature of these vṛttis? Maharṣi Patañjali is going to tell us now.

Honoring the Practice

abhyāsa-vairāgyābhyām tat-nirodhaḥ || 12 ||

अभ्यासवैराग्याभ्यां तन्निरोधः ॥ १२ ॥

They (the modulations) can be restrained by practice and dispassion.

Can you imagine, thousands of years ago, the Maharṣi went to the finest details of defining what sleep is, what memory is, what proof in the mind is? Isn't this mind-boggling? How the seer or the subject has to withdraw from the scenery or the object, back to their consciousness and be established in the source—that is the union of oneself with oneself; that is yoga. It is an amazing way of describing the most indescribable truth in the universe, the most indescribable phenomenon, called consciousness.

How can consciousness be established in the seer? He said there are two ways. One is *abhyāsa*—practice and the other, *vairāgya*—dispassion. When you are passionate, your mind is all over the place. You have lost yourself and you are in that object or person or event or situation that you are passionate about. You lose yourself and you are so totally there. Dispassion alone can bring you back to the seer.

tatra sthitau yatnaḥ-abhyāsaḥ || 13 ||

तत्र स्थितौ यत्नोऽभ्यासः ॥ १३ ॥

The effort to be established there (in the seer) is practice.

Now, what is dispassion and what is practice? Maharṣi Patañjali has described them in an amazing manner!

tatra sthitau yatno'bhyāsaḥ

That which you do to 'be' here and now, in this moment, is abhyāsa. An effort is needed for you to relieve yourself from the five modulations and just be here—Now! Now! Now!—to bring the mind to the present and not dwell on past memories. This effort is called abhyāsa.

You can start by being determined that you are not going to dwell on any logic. You are not going to be interested in any proof. Then, you are free from pramāṇa. If the mind is asking for proof, just know it, observe it and relax.

You are not interested in any wrong knowledge or right knowledge either. Often when the mind holds on to wrong knowledge, it thinks it is right. So, the mind is not even interested in knowing anything, whether right or wrong. Retrieve the mind from knowing and from knowledge. There is no anxiety to see, smell, touch, feel or understand anything. Let things be the way they are. Do not care. Do not pass judgements of right or wrong. Free yourself from viparyaya.

Then vikalpa. Check if the mind is dwelling on some imagination or fantasy. By just knowing that it is imagining or fantasizing, it drops off, thereby freeing you. The minute you realise that you are dreaming—the dream vanishes. That moment is so new, so fresh and so total!

Abhyāsa is just recognizing the moment when you are free, fresh, full and totally in the present moment. Here your mind might try to go into the past. You know that the mind is getting into the five vṛttis, but without any aversion or craving. This is coming back to the centre, to the seer.

Coming back to this moment, again and again and again; the effort to stay focused on the seer, is abhyāsa.

You come back to the seer but you can lose it again because you are drawn by the scenery. Again, when the scenery is not so interesting you come back to the seer. You become more conscious of yourself when you are done with the scenery, with the sense objects. When you are done with the scenery outside, you go within. These moments happen rarely in everyone's life. Now and then, here and there, these experiences come to you. But if you make an effort to stay conscious, to keep mindfulness, that is called practice, abhyāsa.

tatra sthitau yatno 'bhyāsaḥ

To stay there is practice, and it needs effort.

'Never mind' is a very interesting phrase. The mind can never go where you are; a wave can never go to the depth of the ocean. By the time the wave goes to the depth, it ceases to be a wave. So the mind can never come to you. The mind can never be you. That is why 'never mind'! You are never the mind; it is superficial. The moment the mind starts coming towards you, it is not the mind anymore. That is why it is 'never mind'. 'You' are accepted there, never the mind; your mind can never go there.

The mind keeps on asking questions, "Why, Why, Why?" This is an experience all of you have had. You feel that something that is bothering you is your mind stuff! At that moment, alertness and awareness dawn. And then there is relief in the mind. The more you feel that your questions are just mind stuff, the more aware you are. Then the questions just vanish. This is abhyāsa, this is practice.

sa tu dīrgha-kāla-nairantarya-satkāra-āsevito

dṛḍha-bhūmiḥ || 14 ||

स तु दीर्घकाल नैरन्तर्य सत्कारासेवितो दृढभूमिः ॥ १४ ॥

Practice gets established when it is done uninterruptedly for a long time, without a break and with honour and respect.

Now, you have to practice for a long period of time, with dedication and respect. You should honour your practice. Don't just do your practice because you need to. No! When you honour the practice, respect it, give it more importance, it becomes well-founded in you.

Nairantarya—it is very important that the practice be done uninterruptedly. If you receive a *mantra*, chant it for two days and then become irregular, it is not going to work. There should be an uninterrupted practice of chanting. This is very important. Even if it is for a few minutes, it must be uninterrupted. You must do it every day. Only then will it become well established in you.

The effort to be still and steady comes with practice. At some point in time, you may realise that it is 'the moment' and then it vanishes. You feel that the moment came and you lost it. You say, 'Now', and then the 'Now' is lost. It may not be right to say you have lost it but in some sense, you feel you are not in the 'Now'. This effort is not just linear. This effort to be steadily established in the 'Now' is very deep and vast. The 'Now,' the present moment, is not just a point; not just a dot. It is infinite. It is 'Now' in all dimensions and from all sides. Practice gives stability at that moment—that is the purpose of practice. And how can that be arranged? How can that be achieved?

Sa tu dīrghakāla—it takes a long time.

Nairantarya—without a gap.

Satkārāsevito—practising it with honour and respect.

Dṛḍhabhūmiḥ—one becomes firmly grounded.

Anything of value in life takes some time to culture. To master an art—cooking, playing the guitar, sitar, or flute—takes time. Learning to play an instrument takes quite a while and to master it takes longer, but the mind takes even longer for its growth. Constant practice without a gap is essential. If there is no consistency, nothing is gained. Lack of consistency prevents you from learning any art.

Satkārāsevito—doing it with honour and respect. Sometimes, you grumble when you do something. That is not abhyāsa. Abhyāsa is something done with gratitude, gratefulness, honour and with respect. This is something we often lack in our lives. We should do everything in life with honour and respect.

Even if you do something with honour and respect, it lasts for a very short period. And if you have to do something over a period of time, you tend to lose that honour and respect. If you have to arrange a stage and if you are doing it for the first time, you do it with all honour and respect. You put in much attention, love, your heart, and awareness into doing it. But if you have to do it every day for the next six months, you just do it without the spirit with which you did it on the first day.

As time goes on, you lose that alertness, attention, attentiveness, and honour. You feel wonderful when you sit for meditation the first day because you are doing it with honour. But after some sessions you feel bored. You just sit and close your eyes and it doesn't have the same effect.

If any day, your meditation or *Sudarśana Kriyā* is a little low, it is because you have lost respect for it, not that you disrespect it, but the attentiveness and alertness towards it has reduced.

When you come to do a course, your meditation is deeper because you are receiving it with honour. You are honouring that knowledge. You are honouring yourself.

What is honour? Have you ever thought about it? Honour is total attentiveness to the present moment, with a tinge of gratefulness.

Respect and honour every moment of your life. Then that becomes a practice. You respect your own body. That is practice, abhyāsa.

What are āsanas? Āsanas are respecting your own body consciously, every moment.

Respecting and honouring your breath is *prāṇāyāma*.

So, be determined to honour. Consider all the other events to be trivial. Just honour the moment. However the moment may be, it is very precious. Honour the word the Master has given you.

It is very precious. Honouring the Master is honouring the Master's word. If you do not have honour or respect for the Master, your meditation will not work. This is because that honour and the respect awakens the consciousness and raises awareness in you. It helps you to focus on the moment totally. If you do not honour the Master, the Master will not lose anything. Your own mind will be unable to be in the moment totally and to dive deep into the source.

Is this enough? Is just abhyāsa, practice, enough?

No, it is not. There are two oxen that are needed to pull this cart. One is abhyāsa and the other is vairāgya.

Dispassion

dṛṣṭa-anuśravika viṣaya-vitṛṣṇasya vaśīkāra-

sañjñā vairāgyam || 15 ||

दृष्टानुश्रविक विषयवितृष्णस्य वशीकारसंज्ञा वैराग्यम् ॥ १५ ॥

Dispassion is having a say over the thirst that arises from sense objects, either experienced by oneself or heard of from others.

So the Maharṣi says that you need to do two things—one is to practise and the other is to cultivate dispassion. To stay there in that presence, you need to practise uninterruptedly, over a long period of time, with devotion, with respect and honour for the practice. Then it becomes a very solid ground for you. It makes you stronger. Now, what is vairāgya, dispassion?

dṛṣṭa-anuśravika-viṣaya-vitṛṣṇasya

vaśīkāra-sañjñā vairāgyam

The mind gallops towards the world of five senses. Whether you are quiet, have your eyes closed or open, or doing anything, where does your mind go? It goes towards the five senses.

You have experienced many things in the world through the five senses. You can see, hear, taste, smell, and touch. If whatever you experience through these five senses creates craving or aversion inside you, then you lack dispassion. It takes your attention away and rattles the mind. What rattles the mind? Craving! When you are craving for something, you are stuck with the object, the scenery, and are not with the seer. Craving for any of these experiences can prevent you from being in the present moment.

Vairāgya is controlling the craving for objects that you have experienced or heard of. When you have relished nice food, you crave it. You crave sex; you crave appreciation, recognition, praise, and flattery.

Then there is another type of craving—for that which you have not experienced but have only heard of. Jihadis are told that by killing certain people they will go to heaven. They have no idea, but they have only heard from some people that when you do such-and-such things, you will get first-class treatment, super luxurious comfort in heaven. So, people get swayed by what they hear.

All crime and conflicts happen in society because of such cravings. What is conflict? It is self-righteousness and selfishness to possess; a self-centered attitude. In English, we call it self-centered. It is not the same Self that Maharṣi Patañjali is talking about. It is the complete opposite. He talks about being non-self-centric.

Vairāgya is to have a say over these cravings; reining in these tendencies in you, bringing the mind back to its source. Then you will feel that however beautiful a scene is, however great the food, however melodious the music, you are not interested. Vairāgya may be present for even a few moments. This is another basic requirement for meditation. Dispassion has to arise in your mind whenever you want to meditate. Without dispassion, your meditation is no good. It cannot provide you the rest that you are longing for.

Your mind is tired and burnt out because it is galloping towards one desire after another. Just look back and check all the desires that you have fulfilled. Have they given you rest? Have they given you any fulfillment? They have not. They have just created some more desires in you. They have just given you a greater hope that you can achieve more; you can have more. And that has sent you on another pointless trip. You are on a merry-go-round. It is not even merry but just goes round and round. A merry-go-round has dummy horses that you sit on. The horses do not go anywhere. They just go round and round in the same place but give you the illusion that you have traveled miles and miles.

Life has been such a journey where you are galloping and galloping, reaching nowhere. This is what desires do to you. The mind which is obsessed with desires cannot meditate.

On the other extreme, some people feel that the mind should not have any desires and this becomes another desire. They are on this trip to destroy their desires. They keep beating around the bush and achieve nothing.

The craving for any of the sense objects, celestial or heavenly places, which the mind gallops towards is an obstruction. Any expectation in meditation is an obstruction. You may have heard that someone saw a light in their meditation or saw somebody coming from heaven and taking them by the hand. So, you sit with your eyes closed and wait for an angel to come or for a light to shine on you and then to burst into a million stars. All these ideas and thoughts become an obstruction. Your desire for pleasure or happiness will make you unhappy.

If you examine yourself whenever you are miserable or unhappy, you will find that the misery is due to your desire to be happy. Craving happiness brings misery. When you do not crave for happiness, you are liberated and when you do not even care for liberation, you attain love. This is *parama vairāgya*. But that is the second step; the first step is when you do not crave for happiness. Then you are free. You are liberated.

Happiness is a mere idea in your mind. You think if you have a particular thing, you will be happy. If you have whatever you want, are you sure you will be happy? Then, you will think it was not the way that you had thought it would be.

What great happiness do you want? How long can you have it? You are going to leave this life at some time or the other. This is certain. It is all going to end. Before this Earth eats you up, become free.

You need to shatter all your dreams and fantasies. Offer them to the fire, burn them down. Free yourself from the feverishness that is gripping your mind. Free yourself from the craving for happiness. Every object of pleasure that you have experienced will become like styrofoam—absolutely tasteless!

All these objects, such as food and sex, that titillate the senses have their limitations. But your mind is not ready to accept these limitations. It wants unlimited joy and pleasure which the five senses cannot give you. Vairāgya is putting a stop to the craving for happiness.

This does not mean that you have to be miserable. It does not mean you should not enjoy life. But if you can retrieve your mind from the craving for joy, you can meditate. Then you can have all the five modulations, and still yoga happens.

Often, people who think they have dispassion keep blaming the world and the objects of senses. They are afraid of the objects of the senses and try to run away from them.

Vairāgya is skillfully reaching the Self by honouring all the objects of the senses and not blaming them.

Question: Dear Gurudev, is it possible to get stuck in achieving a mood of dispassion, turning one's attention to the separation between the Self and the thoughts, emotions and sensory data, and is it possible to see more clearly who one is? If a habit of separating oneself from everything is developed in an artificial way, will one not lose spontaneity, attunement with nature and be unable to fully engage in life by giving it their hundred percent. How do you walk this tightrope, and how do you know if you are too far on one side or the other?

Gurudev: Dispassion does not divide you. In fact, it connects you. It connects you to the present moment so totally that you can be one hundred percent in anything that you are doing. When you are not dispassionate, then what happens? You are linked to the past or the future. You are not one hundred percent connected to the present and are more divided. So when your mind is hoping for something in the future or regretting the past, it is not hundred percent with the moment; it is divided already.

When you are fully centred while doing anything, then you are hundred percent with every moment. You may be eating and you are eating one hundred percent. You enjoy every bit of it. You can feel every sip of the soup you are having. Every bite of the food tastes great. Every sight is fresh and new. Your love is like the first love every moment. When you look at anybody or anything, it is charming to the very core; as if you are seeing it for the first time.

Dispassion does not take away the joy from you. Dispassion gives the joy which nothing else can give. There is a verse by *Ādi Śankarācārya* that says, "*Kasya sukham na karoti virāgaḥ!*" What pleasure can dispassion not give you! It gives you all possible pleasures because you are so totally in the moment. It puts you a hundred percent in the moment. Every moment is a peak experience.

The so-called dispassion in the world seems so dry. People who think they are dispassionate are melancholy; they are sad. They run away from the world and call it dispassion. Then they say that they have renounced the world. This is no renunciation or dispassion. People who escape because of failure, misery, sorrow, or apathy feel that they have dispassion. Dispassion is something far more precious, more refined, and more valuable in life. If you are dispassionate, you are always centered—full of joy and contentment. Anybody would like to be like that.

Before Alexander the Great came to India, people in his country had told him that if he found some sanyāsīs, he should bring them back with him; they were very precious and were to be found only in India. When he was in India he ordered that some sanyāsīs come to him but nobody came. He then sent a message threatening to chop off their heads. Even then, nobody came! Next, he said that he was going to take away their books—the four vedas and other scriptures too. The *pundits* agreed and said that they would give him all their books the next day. Overnight, the pundits made their children memorize all the manuscripts, and then they gave them to Alexander. They told him that they did not need them anymore.

Alexander got the manuscripts but he wanted a sanyāsi, and a sanyāsi would not come. Finally, he went to one and threatened him saying that he would chop off his head if he did not go with him. The sanyāsi replied that Alexander could do so if he wanted to. The mighty emperor could not even look into the sanyāsi's eyes. He could not stand the power of dispassion that he saw there. Here was a person who, for the first time, did not care for an emperor.

Once, some people presented him with golden bread on a plate. But he said that he was hungry and wanted some real bread. They replied that he was an emperor, how could he eat mere wheat bread? They had prepared golden bread for him. Alexander said that he was starving and wanted real bread. Hearing this, they got some real bread for him. They asked him if such bread was not available in his country. They wanted to know that if he ate the same bread which was eaten in India, then why had he conquered so many places. Was it to get bread?

This question shook Alexander. The power of the truth hit him. What was the point in conquering country after country when all that he needed was to live peacefully and happily? Devoid of happiness and peace, without care and concern for his people, putting his stamp on all the villages and towns he was conquering, had no meaning.

So, Alexander said that when he dies his hands should be kept open. He wanted people to know that though he had conquered so many countries, Alexander the Great left this world empty-handed!

Dispassion is the strength in you. Even if the Lord of Wealth comes, you do not need to take anything from him. That is the strength of dispassion. It is not arrogance. It is centred-ness. If you are centred and calm, then you can understand that everyone has come to this world to give something, not to take anything from here. A great shift takes place.

Types of Samādhi

tatparam puruṣa-khyāteḥ-guṇa-vaitṛṣṇyam || 16 ||

तत्परं पुरुषख्यातेर्गुणवैतृष्ण्यम् ॥ १६ ॥

Higher than that (dispassion) is the centeredness that comes from knowing the glory of the Self.

To control the mind from craving and aversion appears to be very difficult. Then, Patañjali says a beautiful thing—if you have had a glimpse of the Self or Puruṣa, it becomes very easy for you to get over these cravings. These cravings simply drop off at the mere taste of the Self! When people come here for the first time and do one simple meditation, their craving for many things spontaneously disappears.

Tatparam puruṣa-khyāteḥ—just an interaction, an encounter with the glory of the Being and your interest in the material world starts diminishing.

You do not make an effort to let go of the cravings. The moment you get that inner joy, the moment something clicks within, you get a little glimpse of something, the craving for the sensory objects starts diminishing automatically. It happens spontaneously.

tatparam puruṣa-khyāteḥ guṇa-vaitṛṣṇyam

The thirst for the sensory things starts diminishing because the Puruṣa, the Self, is much more joyful, much more glorious and is much more charming than anything else.

This is the experience of every *sādhaka*. Anyone who enters the spiritual path gets a little glimpse of it. Just a little glimpse reduces craving, and brings you back to the Self. It creates awareness, the sense of WOW! When you are in a sense of WOW, it is not related to the scenery but to the seer. You can be lost in the scene around you and have a sense of WOW but when you get this WOW about the seer, about the consciousness, it is a very different situation.

vitarka-vicāra-ānanda-asmitā-rūpa-

anugamāt samprajñātaḥ || 17 ||

वितर्कविचारानन्दास्मितारूपानुगमात् संप्रज्ञातः ॥ १७ ॥

(Samādhi) with awareness can happen through logic, thoughts, bliss or a sense of 'I am'.

This state of consciousness, the WOW in you, which creates alertness, which is full of mindfulness, leads to what is called *samādhi*. What is samādhi? It occurs when there is equanimity in the intellect.

There are four different types of samādhi—*vitarka, vicāra, ānanda and asmitā anugamāt samādhi*. All these are types of *samprajñāt samādhi* where awareness still remains.

Tarka means logic. *Kutarka* means wrong logic. When the intention is not right and logic is applied only to find fault; when you know deep within you that something is not right, but you still logically prove that it is right, it is kutarka.

Vitarka is specialised logic. It is not normal logic. 'Who am I?' is vitarka. When you just say, "Who am I?" it is a thought, but this thought that leads you to infinity, to Self-knowledge is vitarka. You ask, "What is this universe?" and don't get the answer, but this question, 'What is this universe?' is called vitarka. So, this qualified logic that comes up and takes you right back to the Self is one type of samādhi. Certain thoughts that we have, certain suggestions that we give in a guided meditation, take us into deep samādhi.

When there is no thought, but you are doing self-enquiry, it is *vitarka samādhi*. When I do not give any suggestions but tell you to ask yourself a question, 'Who am I?' Then, you sit with your eyes closed and drop down into samādhi. This is vitarka samādhi.

This is another type of samādhi. When I say, "Ok, now sit with your eyes closed and listen to the fan, listen to the birds chirping", you keep listening to these words. These lead to *vicāra samādhi*.

In *vicāra samādhi*, your mind is in equanimity, but thoughts are moving; there are thoughts coming and going within.

When I say, "Now your body is all hollow and empty", this is a thought. With this thought you get into an empty space. So, through thought, you get into samādhi.

In vicāra, there are all the experiences of smell, sight, vision, taste or sounds. When you meditate, observing the thoughts that come and go—this is called vicāra samādhi. There are two states of mind that often surface in you. One is a thought which disturbs you and the other is a thought which does not disturb you, but just hovers around in your consciousness and you are aware of it. You are in samādhi, in an equanimous state of mind and at the same time, there are thoughts hovering. It is a part of meditation—thoughts exist, experiences exist.

In vicāra, words, sentences, and thoughts lead you into samādhi. In vitarka, qualified logic or the spirit of enquiry also leads you to samādhi.

Ānanda anugamāt samādhi happens when a bhajan is being played and you feel so blissful that you don't even want to open your eyes. You dissolve in that music; you are in a blissful state. Have you noticed that after you do Sudarśana Kriyā, you are in a different space? The mind is still elevated. The consciousness is still elevated and equanimous but it is in ecstasy. That is ānanda. You feel very happy. Happiness leads you to a space of void or samādhi.

Asmitā anugamāt samādhi is what happens to most of you in deep meditation. Sometime or the other, all of you have experienced that in meditation you just feel that you are present but you don't know where you are. Just the feeling—'I am' exists, nothing else! Without any of the characters or roles you play and the qualifications you have, you simply experience 'I am'. All other characteristics of your personality are shed. It is commonly translated as ego, but it is not the ego. It is 'I am-ness'; being aware of the presence. This is asmitā anugamāt samādhi.

All these four are called *samprajñāta*, which means that there is consciousness in all this. There is an outflow of awareness throughout.

virāma-pratyaya-abhyāsa-pūrvaḥ

samskāra-śeṣaḥ-anyaḥ || 18 ||

विरामप्रत्ययाभ्यासपूर्वः संस्कारशेषोऽन्यः ॥ १८ ॥

The mind comes to a state of rest by practice done earlier (in this life or in earlier lifetimes) and in this state, only residual impressions remain. This is another type of samādhi (without awareness).

Different types of samādhi have been described here. There is another type of samādhi where through practice you put an end to all the chattering that is happening in the mind. *Virāma* means to put a full stop, to put an end to all the content in the mind. There could be some old impressions in the mind that may be lingering on and we are not even mindful of that.

For some people, this comes through old *samskāras*, due to some old impressions of past lives, while others have to do a lot of practice in order to be calm and equanimous and to bring up more awareness in them.

Some people start opening up right from their birth while some suddenly open up to a spiritual experience after they are thirty or forty years old. But unfortunately, most of them get misguided. The experience seems so real to them that they think they see visions and they begin to make prophecies about the end of the world, that they may have read somewhere.

This is because they have no knowledge of the root of yoga. They may see a white light coming down and exclaim that something is happening. People get misled by such evangelical experiences. But someone who knows the roots will be aware of all such experiences.

Do you know that when you do tai-chi, qi-gong and *yogāsanas* mindfully, what you are doing? You are putting an end to all the chattering in the mind. When you listen to the big metallic gong of a Buddhist temple or to the bells in a Hindu temple, at that time, all other thoughts and constraints in the mind are put to rest. Everything stops. Though there may be some old impressions in the consciousness, it definitely leads you into a deeper samādhi.

bhava-pratyayo videha-prakṛti-layānām || 19 ||

भवप्रत्ययो विदेहप्रकृतिलयानाम् ॥ १९ ॥

For those who are immersed in nature or (are) without a body, the world is the content of the mind.

Bhava-pratyayo—the whole world becomes the content (*bhava* means the world, *pratyayo* is the content) of consciousness. See, if you are thinking only about yourself, your thinking is limited. Your limited worry is different from the worry about the entire planet. The entire universe is the content, for whom? For the *videha* and the *prakṛtilayānām*. Videha are the angels and gods who are beyond physical appearance. Prakṛtilayānām are those who have dissolved into nature. For both of them, bhava pratyayo—the whole universe is the content. That is samādhi here. For the angels, gods, and spirits samādhi is the entire universe.

bhava-pratyayo videha-prakṛti-layānām

Similarly, for those who are deeply immersed in prakṛti, being in the universe itself is samādhi.

Samādhi does not belong to just a particular level of existence. It surpasses that level too. It goes into other worlds also. Those who do not have a body also can be affected by meditation. When you meditate, you are not just bringing harmony within yourself but you are influencing the subtle layers of creation and the subtle bodies at all the different levels of existence in the creation. So, your meditation influences those people who lived hundreds of years ago, their consciousness and their minds. It influences the minds and consciousness of people who would be living in the future too. Though life is there in every moment, it is also infinite. Your life has been here for centuries and will continue to be here for a few more centuries.

Prakṛti layā means those who are completely submerged in nature. Suppose someone is totally dedicated to saving the ocean. Day and night, they think only about the cleanliness of the ocean. Someone who is thinking about the Earth, only thinks about the betterment of the Earth and nothing else. Immersed in these thoughts, they get into a state of awareness. They don't have any other wish, any other desire in life. They are totally focused on their work. They don't even know whether they are eating or sleeping. They don't have time for family and friends either. They are so totally immersed in work. They are so far away from the material existence that they are not even aware of it. They also attain the state of equanimity. This is prakṛti layā. This also leads you to a state of samādhi.

Prakṛti layā is a big practice. People sit in solitude for years till all thoughts disappear. And that is when they attain emptiness.

When you look at a mountain, sometimes you forget yourself. You have no awareness of your thoughts, mind or body, no awareness at all. You are merging with nature at that moment. You are looking at the sunset. You are there along with the sun and then in a while you are not aware of yourself. You are just aware of the sun. This is *prakṛti layā samādhi.*

You can try doing this as an experiment. When you are very worried or tense, just sit by a flowing river or stream and keep looking at the water. Within a few moments, you feel as though there is a magnetic pull; your mind is being pulled in the direction of the current.

Then, sit on the other bank and do the same thing and you'll see that your mind is being pulled in the other direction. That is why many people who want to jump into a river and commit suicide, cannot do so once they look at the flowing water. Something happens within them at the sight of the flowing water. There is a shift, and they can no longer commit suicide. This happens because, by looking at the water, there is a change in the vibrations of their mind, the *prāṇa* in the system. In a short while, all their anguish, delusions and whatever was tormenting them flows away. They become fresh.

People love the ocean because there is more prāṇa there, more ozone. When you go on looking at the waves one after another, it washes something away. This is prakṛti-layā meditation, where you dissolve yourself in nature.

Bhava-pratyayo—for them, the content is this whole universe. It is the same with the gods and goddesses who take care of the world. Taking care of the world itself is their samādhi.

śraddhā-vīrya-smṛti-samādhi-prajñā-

pūrvaka itareṣām || 20 ||

श्रद्धावीर्यस्मृतिसमाधिप्रज्ञापूर्वक इतरेषाम् ॥ २० ॥

Other ways to obtain samādhi are through faith, valour, memory of your origin and awareness of a previous experience of samādhi.

Now, we will look at the other types of samādhi.

Śraddhā—faith—creates good qualities in your consciousness. It is made stable, steady and solid. Doubt in the consciousness makes you very vulnerable, fearful and uncertain. It scatters and destroys you. It pulls you apart. Doubt disseminates your energy, while faith consolidates it. The feeling when you have faith is a form of consolidation, a strength. It makes you strong. Faith brings totality in you. It pulls together all the loose ends of your consciousness. It integrates your whole personality.

That is why Jesus also said that faith is your strength. They are synonymous—faith and strength. When you have faith, you are strong and bold. When you are weak and feeble, you have doubts. Doubt and uncertainty are signs of weakness.

Meditation takes place just out of faith. When there is unshakeable faith, that also leads a person into a state of void and he attains samādhi.

Vīrya is valour, vigour or force, courage and vitality. It is total courage and valour with which a country is defended by its army. We fight for our country when it is in danger. All the energy in the system comes together during that time. This is how valour rises in people.

In that moment of valour and extreme sense of patriotism, there is tremendous joy. That is why this world has wars again and again. If people completely condemn wars and if nobody likes them, then they cannot take place. Though the after-effects of war are very unpleasant, its course is very thrilling. People enjoy thrilling movies for the same reason.

Every cell in our body becomes united and the whole consciousness becomes one. The defence system gets awakened in you. This is strength. When the defence system peaks, it is very joyful because there is equanimity too. There is a sense of patriotism, devotion and gratitude. That sense of patriotism, valour or vigour also takes you into a state of meditation.

When someone goes to climb Mount Everest and has the feeling of, 'I want to achieve it', that is valour. When someone travels around the world in a sailboat and has a sense of 'I will do it', that is valour.

When a soldier at the border puts his life at risk, that is vīrya, valour. The peak of valour leads you to samādhi. The peak of faith, śraddhā, leads you to samādhi.

Smṛti is the remembrance of your origin. Come on, wake up! You are not here for the first time! You have been here a million times. When you 'wake up', you become aware of your true Self; of who you are. You are not what you think you are today. You are not the nationality. Today you are an American or Spaniard or Russian or Indian but 100 years ago, 200 years ago, 500 years ago you were different. This is not the only identity you have. When you remember your true identity, your true nature, even then you reach a state of samādhi. Smṛti, the memory of your origin, your past, can lead you to samādhi.

Smṛti also means the memory of a very peaceful and beautiful state of mind. The very memory of the experience will make you relive that experience. The memory of samādhi reproduces the memory of one's Being, of the Self, freedom, devotion, surrender, love, and joy. This takes you back to the Self.

Often, we do not remember nice things. What we remember are negative things. We do not remember compliments but we remember insults. Yoga is turning the wheel around to remember those wonderful moments you have had. Sit and be with them, and with those very memories your entire being gets back to that wonderful state.

Śraddhā-vīrya-smṛti-samādhi—here again, samādhi is a balance of the mind. If you have total balance of mind, it leads you to this deeper samādhi.

Prajñā is mindfulness, total alertness. Awareness of mind, presence of mind also leads you to samādhi. *Samādhi-prajñā* means awareness of the samādhi that you have experienced. Even if you experience deep serenity inside you once, the memory of that wonderful experience can rekindle that experience in your life again and again and again.

tīvra-samvegānām āsannaḥ || 21 ||

तीव्रसंवेगानाम् आसन्नः ॥ २१ ॥

Through intensity of practice, it (samādhi) is expedited.

Here it is very important to note what Maharṣi Patañjali is saying. You need to have passion, an intense longing.

tīvra-samvegānām-āsannaḥ

Earlier the Maharṣi said, "You have to shun passion. You have to slow down," but here he says, "You should have 100% passion for it, only then can it happen." With passion, success comes very quickly. If there is a one-point intent and an intense desire to do it, then it will happen.

On the other hand, he says, "Rein in your desires." You have to now balance these two things. They appear to be opposites but they are not. They complement each other. You cool down your craving for the outer world but if you put 100% attention and go deep within, then success is for sure.

mṛdu-madhya-adhimātratvāt tataḥ-api viśeṣaḥ || 22 ||

मृदुमध्याधिमात्रत्वात् ततोऽपि विशेषः ॥ २२ ॥

Even among that (intensity of practice) it is qualified as mild, medium or intense.

People put varied efforts in their practice. Some just do it mildly, others do it a little more intently, and the third type of people do it with the utmost intensity.

Some people just do *sādhanā* thinking that they have to do a little while looking at the phone, doing this and that. They are just doing sādhanā for the sake of doing it.

There are others, who are a little more serious. They think, “Yes, I must do it, I must practise.”

Then, there are those who are dedicated to it. So, there are three different levels of people and the result of their effort is according to their intent. Each one will get something. The effects will also be at different levels—supreme, medium and mild.

Who is God?

īśvara-praṇidhānād vā || 23 ||

ईश्वरप्रणिधानाद् वा ॥ २३ ॥

Or (one can achieve samādhi) by surrendering to the Divine.

Surrendering to the Lord, you can achieve the full blossomed state of consciousness.

Now, what is the Lord? Who is the Lord? Where is He? It is easy to say surrender to God but what is God? Where is God? Nobody has ever seen God. What is it that rules this world?

You will find that it is love that rules the world. Just like the Sun is the centre of the solar system and rules all the planets, love is the core of your life. Love is beyond your changing body, changing thoughts, and changing feelings. It is the very centre, core of your existence, which is very subtle and delicate. That consciousness, the core of existence, is responsible for this whole creation. There lies the lordship.

A bird feeds its young ones because of love. A flower blossoms because of love. Ducks hatch eggs because of love. Cows take care of their calves because of love. Kittens are taken care of by their mothers because of love. Have you seen how monkeys care for their young ones? Love is in-built in creation. This is how the creation functions. That is why Jesus said, "Love is God. God is love." They are synonymous.

Here Maharṣi Patañjali says that dedication or devotion to the Divine can also lead you into samādhi. Now, who is the Divine? What are the characteristics of the Divine?

kleśa-karma-vipāka-āśayaiḥ-aparāmṛṣṭaḥ puruṣa

viśeṣa īśvaraḥ || 24 ||

क्लेशकर्मविपाकाशयैरपरामृष्टः पुरुषविशेष ईश्वरः ॥ २४ ॥

Divinity is that special consciousness which is untouched by misery, fruits of actions and desires (latent and manifest).

What is the sign of Divinity? The divine energy is untouched by *kleśa*—misery, untouched by any impact of *karma* and by *vipāka*—the fruit of action. That consciousness, that special being is *Īśvara*. Patañjali says that Īśvara is also a being. Being is that which IS; the consciousness which IS. That special consciousness which is free from misery, karma, the fruit of karma, *āśayaiḥ*—its impressions, implications—that *puruṣa-viśeṣa* is Īśvara.

There are four types of karmas.

1. The karma which gives merits. You may do something good for somebody and they feel good about it and may thank you for it. They thank you from their heart, and that brings you good karma.

2. There is another type of karma which brings you demerits. You might do something bad to somebody and they suffer because of it. That brings you karma of demerit.

3. There are certain karmas which are a combination of merit and demerit. This is the third type of karma.

4. Karmas devoid of both merit and demerit. These actions have no merit or demerit. They are just actions. For example, you go for a walk in the evening or you vacuum the hall. But if you are doing it for somebody then that is an action of merit. If you are helping someone in the kitchen, cutting vegetables and cooking food for everybody, then it is an action of merit.

Actions which give merit, which give demerit, which give mixed results and which have no results at all are the four types of karmas. At the very core of your existence, the Being is free from all these karmas; it has no karma. Whatever action that comes forth from the Lord is not attached to any karma.

Vipāka is the fruit or consequence of the action. The fruit (enjoyment or suffering) of an action does not touch that core of your being and existence, which is the Lord of the creation. That consciousness is free from this.

Āśayaiḥ means latent desires or impressions, seeds, opinions, etc. So when a being is free from kleśa, (misery), karma, vipāka (the fruit of action), and āśayaiḥ (the impressions of actions), then that being or consciousness is Īśvara or Lord. And the Lord is not somewhere in the sky but in your heart. It is in every being's heart. Your actions and the events taking place around you do not touch the central point of your life. That central core remains a virgin. Jesus was born to a virgin. This means that Jesus, the Lord was born to an area deep within you which is untouched by any events or happenings in life.

Puruṣa-viśeṣa—that special being is the Lord. All worship is done by the mind for its Being. It is like the circumference collapsing into the centre. What happens when a boundary collapses into the centre? The area, which had been enclosed by the circumference, becomes infinite, limitless. When our little chattering mind prays, it does so to the Infinite Being that you are. Your external mind worships the core of your being. That is prayer—when you ask your Lord to help you.

Kṛṣṇa meant this when He said that one may pray to whoever he wants but the prayer goes to only Him because He is the core of existence. You may worship one form of God. Another may worship a different form. A third person may worship yet another form. Essentially, worship is just an act of dissolution—a sugar doll or candy getting dissolved in water. It does not matter at which point it gets into the water. It is going to dissolve and merge. Similarly, worship dissolves the mind of the worshipper. It is the act of dissolving the mind into its being; the Being which is free from *kleśa karma vipāka-āśayaiḥ*. This takes place almost instantaneously. That is why there is no difference between God, Guru and the Self.

In the Dakṣiṇāmūrti stotram it is said,

īśvaro guruḥ-ātmeti murti bheda vibhāgine

vyoma-vad vyāpta-dehāya dakśiṇā-mūrtaye namah

ईश्वरो गुरुरात्मेति मूर्तिभेदविभागिने ।

व्योमवद् व्याप्तदेहाय दक्षिणामूर्तये नमः ॥

It is just a matter of using different words which are synonymous. The Master is the core of your being. And so is the Divine who rules this entire creation.

tatra niratiśayam sarvajñatva-bījam || 25 ||

तत्र निरतिशयं सर्वज्ञत्वबीजम् ॥ २५ ॥

The seed of all knowingness abides in that (Lordship).

In that state of consciousness the seed of all-knowing is present in a very subtle manner. It means that you have the key to the entire library. The key to the library is present in this consciousness.

If Kṛṣṇa knew everything, why did He try to pacify all concerned, and try to stop the war thrice? He knew that a war was going to take place but He never told Arjuna this, and also that he was going to win. Instead, He told Arjuna that if he won the war, he would rule the world. And if he lost it, he would go to heaven. It did not seem as if He knew everything. The way He gave answers and instructions, it did not indicate that He knew the future. So if Kṛṣṇa was the Lord and knew it all, why did He not reveal it? Many such questions are still being asked.

Tatra niratiśayam sarvajñatva-bījam—this seed of all-knowingness is present. For example, if you have a dictionary, you can check the meaning of any word you want. You don't need to memorize every word there. Nor do you need to know all the words in the dictionary all the time.

You may open yourself up to this highest form of your consciousness. At that moment, you have all the knowledge—you can know and feel all the beings in the world. You can know how many beings there are and what they are doing—some may be waking up, some going to bed, some taking a bath, some in their cars, some fighting, some eating and some doing other activities. This is just about people.

But take into account the entire creation. There are so many connected activities—so many chickens are hatching, so many are being slaughtered, so many buffaloes are wandering around and so many cows are chewing cud, so many monkeys are jumping from tree to tree. There are so many ants, cockroaches, flies, mosquitoes, amoeba, etc. There are billions of viruses and bacteria. Many are dying and many are being born. There is enormous activity going on at any moment. But amidst this enormous activity, you just wonder what a particular person is doing. This takes so much effort and is not worth it.

Sometimes, people ask me how I know their most well-kept secrets, those which they have not told anybody. I tell them that I do not know how but I know. And then sometimes, I search for my own keys which I have misplaced! This is even more confusing to people. They wonder how I know what they have never told anybody but how do I not know where I have kept my keys! I tell them that it is possible—just like they know they have hair on their head but do not know how many.

Knowledge and ignorance co-exist. That is why it is said *tatra niratiśayam sarvajñatva-bījam*. This seed of all-knowing-ness is present in the Lordship, in that state of consciousness.

pūrveṣām api guruḥ kālena-anavacchedāt || 26 ||

पूर्वेषाम् अपि गुरुः कालेनानवच्छेदात् ॥ २६ ॥

That (Lordship) is the Guru for those who came before too, as it is unobstructed by time.

This consciousness is the Guru, even for the Gurus of the past, because time has no role to play in this consciousness. This consciousness is beyond time. It continues, uninterrupted by time. That consciousness is the *Guru tattva.* The Master is the core of your being. And so is the Divine who rules this entire creation.

There is something similar in the Bible. Jesus said that He had taught people who came even before Abraham. The same thing is touched upon by Kṛṣṇa when he told Arjuna that He had taught Ikṣvāku and Manu. And Arjuna wondered how Kṛṣṇa could have taught them. They had been born long ago and Kṛṣṇa was his contemporary. Arjuna exclaimed that he was terribly confused already and that he could not understand how Kṛṣṇa was a Guru to people who lived thousands of years before Him. How could it be possible?

Then Kṛṣṇa said that Arjuna did not really know Him. That He had come so many times to this world and Arjuna too had come many times. He had forgotten but Kṛṣṇa knew it all. He had taught at that time and he was teaching right then too and would continue to teach in the future.

The Guru principle is the same because there is no break in time. It continues. Jesus is continuing throughout. It is not that he stopped somewhere. People may think that He will come in the future.

Purveshām-api guruhu—that Being was, is and will be the Master at all times because there is no break in time.

tasya vācakaḥ praṇavaḥ || 27 ||

तस्य वाचकः प्रणवः ॥ २७ ॥

That is addressed as 'Om'.

This *Om* is your true name. All other names are just for one lifetime. Your real name, for all lifetimes, is Om. When you realise that your consciousness is eternal, it has been here for millennia, that awareness of your consciousness is the *puruṣa-viśeṣa*. It is the special puruṣa, the special aspect of your being and it is addressed by Om. That is Īśvara.

Om is the nearest sound that It could be addressed by because when Om is chanted, the prāṇa and the consciousness is complete. Om is made of 'aa', 'oo' and 'mm'. When you say 'aa', the prāṇa is in the lower part of the body, with 'oo' it is in the middle and with 'mm' it is in the top part of the body. When you say 'Om', the prāṇa is total; it is complete.

Om is the one sound which is accepted by all the religions in the world. Christians say 'Amen' and Muslims 'Āmeen', sounds very close to Om.

So, *jeevesvara, jeeva*—the being (the individual life) and Īśvara (the Divinity) are not different. They are one and the same. When you realise a part of your deeper consciousness is uninterrupted by time, and when that comes to play in you that is the Guru tattva, the Guru. So that consciousness has been the Guru from the very beginning.

tad-japaḥ tad-artha-bhāvanam || 28 ||

तज्जपः तदर्थभावनम् ॥ २८ ॥

Its repetition and feeling its meaning.

The repetition of Om reveals its meaning. When you sit and repeat Om, the meaning of Om, which is eternal or eternity, which is infinity, simply starts manifesting in you.

For example, if you say mango, the word itself makes your mouth water. Immediately there is a reaction and there is a feeling. Saying 'Christmas' immediately generates a feeling of celebration, of giving and receiving gifts.

Taj-japaḥ tad-artha-bhāvanam—when you say Om, you remember that totality of your being, that Being which is at the very core of this existence, that life which is free from misery and which is all unconditional love. The sound Om reminds you of the Lord of creation.

tataḥ pratyak-cetanā-adhigamaḥ-api-

antaraya-abhāvaḥ-ca || 29 ||

ततः प्रत्यक्चेतनाधिगमोऽप्यन्तरायाभावश्च ॥ २९ ॥

From that is gained the knowledge of consciousness and the destruction of obstacles.

From just contemplating Om and chanting it, the witness consciousness starts taking shape inside you. You start separating from the scenery. You will get *pratyak-cetanā*. The differentiated consciousness in you starts blossoming. You see thoughts coming and moving. You then know that you are not the thought, you are not the feeling, you are not the body. This feeling is generated spontaneously. Doesn't it happen to you when you sit in meditation? You see that your body is different from you, right?

"I am not the body, I am not the thoughts, I am not the emotions, I am not all this." This is pratyak-cetanā. That state of consciousness springs up, and then all the obstacles go away.

Antarāya-abhavaś-ca—obstacles don't rise there at all. Otherwise, there are many obstacles that might arise during the practice, but with the chanting of Om and surrendering to the divine principle, those obstacles simply vanish.

Obstacles on the Path

vyādhi-styāna-saṁśaya-pramāda-ālasya-avirati-

bhrāntidarśana-ālabdhabhūmikatva-anavasthitatvāni

citta-vikṣepāḥ-te-antarāyāḥ || 30 ||

व्याधिस्त्यानसंशयप्रमादालस्याविरतिभ्रान्तिदर्शनालब्धभूमिकत्वा
नवस्थितत्वानि चित्तविक्षेपास्तेऽन्तरायाः ॥ ३० ॥

Illness in the body, mental dullness, doubt, carelessness, laziness, obsessions, hallucination, no experience in practice and instability are the obstacles or distractions (in the practise of yoga).

Vyādhi—bodily illness. When you are sick, you do not want to do anything, any sādhanā, any practice. Illness is a big obstacle. If you are watching television, nothing happens, but if you sit for meditation, your body becomes restless and there are pains here and there. Many times it so happens that when people meditate or do some advanced sādhanā, they get affected by fever, cold, cough, etc. All these are obstacles for deeper meditation and yogic practices.

Styāna—inertia in the mind, mental illnesses, an inability to comprehend, to listen, to understand, to follow and to practise anything.

Saṁśaya—doubt. There are primarily three types of doubts—doubt in oneself, in the Guru and doubt in the technique. These three can clog one's progress.

When you doubt yourself, you wonder if you are good enough. You feel that you cannot do what is required to be done. You might see that everyone else, except you, is meditating in a blissful state. You feel that it is just you who is suffering and that you are no good. You do not think that you can ever make it.

And then doubts arise about the techniques. You feel that they might not do you any good, that you should try some other techniques.

Next, doubts arise about the teacher. These three types of doubts can hamper progress on the path.

Your doubt is always about something that is positive. You never doubt the negative. You never wonder if you are really depressed but you will certainly doubt your happiness. You wonder if you are happy; if what you wanted is really making you happy. Doubt is the third obstacle.

It is detrimental to anyone's progress. So, doubt has to be done away with. When you are doubtful, that means your prāṇa is low. When your energy is high, you do not get doubts.

Pramāda—doing something wrong willfully; doing it with some motive is pramāda. You know that a certain thing is not good for you. Despite that, you continue with it because the mind feels it is going to get some joy out of it. Conversely, you know that something needs to be done but you do not do it. For instance, you know very well that you have to pay tax but you don't pay it. Suppose you are sick and should not eat ice-cream, not overeat, yet you do so. Someone has diabetes and should not eat sugar but they still go on eating sweets or chocolates. Being careless, not being alert and attentive is another obstacle. This is pramāda.

Ālasya—laziness. It is the biggest enemy of mankind. You may be very active but when it comes to doing āsanas, exercises or prāṇāyāma, you feel lazy and do not practise them. That laziness can spread to any aspect of your life. You may intentionally not do something.

Avirati—inability to let go of cravings, to contain the senses; to be obsessed with sensual objects and not let go of them. When you are hungry, you eat some food but after your stomach is full, there is no point in thinking about food the whole day.

It is the same when you see a beautiful place. Once you see it, your want should subside. You should not go on thinking about seeing a beautiful place all the time. The same applies to sex. You have had sex and it is over. You do not carry sex in your head twenty-four hours. People see blue-movies day and night. The body is incapable of functioning and mind is obsessed with thoughts of sex. Even old people have this problem. They are seventy, eighty, ninety years old, but they are still thinking about sex. All the actions of the sense organs should be limited to some time. But thinking about something and being feverish about it all the time is avirati, obsession or non-detachment.

Avirati is a big obstruction in the path of yoga, for it does not allow you to get centered. It just pulls you down and keeps you from moving on.

Bhrāntidarśana—delusion, hallucination. You build a castle which does not exist. You create an image about yourself. You imagine that you are somebody special. Suddenly you think that you are a superstar. This is a problem with many people. Many seekers experience visions after practising for a while. They get caught up in that vision because that vision is neither completely false, nor completely true. It is a mixture of some truth, and some falsehood. So people try to hold on to it.

Many cults have been formed because of bhrāntidarśana. People have never really understood the obstacles that can come up in the path of yoga. This is called *yoga māya*. Yoga māya is a vision that brings an intuitive message. You may be meditating and get an intuitive thought to open the door because somebody is outside the door and when you open the door, you really find that person waiting outside. You get very excited and think that God has told you about it. This will happen again and again because you are not completely hollow and empty. There are residues or traces of desires, hatred, and fears within you. These ideas will come through the form in which you see God or your Guru or through someone else. It will give you ideas which make you suffer. This happened to one of our devotees. She had various visions and most of them happened. She had one vision which indicated that she should not take her husband to the doctor; he would be cured without one. She was already apprehensive about going to a doctor and averse to allopathic medicine. When she had her vision, she became determined not to go to the doctor. Her husband's blood sugar level shot up and due to lack of treatment he lost his eyesight. The devotee became very angry, feeling that her inner voice had deceived her. This happened because of a lack of proper understanding. Most of the factors were alright; there was no impurity in them. But then her own fears and cravings influenced her intuitive thoughts with unpleasant results. This is an obstruction. That is why we should not gallop on the horses of delusions—bhrāntidarśana. Many people get trapped in it.

Your imagination about others can also cause tremendous negativity in your mind. You keep chewing on it and are stuck with it. Delusions, fear, anxiety, megalomania are all part of bhrāntidarśana.

Alabdha-bhūmikatva—inability to attain any state on the path, a state of samādhi, peace, or tranquility. Sometimes people feel that they have been doing various practices for many years but do not seem to be getting anywhere. They feel that they are just sitting and nothing is happening. Their mind is crowded with thoughts and they have not attained any state. They feel completely stuck and think that they are getting nowhere. This state of non-attainment of any state is the eighth obstruction. Despite these thoughts, they do not give up the practice. However, they feel stuck without any progress.

Anavasthitatva—inability to hold on to any state. You have spurts of devotion but you are unable to hold on to it. Some moments of peace and joy come up but you are unable to hold on to it. You are generous, but those few moments of generosity, broad mindedness in your life, simply disappear in a few minutes or seconds. This is the inability to stay in that state. You become very positive, but that positivity lasts only for a few minutes or only as long as you don't see your opponent. The moment you see your opponent, all your positivity is gone with the wind. Someone makes a comment about you and that pricks you deeply. All your equanimity, tranquility, joy, happiness, everything disappears. These are the nine obstacles.

duḥkha-daurmanasya-aṅgamejayatva-śvāsa-praśvāsā

vikṣepa-sahabhuvaḥ || 31 ||

दुःखदौर्मनस्याङ्गमेजयत्वश्वासप्रश्वासा विक्षेपसहभुवः ॥ ३१ ॥

Sorrow, bitterness, lack of control of the body, and imbalance in breathing manifest along with the distractions.

So, what comes along with the obstacles?

Dukha—pain in the body and mind.

Daurmanasya—bitterness in the mind which comes from the obstacles in one's life. Duḥkha or sadness gives way to bitterness, daurmanasya. You do not feel good with anybody. There is bitterness for others and oneself.

Bitterness, dejection, depression are the by-products of the nine obstacles.

Aṅgamejayatva—restlessness and inability to control your body. It means that your body is not obeying you and behaving like a drunkard. A drunkard wants to go to the left but his body goes to the right. He wants to walk straight but his body goes elsewhere. He tries to reach for his glass but goes on putting his hand on the table away from the glass. This lack of coordination between the body and the mind is aṅgamejayatva. The body does not listen to you. You want to walk but the body does not move.

Śvāsapraśvāsāḥ vikṣepa—your breath is irregular, unsettled, shaky and uncomfortable. Have you observed the breath of frustrated people? Their inhalation is staggered and exhalation is also not normal; this indicates vikṣepa. Vikṣepa means the disturbed state of mind or wrong perception of reality.

When you are disturbed, if you observe the incoming and outgoing breath, you will notice that there is a complete imbalance. You often let out a big sigh, when you are unhappy, indicating heaviness and sadness. When you are happy or excited, the incoming breath is longer and you are more aware of it. It is more prominent.

Overcoming the Obstacles

tat-pratiṣedha-artham eka-tattva-abhyāsaḥ || 32 ||

तत्प्रतिषेधार्थम् एकतत्त्वाभ्यासः ॥ ३२ ॥

To counter these (obstacles) practise one principle.

How do you get over the obstacles? By practicing one pointedness, holding onto one principle.

Which principle? It could be Om. Maharṣi Patañjali asks to chant Om and feel it. Om has many meanings—purity, clarity and sincerity, not just one. Om is the essence of creation. It is unconditional love. Om is everything, and the true name is Om. Put your attention on the one principle, one Divinity, one non-changing, eternal, blissful consciousness.

There are many ways to look at that one Principle. Within one, there is diversity. One principle could mean that you just focus on the air element or fire or the earth element. Know that this body is the earth element that goes back to the Earth. The earth element has all the other elements in it.

The one tattva could be the Śiva principle or the Guru principle—nothing other than the Guru. What happens when you keep doing one thing? Boredom arises, restlessness will surface. That restlessness and boredom take you to a peak that brings clarity. This is the only way out. Our mind is troubled because it is dwelling on duality. It has innumerable choices and is further confused. It wonders if it should do this or that. Then it jumps all over the place and gets further divided. A divided mind is misery and a one-pointed mind is joy.

In all those moments when you have been very happy, you experienced life itself in totality. If you notice what happiness is, it is the mind becoming one whole. It becomes so total and then you experience joy, peace, and bliss.

Duality, or a divided mind, is the cause of fear and misery. If you keep doing two things or too many things, it is not *eka-tattva-abhyāsaḥ*; it is not one practice.

What is eka-tattva? It is attending to one principle. This one principle could be God, could be matter, could be Guru or the Self. It could be anything but you need to practise just that one thing—*eka-tattva-abhyāsaḥ*.

You can attend to one principle only if there is a certain degree of calmness and subtleness in the mind. Otherwise, that does not seem possible.

You see that One Principle in everybody.

'It is the Self that is present everywhere.'

'It is my Master who is present everywhere. There is nobody other than my Master. He is everything for me.'

'God is everything for me.'

'It is all me only. There is nothing other than me.'

This is the skill in life—holding on to one principle and seeing that principle in everything.

Our life has to be lived in the realm of multiplicity. In the world, you live with many people and everybody is not the same. But how can you see the same thing in everybody? Nothing appears to be the same. No two people appear to be the same. But here, Patañjali says, "See one thing in every one. Focus on that one principle. Then, you get over all the obstacles."

maitrī-karuṇā-mudita-upekṣāṇām
sukha-duḥkha-puṇya-apuṇya-viṣayāṇām
bhāvanātaḥ-citta-prasādanam || 33 ||

मैत्रीकरुणामुदितोपेक्षाणां सुखदुःखपुण्यापुण्यविषयाणां
भावनातश्चित्तप्रसादनम् ॥ ३३ ॥

We attain a pleasant state of mind by cultivating feelings of friendliness towards those who are happy, compassion for those who are suffering, goodwill towards those who are virtuous, and indifference towards the unethical.

How to keep the pleasantness of the mind? It is not that there are only good and happy people in society but all kinds. There is misery in the world, there is joy, there are both good and bad things in the world. How do you deal with all of them? What is the attitude you should have? Here, Maharṣi Patañjali gives you a great formula:

maitrī-karuṇā-muditā-upekṣāṇām-sukha-duḥkha-puṇya-apuṇya-viṣayāṇām bhāvanātaḥ-citta-prasādanam

For your consciousness to be pleasant, to be in a state of equanimity, what do you need? You need to have four kinds of attitude.

Maitrī—friendliness. Towards those who are happy. If your friends are happy, don't you feel happy? If you don't feel happy with your friends, that means they are not your friends. If you're not friendly with happy people, you will become jealous of them. You are jealous of people who are happier than you. But if you feel that they belong to you, it does not bother you when they are happy. You are never jealous about the happiness of someone very close and dear to you. Jealousy arises when the happy person is not connected to you totally. It might be difficult in the beginning to feel the connection. Intellectually you may feel that it is only you who is in the other person but your feelings still have their preferences since they are not fully cultured and established in the Self. So, friendship with those who are happy will help you get over jealousy.

Karuṇā—compassion. Towards those who are suffering, have compassion, not friendliness. This is a secret! Don't be friendly with them because this friendship will drag you down and make you unhappy too. Then you will be unable to help them. You might think that you should share the unhappiness of your friend but then, you will not be able to share your happiness with them. So, you should not be friendly with unhappy people but be compassionate with them. There is a difference here. Karuṇā is compassion. If someone is suffering, they are suffering because of their karma. Be compassionate to them, not friendly. If you do not know how to deal with people who are suffering, you make their beliefs, that God has been unjust with them and that nature has been unkind to them, stronger.

When you agree with them that they are suffering, you push them lower down. Actually, you should be trying to pull them out of the rut they have pushed themselves into. Instead, you do the opposite and you do it unconsciously.

You should not pity people who are suffering. There is a big difference between pity and compassion. When you pity a person you push him further down. With pity, you make the belief of the suffering person, about his sorrow, more concrete. If someone thinks that a great injustice has been done to them and they are on a self-pitying trip, you are not helping them in any way if you pity them too. You will not help them in any way to wake up to the truth. You should have compassion and not friendliness, for people who are suffering.

In many āśramas, if someone is unhappy or negative, everybody ostracises them. Nobody talks to them, in order to avoid their negativity. The scriptures also tell you not to sit with one who has too many doubts—doubt about the practice, about the Guru, about knowledge. If you sit with them, you will also go down with them. Their energy is low and they will pull your energy down also. In Hindi there is a saying, don't even shake hands with those who are negative about the path, about the knowledge, about the Master. Because those negative vibrations will come to you and that is considered a sin. In ancient days if someone said something negative, people would close their ears and start chanting, "Śiva-

Śiva-Śiva-Śiva let my ears not hear these sort of things. Let me plug my ears because it is going to destroy my own consciousness."

Muditā—feel happy for those doing good work. You should become one with them and feel that you are doing a good job with them. Then, the sense of competition disappears, anger and jealousy subside. The tendency of finding fault with people who are doing good things will disappear.

The people who complain would not have done much themselves. Criticism comes from people who do not work. You should not find fault with people who are doing good work. You can do this only when you become one with them. Muditā means happiness for people who are doing a wonderful job. Share the happiness, feel happy.

Upekṣā—just be indifferent to the people who say or do negative things. If somebody says something which is not true, just brush it off. It is not even worth thinking about. But you do the reverse. You do not think of people who are doing meritorious work. Instead of ignoring people who do sinful things, you keep on thinking about them.

So, when you see people doing sinful things, you should educate them and then ignore them.

You educate out of compassion and then ignore. Otherwise, you will think about their actions and get bothered. You may think they're imperfect. If you go on thinking so, you will become imperfect. Then, you will become like them, maybe even worse.

Secondly, you think that the other person is wrong and you are right. If you look honestly at yourself, you will realise that you may be wrong too. If you point an accusing finger at somebody, then there are three fingers always pointing at you. But if you stop differentiating between yourself and others, then you can just turn inward.

If you keep these four attitudes in your mind, your mind will blossom—*cittaprasādanam*. Grace will dawn in your mind.

pracchardana-vidhāraṇābhyām vā prāṇasya || 34 ||

प्रच्छर्दनविधारणाभ्यां वा प्राणस्य ॥ ३४ ॥

Or by breaking and elongating the flow of prāṇa.

The mind is also calmed by regulating the breath, particularly attending to exhalation and the natural stilling of breath. By consciously changing the pattern of breath and holding the breath, the state of mind can be changed. *Bhastrikā*, prāṇāyāma and Sudarśana Kriyā are all an indication of *pracchardana*.

Patañjali has not mentioned Sudarśana Kriyā directly. But in this sentence, there is a clue. You can trace our practices to that one sutra. We are not just breathing any way we like. We are consciously breathing in a definite rhythm. That is pracchhardana—splitting. We are splitting the breath, dividing it and holding it with different rhythms.

That is *pracchardana-vidhāraṇābhyām vā prāṇasya.*

We are modulating the prāṇa and the breath. This also makes our mind focused.

viṣayavatī vā pravṛttiḥ-utpannā manasaḥ

sthiti-nibandhinī || 35 ||

विषयवती वा प्रवृत्तिरुत्पन्ना मनसः स्थितिनिबन्धिनी ॥ ३५ ॥

Or by arresting (holding) the mind in that state which arises through contact with the sense objects.

If your mind is engrossed in any of the five senses, through that also you can attain samādhi. Here Maharṣi Patañjali gives a clue of *Vijñāna Bhairava*. In the Vijñāna Bhairava, Śiva tells us that through sight, sound, smell, taste and touch; through all these five senses, you can enter into the state of Bhairava, the higher consciousness.

What happens in the eye-gazing process, during the Advanced Meditation Course (The Art of Living Silence Retreat)? You look at somebody for a few minutes, you gaze at that person from the bottom of your heart. At that time, your mind does not run here and there. The mind comes to a standstill and is completely settled.

Here Maharṣi Patañjali says that by paying attention to any of the five senses, your consciousness can perceive subtle sensory experiences. It's not just the gross sensory experiences. In the state of sleep, you are experiencing all the five senses but in a subtle way. You are not using your eyes, you are not using your ears but in the deep state of sleep or dream, you are experiencing them.

For example, if you see a baby eating a lollipop, it is totally engrossed in it. It is very different from the way you eat food. A bird chirping is totally into chirping and it does only that at that time. When it does other activities, it does not chirp. Similarly, if you put your 100% attention on any one of the senses, that also brings stability in the consciousness, stability in the mind.

viśokā vā jyotiṣmatī || 36 ||

विशोका वा ज्योतिष्मती ॥ ३६ ॥

Or by the sorrowless state attained through the glowing intellect.

If you are, even for a few moments, with a person who is very unhappy and sad, then you also start feeling depressed. And if you are with someone who is very joyful and is bubbling with joy and enthusiasm, then you start feeling joyful too. You have trained your mind to be happy or unhappy. If you have acquired the habit of being unhappy, then it becomes your second nature. You feel at home having a long face all the time.

Viśokā vā jyotiṣmatī—when you focus on a state which is devoid of sadness or sorrow then the effulgent intellect dawns within you.

Viśokā means getting rid of unhappiness. Feeling sad is just a habit. If you look into your mind and see that the sadness is simply unfounded and self-generated, it will disappear and you will become free of it. It is just a concept. It is baseless. You may feel that you are not smart enough; nobody cares for you, people do not respect you. Why should you think so? All these self-imposed ideas make you unhappy. Your comparisons can disturb you and make you sad. Do not compare yourself with anybody. You should feel that you can be happier than you are now. Make your mind free of sadness which is born out of your concepts.

Jyotiṣmatīprajñā—consider your mind as light, as a flame. Your consciousness is a flame. Your entire body is functioning because of the presence of the mind as a flame in you. Otherwise, you will be like an unlit candle.

How does a flame work? A flame burns because of oxygen. There is a combination of matter and oxygen and a flame comes into being.

What is life? Life is also the same. It uses oxygen and lives on some matter. Just as a flame lives on wax, the wick and oxygen, your life and the mind uses the body and the food in the body as wax. The air is like the oxygen and exhibits activities in the body just as the flame exhibits its activity.

Life and light are very similar. If you put a bottle over a burning candle, it will be extinguished in a few moments. Similarly, if you are shut in a room, without any windows, you can live only for a few hours due to the lack of oxygen. If you do to your body what you do to the candle, the reaction will be the same. If you put more wax into the candle, it will burn for a longer period.

Similarly, if you put food into your body, then it will live longer. If the wick is burnt out, no amount of wax will make the candle burn. The wick has its own limitation. Similarly, no amount of food will sustain the body after some years of life. The body functions just like the wick. This body is holding on to the jyotiṣmatīprajñā.

Viśokā vā jyotiṣmatī—get rid of unhappiness and be happy. At the same time know that your mind is made up of light and not matter. Your mind is energy. You ARE energy.

vītarāga-viṣayam vā cittam || 37 ||

वीतराग विषयम् वा चित्तम् ॥ ३७ ॥

Or by remembering the one who is devoid of craving.

Your mind is like water. I said earlier that your mind is like a flame. I tell you, your mind is also like water. Just as water assumes the shape of its container, your mind becomes like the thought you engage in.

Vītarāga—one who is liberated from cravings. If you think of such a person, then your mind also gets those qualities. It develops all the qualities of whatever thoughts you put into it.

Putting your attention on the enlightened, on a saint, on one whose mind is still, your mind becomes stable and you attain samādhi. This is the principle that is used by Jains and Buddhists. The Hindu philosophy asks to put the attention on the Guru, on the Buddha, on the Jain *tīrthaṅkara*, one who is still, who is just there. Whomsoever you think of, your mind assumes their state. If you think of a person who is agitated or negative, your mind assumes that agitation. If you think of a calm person, your mind also begins to develop those qualities. It starts feeling that peace and that quietness. This is because the mind is also like air. Air does not have a location. It is not just fixed anywhere. The cool breeze, that energy enters your system.

The mind is also like ether because it is all permeating. Your consciousness is like ether, all-pervading.

But if you have *rāga* and *dveṣa* (craving and aversion) with someone who is vītarāga, then it defeats the purpose. That is why they say not to see a Guru or an enlightened person as a human being, as a person with likes and dislikes. Otherwise, your mind goes on a big trip, "What will they like? What will they not? Why this and not that?" Instead, see them as pure consciousness, as peace, as joy. Then, you also start radiating these. But even if any thoughts come or likes and dislikes arise, do not struggle with them, "I shouldn't think that." Just let go and relax.

It is very simple. When you think of someone who is without craving, then immediately you draw on that energy and assume that form. You should try this on your own and experiment. Just think of somebody nasty and you will begin to feel nasty emotions inside. If you think of somebody who is jealous of you, you will feel uncomfortable. If you think of somebody who is into drugs, alcohol and who is very miserable, then you will feel all these knots coming up in your body, in your system. Think of somebody whom you love very much, and you will have nice feelings and sensations arise in you.

If you think of the enlightened, your consciousness becomes more and more alive and filled with light. That is why Jesus said, "If you have to go to my Father, you have to go through me. There is no other way." You have to go through the Master, because the

Master is an example right there. You have to pass through your mind. And what can help? The doorway with those vibrations and sensations. And these vibrations and sensations manifest in that body where the citta is vītarāga, fully blossomed, without any hindrances.

svapna-nidrā-jñāna-ālambanam vā || 38 ||

स्वप्ननिद्राज्ञानालम्बनं वा ॥३८ ॥

Or through the knowledge of sleep and dreams.

By focusing your attention on sleep you can attain samādhi. We sleep every night but we have never met our sleep. We don't know what sleep is. If you happen to know what sleep is, that very moment you will attain samādhi. When you dream, the dreamer is not there, only the dream is there. But if you realise "I am dreaming", this knowledge of dream and deep sleep can also still your mind.

What happens when you sleep? You let go of everything. If you hold on to even one thing, you cannot sleep. In sleep, all your identities disappear. You are neither male nor female, neither rich nor poor, neither stupid nor intelligent; sleep is just sleep.

In sleep, all your likes and dislikes disappear. You cannot carry anybody into your sleep. However dear somebody is, you cannot take them with you in your sleep. In your sleep, you are devoid of all your identities, your cravings, your aversions, etc. You let go of all of them and just rest. You do not do anything.

This is exactly what meditation is—doing nothing. In meditation, you do not do anything even for God or for yourself. You just let go of everything, just as you do when you sleep. The knowledge of sleep leads you to samādhi.

Ignorant people take dreams as the reality and enlightened people see this reality as a dream. Trying to interpret what you saw in your dream is utter ignorance. Enlightenment is to realise that this reality itself is a dream. If you tell an enlightened person about your dreams, he will tell you to forget about them and to wake up.

However, somebody who does 'dream interpretation' will give you various meanings for your dreams. They will put more ideas in your head. This is ignorance.

There are five types of dreams. The first are those that are the fulfilment of your cravings and your unfulfilled desires. You wanted to have an ice-cream or a pizza but you couldn't. Then, when you are asleep you have a dream in which you are eating a pizza or having a big scoop of ice-cream. You may have wanted to go for a walk with somebody and you could not do it. Then you dream that you are on such a walk. Your latent desires come up in dreams. Desires and fears are seen in dreams.

The second type of dream is when there is some stress being released from the past. Past experiences are seen in such dreams.

The third type is an intuitive dream. It could be about what might happen in the future—an intuition.

The fourth type of dream is a combination of all the three—fulfillment, stress-release and intuitiveness.

And the fifth type of dream has nothing to do with you; it is about the place where you are sleeping. You may be in a hotel in Italy and you dream of the unfamiliar Italian language, and all the unfamiliar sounds that you have been hearing in that country.

So, any of these five types of dreams can occur and you may not be able to categorize your dreams. Usually, it will be the fourth type, which is a combination of all types. Therefore, a wise person will just brush them aside. He will consider a dream to just be that, and nothing more. Even the reality of wakefulness is a dream. You may be in a place on one day and in another the next and in a third the day after. Your presence in a place in the past will seem like a dream.

Similarly, what you are planning to do next week is like a dream right now. Your mind is more in a dream than in wakefulness. You could say that there are only two states of consciousness, not three. One is deep sleep and the other is dreaming—dreaming in the day or in the night. Daydreaming, building castles in the air goes on and on in the mind all the time.

But once you know that you are daydreaming, there is a gush of energy in you. You become alert. This alertness wakes you up to reality; you are awakened. This awakening is prajñā. It is samādhi. Only at that moment are you fully alive. Only then are you awake to the truth of what IS. The rest of the time, you are asleep. You wake up even when you know that you have been in deep sleep and dreaming.

Patañjali has done a marvelous thing just quoting this one sūtra. Knowledge of sleep awakens you. This is because when a person is asleep, he is not at all aware of it. The moment he knows that he is sleeping, he is already awake. A person who is daydreaming does not know it. The moment he knows that he is daydreaming, he wakes up to reality instantly. When you do Kriyā and prāṇāyāma and nothing happens to you, you begin to daydream or sleep. There can be only these two possibilities. If you are daydreaming, the prāṇāyāma cannot help you because the mind is galloping on a dream, 'I'll be president'. You don't know how much of a headache it is to be president. It is very difficult to get into any sādhanā when the mind is in a constant state of daydreaming. The pity is people do not even know they are daydreaming and their dreams are worth nothing really.

svapna-nidrā jñāna-ālambanam vā

The knowledge of dreams and sleep can also awaken you to the truth.

yathā-abhimata-dhyānād vā || 39 ||

यथाभिमतध्यानाद्‌ वा ॥ ३९ ॥

Or by meditation according to one's liking.

Meditation also happens effortlessly when you put your attention on whatever you like. If you are walking around enjoying the garden, just staying in the garden can still your mind. This is a very important sūtra.

In Indian temples, the deities are dressed up in beautiful clothes, jewellery, flowers, and the like just to capture your mind.

Sometimes, when you have nothing else to do, you just go around window shopping because the mind likes to see things that are charming. Whichever objects charm the mind, put all of them in one place—this was the trick the ancient *ṛṣis* resorted to, in order to arrest the mind in a place. That is why in temples, all nice food items are served as *prasāda* and beautiful garments, jewellery, flowers, clothes, and other things adorn the deity and your mind says, "Wow! So beautiful!" Your mind is arrested there and becomes stable. If your mind is still going here and there, it is quietened by the sound of loud bells and drums. Especially during the *aarati*, beating drums and clanging bells make your mind go blank. When the mind goes blank, that is the time it has access to the infinite energy deep within.

yathā-bhimata-dhyānād-vā

Wherever the mind goes, you arrest it right there and you can go deep into meditation. Does it mean you just flow away with the attractions? Whenever you feel attracted to something, you want to possess it and when you go to possess it, you destroy it. That is not *dhyāna*, that is *bhoga* (enjoyment). Yoga is the complete opposite of bhoga. Yoga is appreciation, adoring the beauty, honouring the beauty and staying centered. Do you see what I'm saying? There is a difference. This is not waywardness, doing whatever you want. Maharṣi Patañjali says whenever the mind wanders, use that moment to turn inwards and go deep into your origin—*dṛṣṭā svarūpa*—the nature of the seer.

The Fruit of the Practice

paramāṇu parama-mahattva-antaḥ-

asya vaśīkāraḥ || 40 ||

परमाणु परममहत्त्वान्तोऽस्य वशीकारः ॥ ४० ॥

One gains control over the smallest as well as the largest.

What happens when you go inwards? You gain the ability of vastness and subtlety.

Parama-mahattva means the vastness of consciousness. You realise that the nature of consciousness is vast and at the same time very subtle. It is smaller than the smallest and bigger than the biggest. This experience comes to you when the mind becomes stable, calm and serene.

When you are sad and upset, when your mind is all over the place, you feel neither the expansion nor the subtlety of consciousness. But when your mind is calm, you experience the most delicate and the subtlest aspect of your consciousness and also the vastness of the consciousness. You experience both. Then you are able to influence the tiniest aspect of your consciousness and the largest manifestation of it.

kṣīṇa-vṛtteḥ-abhijātasya-iva

maṇeḥ-grahītṛ-grahaṇa-grāhyeṣu tat-stha-tad-

añjanatā samāpattiḥ || 41 ||

क्षीणवृत्तेरभिजातस्येव मणेर्ग्रहीतृग्रहणग्राह्येषु

तत्स्थतदञ्जनतासमापत्तिः ॥ ४१ ॥

When the modulations of the mind are diminished, it becomes like a polished transparent crystal and alignment (samāpattiḥ) is established between the perceiver, perception and the object of perception.

If you keep a crystal in front of you and focus a light on it, the crystal will reflect, radiate the light and it will assume the colour of the light also. In the same way, when our consciousness becomes crystal clear, it is able to perceive things with much more clarity than before. The perceiver, the perception and the object that it perceives, all the three dimensions of the one consciousness come into play. When you are moving in a car, so many cars are reflected in the side mirror. Do any of the images leave an imprint on the mirror? No! When your mind has inner stability, then nothing stays there. Your mind becomes like a mirror, like a crystal. This is *samāpattiḥ*.

Just like the crystal that remains unstained while reflecting and holding the light, the pure mind reflects the objects of perception and yet does not get stained with them.

When the mind is not that pure, the stain of all the events or the sceneries or objects on the mind becomes its karma. Suppose an image gets imprinted in a mirror, it is its karma. But if the mirror is clean and it just reflects the image, nothing gets imprinted, that is samāpattiḥ.

No doubt the object is being reflected in the mirror, but the mirror does not hold onto the object. Similarly, though the consciousness perceives everything more clearly, nothing stays on or sticks to it. That is samāpattiḥ.

It's like a child's smile. One moment the child is angry, the next moment it is smiling. But when you get upset, it probably takes several days to pull yourself out of it. When the consciousness becomes very clear and pure, you enjoy everything in the world much more than before. Every flower appears to be more beautiful, all colours appear to be brighter, and every bit of water you drink appears to be tastier. So, every move of your life is enhanced with bliss. Yet no cravings for it will ever get imprinted on the mind. That is samāpattiḥ.

tatra śabda-artha-jñāna-vikalpaiḥ saṅkīrṇā

savitarkā samāpattiḥ || 42 ||

तत्र शब्दार्थज्ञानविकल्पैः संङ्कीर्णा सवितर्का समापत्तिः ॥ ४२ ॥

That state when the gap between the word, its meaning and its experience, becomes insignificant, is called savitarkā samāpatti—alignment with a special logic.

In this state of equanimity, words, meanings, and experiences are still there. Though there is engrossment, it is *savitarkā*. It contains a logical, sequential understanding.

smṛti-pariśuddhau svarūpa-śūnya-iva-artha-mātra-

nirbhāsā nirvitarkā || 43 ||

स्मृतिपरिशुद्धौ स्वरूपशून्येवार्थमात्रनिर्भासा निर्वितर्का ॥ ४३ ॥

When the memory (latent impressions) is purified, the 'I' seems as if void and only 'am' of the 'I am' exists. That is called nirvitarkā samāpatti.

Vitarka is when you ask, "Who am I?" *Nirvitarkā* is when you are not even asking the question. When your memory of who you are, is crystal clear then your memory has deepened. You know this life is only a part of a stream of lives that we have had on this planet, "My consciousness, 'I am', has gone through various bodies but I am not this or any of these identities." That state of mind which is devoid of even thoughts and is just a presence is called *nirvitarkā* samādhi. Savitarkā means there is an understanding, a thought. *Nirvitarkā* means only the presence exists, there is no thought. Sometimes in deep meditation, you experience that you 'are' but you don't know where you are, who you are, nothing! You are not aware of anything else, just this presence 'I am' that is all. That is called *nirvitarkā* samādhi.

etayā-iva savicārā nirvicārā ca sūkṣma-viṣayā

vyākhyātā || 44 ||

एतयैव सविचारा निर्विचारा च सूक्ष्मविषया व्याख्याता ॥ ४४ ॥

When the word-meaning-experience is about subtle objects, then savicārā and nirvicārā samāpatti are similarly explained.

We've seen savitarkā and nirvitarkā but *savicārā* and *nirvicārā* are even subtler.

In savicārā samādhi there are some traces of experiences. Here, vicāra means *anubhūti,* experiences.

Nirvicārā means devoid of any experience, just the presence. At that time there is no duality. There is no knower and things to be known. That type of total merger is nirvicārā.

sūkṣma-viṣayatvam ca-aliṇga-paryavasānam || 45 ||

सूक्ष्मविषयत्वं चालिङ्गपर्यवसानम् ॥ ४५ ॥

And the realm of these subtle objects extends all the way up to the Unmanifest.

When this samādhi goes deeper, it extends till all the deeper impressions are removed and merger with the unmanifest Prakṛti happens.

Prakṛti manifests objects around us. It is the primal cause behind the subtle manifestation too. Like this gross world, there is a world of energy which is subtler than this. This is *sūkṣma-viṣayatvam*. In the subtle world of energy too all the five senses are operating. These are called *tanmātrā*—the subtle aspects of all the five gross elements.

tā eva sabījaḥ samādhiḥ || 46 ||

ता एव सबीजः समाधिः ॥ ४६ ॥

All of these (mentioned above) are samādhi with a seed.

You have experienced samādhi but when you come out of it you still have some impressions in you. This is *sabīja samādhi*. Though you have experienced samādhi, the seed has not been annihilated and still continues to exist. The impressions of lifetimes are still there in seed form.

Most of you have experienced sabīja samādhi during activity, especially in childhood. Have you noticed a child? Its eyes are not flitting here and there. They are very steady. When a child looks at things s/he stares at them and there is a depth in its eyes. This indicates steadiness and stability of the soul. The eyes are the windows to the world and for the world to see your soul; to see its steadiness.

If someone is very ambitious and greedy, their eyes will tell it all. The eyes of a person who is kind and compassionate, reflect very different qualities. Eyes reflect the senses, the behaviour and everything else. Your appearance, your walk, your behaviour, your words and your entire life reflects what you are deep inside. The job of the senses is to give you knowledge of the world. When you polish the senses and make yourself hollow and empty, you become like a crystal. The soul in you reflects the Divinity, the Lord. The senses in you reflect that soul, that Lordship in you. When you look at a flower, you are not just looking at it, you are touching it, feeling the flower and listening to it. All your senses become totally active. The being in you, your senses and the object of your senses, reflect one Divinity like the crystal.

This reflects the purushā in you. This is sabīja samādhi.

You look at a mountain and it reminds you of the Self, the consciousness. You look at a flower and the flower reminds you of consciousness. You look at the sun, moon, water, etc. and these give you an idea of the formless energy, the Self. And at that very moment, you are in samādhi. You may be looking at a sunset and you are in samādhi because the mind and the senses are steady. Steadiness is dignity, strength and dispassion. You can experience this. For a few moments, keep your body and eyes steady and you will see, almost immediately, the mind will also become steady. If you stand still, the mind will become still and the breath will become steady. This is when time stops, death stops and immortality begins. You wake up before time swallows you and before this earth gulps you. Then, you swallow time. This is samādhi. Samādhi is the state where you feel you can stay like that for a million years. It is a state where the mind freezes. Things remain fresh when you put them in a fridge. Samādhi is the refrigerator of your life. It is the secret of youthfulness, the secret of bubbling enthusiasm and the secret of renewal of life. It is steadiness.

People wrongly associate samādhi with fasting, skinny bodies, applying ash on the bodies, etc. These are incorrect perceptions.

When you are in samādhi, every experience of your senses becomes very bright, colourful and complete. When you are happy, you feel expanded. You are not aware of your body. When you are sad, you feel contracted and sorrowful. There seems to be a tightness or reduction in you.

When you feel expanded and your awareness is expanding, you tend to fall asleep. And when you want to have a keenness of awareness, you seem to be more uptight and not relaxed. It takes alertness to thread a needle. A drowsy or drunk person cannot do it. It needs keenness of awareness to do something very delicate.

There are many people who are very skillful. They can carve things on one grain of rice. They have a lot of sharpness of awareness. Yet, when there is keenness of awareness, there is no relaxation; there is no expansion of awareness. And, when the awareness is expanded, there is no keenness of awareness. The combination of both these is sabīja samādhi—when you are totally relaxed, happy and expanded and when, at the same time, you have that sharpness of awareness and intelligence. Your senses become so clear that they can see, hear and perceive better. Ninety-five percent of the population in the world does not hear properly. If you tell people something and ask them to repeat it, you can bet that they will not be able to do it. Or, if you talk to them for fifteen minutes and ask them to repeat what you said, they will never be able to repeat what you said for more than a minute at the most. The rest of what you said has just passed them by. They have not heard it.

This happens with sight too. People are not able to see things as they are. We are insensitive to people's feelings because we do not see or hear properly. Samādhi is being sensitive to other's feelings too. When you become sensitive, the world and nature become sensitive to you. Nature listens to you.

nirvicāra-vaiśāradye-adhyātma-prasādaḥ || 47 ||

निर्विचारवैशारद्येऽध्यात्मप्रसादः ॥ ४७ ॥

Of these, when one attains proficiency in nirvicāra samādhi, that brings spiritual fulfillment.

When the mind is free from the thought constraints, then it attains the grace or the blessings of spirituality.

Ādhyātma-prasādaḥ means self-illumination happens to you. Whenever you hear spiritual discourses your mind becomes free. It becomes illumined, quiet and pleasant. This is ādhyātma-prasādaḥ. The more we practise deep meditation, the less thoughts chatter. What happens then? The energy, the light dawns in you.

ṛtambharā tatra prajñā || 48 ||

ऋतंभरा तत्र प्रज्ञा ॥ ४८ ॥

In such a state, the consciousness is filled with awareness of truth (intuition).

Ṛtambharā tatra prajñā is that awareness which has the depth of truth, depth of wisdom. It is intuitive knowledge. *Satya* means truth, *ṛtam* means the deeper truth, the subtle truth which is connected to the causal existence. Like the gross and subtle existence, there is a causal existence. That consciousness which is connected with the causal existence, that wisdom, that awareness, is called ṛitam. This consciousness will be filled with that ṛtam, so mistakes don't happen through it.

śruta-anumāna-prajñābhyām anya-viṣayā

viśeṣa-arthatvāt || 49 ||

श्रुतानुमानप्रज्ञाभ्याम् अन्यविषया विशेषार्थत्वात् ॥४९ ॥

The awareness (or knowledge) that comes from such a state is special compared to knowledge arising from the senses or the intellect because it is based on a different source (spiritual fulfillment).

This is what happens in our Intuition Process. The children close their eyes and it is *ṛtambharā prajñā*. From that inner state of consciousness, they predict, they tell the truth, they write things which they have never heard of or seen. A child from India writes Chinese. A child in China writes Samskṛta. How is this possible? This is possible by getting into the deeper core of our being. This is ṛtambharā which is full of intuitive wisdom and it can never be wrong.

tajjaḥ samskāraḥ-anya-samskāra-pratibandhī || 50 ||

तज्जः संस्कारोऽन्यसंस्कारप्रतिबन्धी ॥ ५० ॥

The impressions born of such samādhi overrule the impressions generated from other experiences.

This is quite obvious in our life. A greater joy always sublimes the smaller joy. The taste of ecstasy in meditation can take you out of all types of addictions. Ādhyātma-prasādaḥ, the blessings of the spiritual energy can lift us above all the other impressions that we are struggling with or are bound by.

tajjaḥ-samskāraḥ-anya-samskāra-pratibandhī

It can override all other impressions.

The impression of that state of consciousness can wipe out all other impressions in the mind which are useless and not necessary for life. Something of the past is erased in your first meditation. You begin to feel that you are a new person. The deeper you go, the more hollow and empty you become. You feel that you are a different person.

What exactly has happened that makes you feel different? The old samskāras and impressions have been erased from your mind. It has made you new. It renews you again, and again, and again, and again.

Often, when you reflect on events of the past, you feel that you are not the same person you were then. You even feel that it was not you at all; as though you are not at all connected to those events. This is because this samskāra of your consciousness has been erasing those things of your past continuously and has been making you a new person every day. This is the grace of pure knowledge. If someone holds you to something you did in the past, you should laugh at them. This is because you are not the same person now. You should see it as if somebody else had done it.

Once Buddha was in an assembly and a gentleman came to him. He was furious. He thought that Buddha was doing something wrong; he was attracting people and making everybody meditate. The people had become very calm and quiet. The gentleman was a restless businessman. He had found that his children were sitting with Buddha and meditating for two hours every day. And he thought that if his children would engage in business, they could make more money and be better off. What would they get by sitting for two hours with somebody with their eyes closed? So he was angry and wanted to teach Buddha a lesson. He walked up to Buddha but as soon as he came near Him all his thoughts disappeared. But he was still shaking with anger and could not speak. No words would come out of his mouth. So he spat on Buddha's face. And Buddha just smiled. However, all the other disciples there became furious but could not react because Buddha was there. So, everybody restrained themselves. The man could not stay any longer because he thought that if he stayed any longer, he would burst out. He went away. He could not sleep the whole night. For the first time in his life, he had met somebody who could smile even when he was spat on. He began shivering. His world had turned topsy-turvy. The next day he went to Buddha and fell at his feet. He asked for forgiveness and said that he was not aware of what he had done. However, Buddha said that he could not forgive him. The disciples were shocked to hear this. Buddha was so compassionate and forgave everybody. How could he not forgive that person! But Buddha explained that the person had done nothing for which forgiveness was required. However, the businessman pointed out that he was the same person who had spat on him the previous day. Then, Buddha said, "The person you spat on is not here now. If I ever meet him, I'll tell him to excuse you." Buddha pointed out that the businessman had done no wrong.

This is compassion. Compassion is not making a person feel like a culprit and then forgiving him. Your forgiveness should be such that the person, who is being forgiven, does not even know that you are forgiving them. They should not feel guilty of a mistake. That is the right type of forgiveness. If you make someone feel guilty about their mistake, then you have not forgiven them. That guilt itself is the punishment. Knowledge takes you away from guilt and puts you on a pedestal where you do not see the world of the small mind and its useless chattering. It appears insignificant.

tasya-api nirodhe sarva-nirodhāt-

nirbījaḥ samādhiḥ || 51 ||

तस्यापि निरोधे सर्वनिरोधान्निर्बीजः समाधिः ॥ ५१ ॥

When even such impressions (born of samādhi) are eliminated, then, everything having been restrained, seedless samādhi results.

One is gross intuition, the other is subtle intuition, an intuition about something higher. When even this is not encouraged and you move on to another state, that is called *nirbīja samādhi*—where there is nothing but total union with the existence, with the Divinity.

The *Samādhi Pāda* is all about the different types of samādhi. The final samādhi is *nirvikalpa samādhi* or nirbīja samādhi, wherein you are not communicable with the universe at all. That's why usually when any saint leaves the body, people say he has attained samādhi.

Nirvikalpa samādhi totally cuts you off from all of existence. You can experience it for a short time and then you have to come back from there. It cannot be held for too long. But before that there are many stages and these are all good enough.

Nirbīja samādhi can be experienced only through grace and not through effort. It is possible to be in that state of samādhi for a short period of time, but then you have to come back from that state to live in the body. The body cannot sustain nirbīja samādhi for more than three years, after that the body will start decaying. That is the end of life.

There are many different states of awareness and types of samādhi described. The path is long. Every step is complete in itself. It is not that you are aiming for a goal after some time.

The goal is in every moment. Yet the path is long. The goal is where you are. You should not be in a hurry and want samādhi immediately. There should be enthusiasm and along with it patience. Those who are very enthusiastic have no patience. People who have patience are lethargic. There is either one extreme or the other. You can sleep but you cannot have a quick sleep; a hurried sleep is not possible. You cannot feel that since you are in a hurry, you should sleep quickly, get up and leave.

In the same way, you cannot remember something in a hurry. This hurry delays it all the more. It is the same with meditation.

If you do not have the time, you cannot have a quick meditation. So this path is a middle path, a golden path, wherein you are enthusiastic, at the same time, you are patient. You are patient and, at the same time, you are not lethargic. You are not postponing things. Often, if people have to do something good, something for their personal development, they will feel that if God is willing, they will do it and it will happen. They leave it to God when it comes to their practices and their development. But if they have to build a house or have a relationship they don't leave it to God. They will put in their 100% for that. So, patience and dynamism is the golden rule.

The first chapter is a little technical. If it goes a little over your head, never mind! Read it several times. It is also quite difficult to convey and it is not right to reduce it to a very low level because then it doesn't do justice to this knowledge. It has to go with the experience of it.

This much you can keep in mind—the nine obstacles, and the four subordinates that come with them. How to get over them? *Ek tattva abhyāsa*. Then Patañjali has given many ways. *Yathābhimata dhyānādvā*—if you're looking at the moon and looking at the moon is taking you into deep meditation, go ahead with that. If you are listening to a flute, and while listening to it you dissolve, go for it! You don't have to sit and chant at that time. He says that the strong pull of any one of these experiences can also lead you into meditation. These are the ways he is bringing you to what he wants you to know.

Questions and Answers

Question: Of the five modulations, one is sleep (nidrā), which means that everything that we do in the waking state falls under pramāṇa, viparyaya, vikalpa and smṛti. However, when somebody is just driving or going about their work, during that activity, they are not wanting proof, they are not imagining and not remembering anything either. I am not sure if this state can be called wrong understanding. Does it mean they are in the seer?

Gurudev: Without pramāṇa, how can they drive? Driving is pratyakṣa, you are experiencing it. Pratyakṣa means that which is obvious in your experience. There is pramāṇa in whatever action you do.

Anumāna—you guess that this is the way you have to go, and you keep driving. If you know that the road is ending at a cliff; would you drive at full speed there? No! Since you know that there isn't any cliff, you continue to drive. The road will not end, to that extent you have pramāṇa. Suppose you drive at the speed of hundred kilometres per hour and that road suddenly ends and you don't know it, what would happen? If you know the road is going to end, would you drive at the speed of hundred kilometers per hour? No, you wouldn't! You would reduce the speed to twenty kilometres per hour and then apply the brakes. There is pramāṇa in whatever action you do.

In any action you do there is viparyaya—wrong understanding.

In any action you do there is vikalpa—you think it is so and it is really not like that. You think somebody is a thief and that person is really not a thief. This is all vikalpa.

Nidrā is not only when you go into deep sleep. Nidrā is also when you are in an inert state. There is inertia and you don't even know what is happening around you. That is what Lord Kṛṣṇa says in Bhagavad Gītā, "A *yogī* is one who is awake when everybody else is asleep, and he sleeps when everybody else is awake." When everyone is nervous, a yogī is asleep. He takes it very easy. And when everyone is asleep, meaning they are not bothered and in a state of inertia, at that time a yogī is very alert. It is not the physical day and night he is talking about, yogīs are not nocturnal. It's just a simile.

Question: On the one hand Patañjali says if you put intense effort for samādhi it comes quickly. On the other hand he says you can also get it by surrendering to God. Could you please elaborate?

Gurudev: Truth is multidimensional. It is confusing and it is opposites put together. You are correct, he has said that. You have to put in your effort. One who puts 100% effort, gets it faster. One who puts in only 70% effort takes a while and one who puts in only 30% effort will also get a little bit. On the other hand, when there is intense devotion, when devotion is 100% then it is easily achieved.

Question: If samādhi is a very personal and subjective experience, unlike any other, how does one know that what they have experienced is samādhi?

Gurudev: Maharṣi Patañjali has described different types of samādhi. Being alert and keeping your awareness sharp needs some effort. But love and devotion do not need any effort. You cannot make an effort to love somebody or something. It is simply there. You can only remove the ignorance, doubts, frustration and selfishness that hides the love. When selfishness is removed then you find that love is already there. So, *layā samādhi* is achievable. Samādhi with devotion is very easy. If your chattering mind does not put up an obstruction, just by listening to music you can easily get into a thoughtless state. So, both are possible. If your head is strong it takes more effort. If your heart is strong, it is no effort.

Question: How do I continue with my normal job and life along with not being in any of the vṛttis?

Gurudev: Why should you not be (in any of the vṛttis)? Maharṣi Patañjali does not say vṛttis should be thrown out. He says they should be controlled. While driving at night, if you do not have control over your sleep, what will happen? Disaster! Right? So, you control your sleep. Suppose someone cannot control sleep at all, what will happen to him? He will go to the grave sooner than expected, correct?

Similarly with smṛti—if you don't forget and forgive, and hold onto people and situations, what will happen to you? You will land up in a mental hospital before going to the grave. You can be stuck in your memories and this can make your life totally miserable.

If you are stuck in vikalpā, you imagine that others are after you, to get you out of whatever position you enjoy, you are going to go crazy. If you do not have control over your fantasies and fanciful imagination, if you do not let go of it again and again, you will be mentally deranged. Isn't it?

This is the science of consciousness, the science of the mind. Maharshi Patañjali is telling you to stand by proof but that also keeps changing. Science is changing all the time.

A couple of years back some doctors said that cholesterol-lowering drugs are useless; you should not take them. Millions of people around the world have been consuming these to control their cholesterol. Today, scientists say dietary cholesterol has nothing to do with your heart and such drugs are more harmful than of use. This is another proof. One proof was given earlier that cholesterol-lowering drugs are essential.

One proof was given that butter is bad, now another proof, another pramāṇa, tells you that butter, not margarine, is good for you. So, what do you say? These are proofs. If you are holding onto a pramāṇa, you will be doomed. You have to control this pramāṇa vṛtti.

You say, I have proof of somebody's wrong doing and you hold onto it forever. You will get another proof to say that there was no wrongdoing at all. This is how cases are fought in the court. Isn't it? One pramāṇa is cut by another pramāṇa. One proof is negated by another proof. These things happen in life.

Viparyaya—wrong understanding. When do you know you have a wrong understanding? Only when you have come out of it. Only the right understanding can make you understand that you had a wrong understanding.

People who are in viparyaya think this is right, this is how things are. But only when they get the real understanding through pramāṇa, do they understand, it was viparyaya!

It is the same with vikalpa. When you are drowned in vikalpā, you don't even know it is vikalpa. Only when you come out of vikalpā do you realise it was a vikalpa.

Similarly, when you wake up from sleep you realise you were sleeping. Only when memories flood your mind, do you feel, "Oh! I remember this."

So Patañjali is not saying these are to be done away with. They exist, just be aware of them and have control over them.

Question: Patañjali asks to cultivate indifference towards people who are negative. What if they are your own relatives or close ones?

Gurudev: You need to be indifferent only to your own relatives or close ones. Those who are not close to you, you are anyway indifferent to them! Whether they are good or bad you are indifferent to them. But with people who are close to you, be indifferent in your mind. Indifference does not mean inaction. He does not say do not act at all. Have an attitude of indifference so that you do not get bogged down by them, your mind does not start boiling with anger and rage. When you get into a state of rage, your communication takes a big beating; it becomes zero. If you are reeling with rage with the person who is close to you then your communication is finished. When your communication is finished, everything is finished. So, indifference should be shown when they do wrong things. Indifference should be in the attitude. Maharṣi Patañjali does not say, do not talk to them and do not make them understand. He does not say those things. Nowhere does he say, be inactive towards wrongdoings. He says indifference in the attitude only.

Question: Gurudev, there are so many types of samādhi. What is the right type of samādhi to do right now, in your presence?

Gurudev: Just listening itself is samādhi. If you are here, 100% and listening, that listening itself is samādhi. Then waiting itself is samādhi. Got it?

Question: Patañjali mentions the knowledge of sleep and dreams. How does one get this knowledge?

Gurudev: Knowledge of sleep and dreams comes by practice. First you need to continue your practice. Practise meditation every day, practise dispassion every day. Practising dispassion means reminding yourself of the impermanent nature of the universe again and again. Remind yourself of the impermanence or the transient nature of everything around you. That is good enough. This leads you to that state.

This is not the end of it. Maharshi Patañjali has given the goal in the Samādhi Pāda. You know, he goes with the highest first. He gives you the highest. If you have taken the second sūtra itself, you don't need any more sūtras.

alpaksharam asandigdham sārawat vishwatomukham

Sūtra means that which is very short, said in a very few words and that which is timely. It is like a formula, which is concise, definite and irrefutable.

Asandigdham means without doubt, that which is for sure.

Sārawat viswatomukham—it is the essence, it is universal in nature and is multidimensional.

The second sūtra itself says, *yogaś-citta-vṛtti-nirodhaḥ.*

You control all these vṛttis. If you control, then what will happen?

Tadā drasṭuḥ svarūpe-'vasthānam—you will be established in the seat of the seer. At other times, you become the vṛttis—*vṛtti sārūpyam-itaratra.*

Otherwise you are not different from vṛttis, you become the vṛttis. Here in the first chapter, first quarter, first pādā, he has enunciated what samādhi is.

Next he will explain the *Sādhanā Pāda*, how to achieve samādhi, what are the means to achieve it. The goal is given to you first and then the means.

Question: Gurudev, the yoga sūtras describe different kinds of samādhi. When one becomes an expert in samādhi, can one choose the kind of samādhi to get into like, "Today I want to experience the samādhi of bliss, today samādhi without thoughts," and so forth or does one have no control over what kind of samādhi will happen?

Gurudev: Yes and no both. You can choose to go into *bhāva samādhi* when there is music. You listen to music, your emotions rise high and then you go beyond the emotion—that's *bhāvatīt*. Going beyond the emotions and just dissolving in that ecstasy.

You can just sit and have total dispassion about everything and still be centred. You can get into that *samādhi—sākshi samādhi* where you are a witness to everything.

When flute music or a stringed instrument is being played and you just dissolve in it, that is *laya samādhi*.

With devotional ecstasy, there is *bhāva samādhi* and with intellectual analysis—knowing this is all a dream—there is *prajñā samādhi*. It takes just a few seconds to realise that this is all just a dream; nothing really exists.

So there are many different types of samādhi. Sometimes it just happens to you. When someone dies immediately you find a vacuum, that brings you so much of dispassion, "Hey, it's all going to finish!" That thought, that memory, that smṛti, remembrance itself can lead you to that type of samādhi.

Not giving up in spite of a thousand attempts to destroy your faith and holding on to that intensity of faith will also lead you to another different kind of samādhi.

Total faith, 100% faith will bring such integrity in your personality. When your faith is not conditioned to the happening around you, then it is real faith.

You wish for something, "Oh I want to get a car, I want to get a job, this particular job." Suppose this does not happen and your faith disappears then that faith is weak. But if it gets deconditioned to whatever that is happening around you, then that is the real faith, that faith is strong.

Suppose you are friendly with someone because they give you compliments but if you can maintain your friendliness even if they were to insult you, then you are their true friend. You just don't bother! It's just like the faith of the mother and the child, and the child and the mother. I keep giving this example again and again. This is very close to one's individual being with the universal Being. That is what it is between the Guru and the disciple. The mother gets angry and slaps the child but the mother does not have any ill feelings for the child at all, does she? No, impossible! Similarly, a child may get thoroughly scolded by its mother but that does not go deep in its heart. It just goes a little bit in the head. You get upset for a little while but then the connection between you and the mother is never lost because she is upset or angry at you or shouting at you.

It happens with the mother-in-law for sure. She may say one-tenth of what the mother would say, and that is enough to destroy your connection or friendliness. But with mother whatever she may be blabbering, it does not really affect you; your connection and understanding are beyond the behaviour. Similarly, a child's behaviour is not what affects a mother's attitude towards the child. It is deconditioned from the outer happenings.

The child may be doing all things wrong yet the mother feels for her. She prays to God, comes to Gurudev, "Let my daughter be on the right path." She is pained by that, she scolds the daughter but their connection just does not disappear. It is the same way with the faith in the teacher, in the Master too. You may find a thousand opportunities to have your faith shaken and if you still hold on, then you reach a higher level. I have heard about a saint who was living on top of a hill and at the bottom of the hill was another saint who would always say venomous things about him. Mostly everybody who would hear the scandalous stories would go away and not visit the saint on the top of the hill. But then one guy said, "No, let me go there and see," and he went up to the Guru on the hill and told him, "Look, that man down the hill is blaming you all the time. He is saying bad things about you." That man smiled and said, "I only kept him there. He is my disciple, so that I can filter out all those with weak faiths and not have to deal with them. I want to have my peace of mind, so I have that guy to filter them all out." The stronger the faith, the deeper the samādhi.

śraddhā-vīrya-smṛti-samādhi-prajñā-pūrvaka itareṣām

Similarly, the soldiers who are working to protect the country, the nation have that valour. It can also help you. One with valour has no tension and anxiety. If you have valour, there is no tension, anxiety, doubt and no weaknesses. People with valour have no doubts. Doubts are only with the weak. One who has valour, has confidence and faith as well. So they move with valour. Hunger, thirst, sleep or no sleep, nothing matters! You hear how Shivaji Maharaj was fighting against the Mughals; how Maharana Pratap was fighting or how Akbar was fighting. You hear many stories of valour, they are very inspiring. When Guru Gobind Singh Maharaj was having so many wounds in the body, he sang,

हाल मुरीदां दा कहना, मित्तर प्यारे नूं

Tell my Lord the state of me, my heart is still full. There is valour in me.

His body was all wounded and he composed a heart-melting song. So valour and devotion lead you to samādhi and samādhi is bliss, is the true joy, the true bliss and it is the source of all energy. Mental, physical, spiritual, and intellectual energy is embedded in samādhi.

Question: Gurudev, *asamprajñāta samādhi*, the samādhi without any awareness and nidrā vritti both seem to be devoid of thoughts. What is the difference between them?

Gurudev: In nidrā, there is inertia, in samādhi there is liveliness, that's it.

Question: Kindly elaborate *ekatatva abhyāsa*. Is it about chanting or focusing on 'Om' or chanting the Guru's name and thinking of the Guru all the time?

Gurudev: Abhyāsa can only be for a limited period of time. If you are practising archery, cooking, swimming or playing sitar, it is time bound. If you practise 24 hours you will go crazy. Similarly, chanting is also a practice but it is time bound. Many people try to chant for 24 hours every day! It's OK to do so once in a while to break the natural cycle of hunger, sleep, thirst and the like.

Question: Gurudev, the yoga sūtras describe different states of samādhi and *Vijnāna Bhairava* describes different techniques to get into that state. Is there a connection between the kind of technique you use and the kind of samādhi that results? For example, do ānvopāyas lead to a different kind of samādhi, and shāktopāyas a different kind?

Gurudev: Different *upāyas* or methodologies are there but the substance is the same. The end is the same and that is You, your Being, your Self. Sometimes when you do yoga, you use props to get to some position. Similarly, ānvopāya is using various methodologies, taking help of other aids. It has some effort in it, shāktopāya has very little effort and shāmbhavopāya means effortless. It simply happens and only recognition is there, you simply recognize. You are looking for your spectacles and suddenly someone says, "Hey, it's on your head!" The memory of knowledge and the result are almost simultaneous. As you are looking for your shawl and someone says, "Hey, it's on your shoulders!" And you say, "Oh, Yeah!" The memory, remembrance of the shawl and obtaining it has no time difference at all. This is called shāmbhavopāya. It means the highest form of awareness. You just become aware, you may be sitting in Bangalore thinking you are in Calcutta when someone says, "Hey, you are in Bangalore!" The very awareness that you are in Bangalore, means you are already in Bangalore. So there is no time gap between the knowledge and its achievement. This is shāmbhavopāya. It's very subtle.

Question: Gurudev when Patañjali says *nairantaryam* (without a break) how often would be considered without a break? Can I do a practice daily or weekly or monthly?

Gurudev: Nairantaryam means daily, to be done every day. That's why it's called *nitya*. *Naimitika* means once every week, month or quarter. Nitya means every day; doing it every day. *Japa* and meditations are to be done every day. Once in a while if you cannot do it on a particular day, nevermind, don't feel guilty about it. Suppose one day you could not do it as you had to hurry up to do some work or you had to go for some funeral or somebody has died or some unavoidable circumstances come up. There is no compulsion for you to do your practices on that day. I remember once, long ago, I was with two German devotees, who were ardent yoga followers. We were travelling from Joshimath to Rishikesh and in the meanwhile the sunset happened. It was time for their practice, so they told the driver to stop the car there. They came out with their yoga mat and started practising yoga and doing meditation by the roadside. The roads were very narrow, it's not a very big wide road, so we found a little curve and stopped the car. Many trucks and cars started honking because our car was standing right there. The driver didn't know English and he was yelling, "You know it's dark, any bear can come here, some lion may come or some cheetah may come, this is a forest area, there will be snakes. These people don't understand, the responsibility is mine." He was shouting and they were happily sitting, doing their prāṇāyāma and meditation. I had a lot of fun between these two. I am talking about the late 70s, 1978 or 1979. So you don't need to do that! I know of a person who would have to do *agnihotra* every day, so he would take the agnihotra supplies in the train also. He started doing agnihotra in the train. There were passengers sitting all around! If they don't mind the fire or smoke it's OK but you don't need to do such things you know! You can meditate inside the train. Even if you want to do a little bit of asanas, and you have your own berth you can do it, nevermind! But if you think that if you do not do it that's the end of the world that is not correct. I remember one lady bought a ticket next to my secretary in the plane because she does not get to see me when I go to her city. She brought the whole aarti thaali. In the plane! I wonder how she came up with all that! She said, "I don't get to do this for you and this is the dream of my life." I had to speak very sternly to her, I do not remember having said anything so sternly but she came with such delicate feelings one couldn't even scold her! I told her, "Look, I promise you when we get down from the plane I will come to the place, wherever and, you can do all, whatever you want aarti and everything. Do not light the camphor here in the plane!" She had the thaali with all the *kumkum* in it and she wanted me to put my feet in that thing! She said, "No one allows me, no one lets me come near so I have to do this." When we got down in Hyderabad from Bhubaneswar, I told my secretary, "Get this lady first, we will fulfil her desire for what she wants to do." So you don't need to do like that and cause trouble for yourself and others. That is not what the practice is all about.

Question: Gurudev, Maharṣi says that practice is the effort to be established in the Self. Is the practice of mindfulness based on the yoga sūtras ?

Gurudev: Yes, mindfulness is just another new name for being more alert and aware. That's all! In the West, people considered meditation to be a taboo. They thought meditation is something different. So they invented 'mindfulness', being more alert and awake, which is a by-product of meditation. I usually say that mindfulness is just the driveway not the home, but nevermind you come to the driveway, that is necessary. However, you can't sit in the driveway; then you will be a fool. You have to get out of the driveway and get into the home. Meditation is the house, is your home and meditating is coming back home. Mindfulness is coming to the driveway, meditation is coming home—homecoming.

Now we will move to the second pāda—the *Sādhanā Pāda*. Samādhi is the end, the result has been enunciated in the Samādhi Pāda. How do you get there? What is the path? What is the way? That is called the Sādhanā Pāda, the path of practice.

Sādhanā Pāda

Kriyā Yoga

When someone is anxious, they are very aware of the passage of time, of every moment. However, when the total focus is on an event or happening, the focus is on that particular event or happening rather than just on time. Someone may be waiting for a train, a bus or a boat. While waiting they go on thinking if it will come or not. The focus is on the concerned object rather than just on time.

But if there is a little shift from waiting for somebody or something, to waiting—Now—this is uniting with time. This is yoga. When you do this, your mind is in the moment and waiting for nothing. However, you are still waiting. This adds a different quality to the consciousness. It sharpens the intellect and softens the heart. This is called the yoga of action or *kriyā yoga*.

tapaḥ svādhyāya-īśvara-praṇidhānāni

kriyā-yogaḥ || 1 ||

तपः स्वाध्यायेश्वरप्रणिधानानि क्रियायोगः ॥ १ ॥

Endurance, self-study and surrender to the Divine constitutes the yoga of action.

samādhi-bhāvana-arthaḥ kleśa-tanū-

karaṇārthaḥ-ca || 2 ||

समाधिभावनार्थः क्लेशतनूकरणार्थश्च ॥ २ ॥

(The purpose of Kriyā Yoga) to bring about samādhi and to minimize the afflictions or miseries.

tapaḥ svādhyāy-īśvarapraṇidhānāni kriyā-yogaḥ

What is *tapaḥ*?

Tapo vai dwanda sahanam—forbearing the opposites is called tapaḥ. Life is full of opposites and to the extent you can bear them indicates your strength. Tapas—penance—brings you strength.

There are three types of tapas—the tapas of the body, the tapas of speech and the tapas of the mind. They are all very closely linked because the body-mind complex is such that one reflects the other. Whatever is in the body is reflected in the mind and whatever is in the mind reflects in the body as well. So tapas is very important in one's life. This is called *kriyā yoga*.

What is kriyā yoga?

Kriyā yoga is the yoga of action. Action is a part of this creation. There is activity in everything in creation—from an atom to the sun, moon and the stars. The entire creation is activity. There is nothing that is immobile in this creation.

The Brahman, the Infinity, is filled with infinite activity. There is absolutely no silence at all. There is activity even in sleep. You may think that when you are asleep, there is no activity but there is tremendous activity then. Your body grows more during sleep than during wakefulness.

That is why a growing child sleeps longer. Every cell is multiplying and in sleep the cells multiply faster. A youth sleeps more than an aged person because there is a lot of metabolic activity in the young. If you deprive somebody of sleep, their growth gets stunted.

Even in silence, there is activity. At the same time, in every activity there is a corner that is very silent. Kṛṣṇa asked Arjuna if he knew who was really intelligent. When he replied that he did not, Kṛṣṇa said that a person who sees silence in activity and activity in silence is really intelligent. How do you see silence in activity and activity in silence? It needs sharpness of awareness, alertness and keenness. And you can have all this when there is skill in your activity. Yoga is the skill in activity.

The first component of kriyā yoga is tapas—forbearance or endurance and acceptance. No achievement is possible if there is no tapas in one's life. You bear what appears to be unpleasant because you know something better is going to come out of it—taking a long flight, driving long distances, fasting, etc. This is tapas. So the tapas of the body, is bearing the heat and cold. That makes your body strong—*Kāyendriyasiddhi*. Kāyendriya siddhi means your body becomes strong.

Nobody wants to lift dumbbells and exercise if it is not going to benefit them. You know it is going to benefit you, that is why you get onto the treadmill, exercise, and sweat it out. You don't look very relaxed and happy when you're exercising but still you do it. That is tapas. Willingly taking on something, against which your mind rebels is tapas. Your mind is rebelling but you are bearing it because you know something good is going to come out of it. This is tapas.

What happens when you do tapas?

Kāyendriyasiddhi—the body becomes very strong.

nāymātmā balahinena labhyo

नायमात्मा बलहीनेन लभ्यो

(Mundakopnishad 3.2.4)

A weak person cannot achieve self knowledge, self realization.

Nātapaskāya[1]—if we don't do tapas, then too self realization will not happen. So tapas is very important and to some extent, everybody has to do tapas in their life. Whether consciously or unconsciously, willingly or unwillingly, tapas falls on you. You have to bear it. You sit in a bus for a long journey, you cannot walk around in the bus, your legs hurt, your back is in pain. Still you sit in the bus, this is tapas. You cannot be in the air conditioning all the time in tropical countries. You have to bear the heat too. Whether heat or cold, pleasant or unpleasant, taking them all on the same platter is tapas. Tapas is willingly doing something that is not very easy. It makes your body, mind and Being strong. The Being is anyways strong, it just makes you realise that!

---

1. idam te nātapaskāya nābhaktāya kadācana na cāśuśrūṣave vācyam na ca māṃ yo 'bhyasūyati (Bhagavad Gītā 18.67)

Three Types of Tapas

There are three types of tapas—of the body, of words or speech and of the mind (*kāyā*, *vacana, mana*).

What is bodily tapas? Keeping physical hygiene, keeping lethargy away, having a say over the senses. If you do not want to watch television, you do not. If you do not want to eat, you just don't eat even if the food served is delicious. Keeping personal hygiene, abstinence, and having control over the senses is called physical tapas.

anudvega-karam vākyam satyam priya-hitam cha yat

svādhyāyābhyasanam caiva vāṅ-mayam tapa uchyate

(Bhagavad Gītā 17.15)

अनुद्वेगकरं वाक्यं सत्यं प्रियहितं च यत्।

स्वाध्यायाभ्यसनं चैव वाङ्मयं तप उच्यते ॥ १७·१५ ॥

Tapas of speech is saying only such things that do not distress people, speaking the truth and speaking the pleasant truth.

Make a note of what you tell people when you are with them; what do you talk about? Do you excite them and do they leave you feeling relieved and at peace or do they leave you feeling angry, jealous, greedy, frustrated or depressed? Often, you are a better person when you are silent. You are more charming and likeable. However, you may have no control over what you say and words just come shooting out of your mouth. You may not even think about their effects. They could be as sharp as daggers or as soft as flowers.

Vāṅmaya tapas—words that do not ruffle feathers. It is different if you want to intentionally disturb another person. Often, what you say creates a disturbance in others' minds but it is unintentional. Those who speak harshly feel that they are telling the truth. They feel that there is no need to skirt the truth. However, what is said can be a pleasant expression of truth. An example often given in Saṃskṛta is that if you meet someone who is blind, you can address him as so. Granted, it is the truth but doing this can greatly hurt the person. Instead you can address him as *prajñācakṣu*—meaning one whose third eye, the eye of intuition has been awakened.

Vāṅmaya tapas is important because as you grow on this path of yoga—your words become more and more powerful. You may call someone a fool and, even if he is not a fool, he will become one. So your words will have the power to bless as well as curse. Vāṅmaya tapas purifies you. Otherwise those things rebound. If you speak harshly, your words will affect you adversely. This does not mean that you should always be goody-goody. That is also self-deception. You do not have to be a hypocrite—nice and cordial outside and just the opposite inside. Then again, you do not need to harshly speak the truth.

This is vāṅmaya tapas.

Manomaya tapas—tapas of the mind.

manaḥ prasādaḥ saumyatvam maunam-

ātma-vinigrahaḥ

bhāva-samśuddhir-iti-etat-tapo mānasam-uchyate

(Bhagavad Gītā 17.16)

मनः प्रसादः सौम्यत्वं मौनमात्मविनिग्रहः ।

भावसंशुद्धिरित्येतत्तपो मानसमुच्यते ॥ १७·१६ ॥

The Bhagavad Gītā says four things

Manaḥ-prasādaḥ—the pleasantness in the mind. It is a big tapas to maintain the pleasantness of the mind. You may feel pleasant but it vanishes in no time.

Saumyatvam—*saumya* means calm and composed. You can feel pleasant, but excited. That is not saumya. Some people feel very pleasant but they do not feel calm. The pleasantness can make them feel very crazy and excited. So, along with pleasantness it is essential to be composed—saumyatvam.

People who are happy create trouble for others. This is because they are not aware that in their excitement and happiness, they say and do things that may adversely affect others. But if a person is calm and composed, he is more aware. There is awareness in a composed mind. You are sensitive to others' feelings and to your surroundings. So, what is required is a pleasant and composed mind.

Manaḥ-prasādaḥ saumyatvam

Maunam—is a silent mind; not a chattering mind. Silence is the tapas of the mind. Maunam is the silence obtained by bringing together the scattered mind and tying all the loose ends.

Ātma-vinigrahaḥ—remaining in the Self; getting back to the Self. This is the tapas of the mind. The mind loses its way again and again. It needs to be brought back to the Self and see the Self in everybody. Feel this person is also you, that person and everybody else is also you.

Normally, we think our mind is in the body but it is not so. The body is inside the mind. Your body of prāṇa, bio-energy is ten times bigger than your physical body. Ten times bigger than the pranic body is your mind-body, your thought-body. Ten times bigger than that is your intuitive-body. And ten times bigger than that is the blissful-body. Our blissful-body is boundless. That is why when you feel blissful and happy you do not feel any boundary. You feel expanded and do not feel any limit. And when you feel sad or unhappy, you feel crushed because your prāṇa has become smaller than your real body. This is the mechanism of unhappiness. It is like trying to put your body through a small hole where it cannot fit. This is the reason why you feel so unhappy. When you try to crush your prāṇa, which is so big, into a small space, you feel unhappy. Whenever you are unhappy in life, know that you have put your love into a small channel. Your love is so great, so big. It needs a royal door to walk through. But you have stuck that big body of love, into a small chimney, or ventilator. It can neither go out nor come in. This is entanglement. That is why that love seems to bring problems to you. You do not understand its magnitude. This is tapas, manomaya tapas.

Ātma-vinigrahaḥ—coming back to the Self, holding on to the centeredness in you.

Fire sustains life and there are five types of fire—*pañcāgni.*

Going through these fires is also tapas.

Bhutāgni—it is the fire which heats your homes and keeps you warm. This physical fire sustains life. It may not be so obvious in tropical countries where it is already warm. Not much importance is accorded to fire here. But it is very important in cold countries. Without physical fire, life cannot survive. This physical fire is present in the body, to some extent.

Kāmāgni—it is the fire of desire, lust or passion. This fire engulfs you. Life continues on this planet because of this fire. The fire of passion is present in all the species in creation.

People who are promiscuous have no kāmāgni. This is because they do not even allow the fire of passion to come up and burn and bake them a little bit. The moment there is a desire for sex, they fulfil it. Then the kāmāgni does not get awakened in them. The desire to eat and have sex are the oldest samskāras. In all your lifetimes, you have certainly done two things—eaten and had sex. These two acts have been done by you even as a cow, a monkey, a donkey, a horse or an ox.

When this passion arises, observe it. It is in every cell of your body. It engulfs you totally. It burns and moves on. There is one hundred percent totality of alertness and awareness. But if you do not allow it to come up then a little desire arises which immediately cools down. Then, your power or *śakti*, the potentiality in you goes down and becomes dormant. You become more inert and less sensitive. There is no vigour, valour, joy, or enthusiasm in anything that you do. This is the reason why people who are promiscuous do not have much enthusiasm. They do not have the force, will or strength to do anything.

Jaṭharāgni—it is the fire of hunger and digestion. This is one of the important principles in āyurveda. If the fire of digestion is less or more, it affects your health and your balance.

When there is fever, we just treat the symptoms. We do not understand the principles involved. Your body, operating its defence mechanism, turns up the heat and burns up all the foreign bacteria and viruses that have entered it. As soon as they are destroyed, the fever comes down. Jaṭharāgni purifies the system by getting rid of the foreign matter.

You keep stuffing yourself with food even before you are hungry. This affects your body and makes it toxic. Overeating is the underlying cause of many diseases in the world. Nowadays, very few people die of hunger, more and more people die of overeating because they have not let the fire of hunger come up. We have never kindled that fire. This is the principle of fasting. When you fast, every cell of your body becomes alive. It is a very good therapy to cleanse your system. The jaṭharāgni can cleanse you of all toxins. When your head is clogged with worry, tension and unpleasant thoughts or nightmares, fasting is of great help.

Much research has been done on fasting. Fasting and prayers are linked in Christianity, Jainism, Islam, and in almost all the religions of the world. This is because fasting touches the deepest samskāra, or impression present in us since many lifetimes—to eat, eat, and just eat.

There are some people who just go on fasting without being aware of the connected factors; too much fire can also burn you down. Fasting should be done but with awareness. There are people who go to extremes. Either they overeat or fast too much. Neither is good. Moderate fasting under proper guidance can cleanse your system and bring balance.

Premāgni or jñānāgni—it is the fire of love. Love can create such a fire in you. The fire of love can really lift you up from the fear of criticism. The fire of love is so strong that you do not mind people's opinions. It consumes you totally. The fire of knowledge and the fire of love are the same. They are synonymous. Fire of love begins with a longing—an intense longing. It feels so new that it can also feel uncomfortable. This fire can be experienced only in human life, in human birth. Fire of love or fire of knowledge creates an unpleasant sense of longing in the beginning. But then it moves on to the blossoming of bliss, the blossoming of fullness.

Baḍavāgni—it is the fire of criticism. When people criticize you, there is a fire which flares up in your system. When you speak before a big crowd, you are uncomfortable and nervous because you fear their opinions and criticism.

Baḍavāgni is the fire of social criticism. Man is a social animal and lives in a society. He has to follow certain rules and cannot live as he pleases all the time.

When you drive, you have to follow the rules. You have to drive on the correct side. When you walk, you have to do so in the proper place. You have to follow certain rules and regulations; certain code of conduct. This gives rise to certain fears in you—the fear of criticism, the fear of being fined, the fear of being punished, etc. Abiding by certain laws brings up certain concerns but if you are greatly concerned about criticism and other people's opinions about you, then you are missing the boat. Certainly, the fear of criticism keeps you within the limits of morality. But if it goes out of control or out of limit, the same fear of criticism can finish your freedom, openness and centeredness. If the fire of criticism is too much, then you will be tense and worried about everything. You should pass through the fear of criticism. It does not matter what people say; their opinions change. And you know in your consciousness that you are not doing any harm to anybody. When life moves through all these fires, it will emerge as gold.

Unfortunately, you have not understood this principle. You do not even allow the fire to come up in you.

Tapa means being fried or baked. You would have read about the *Kumbh Mela* in many magazines. In this religious gathering, you may find somebody standing on one leg with ash smeared all over his body and a pot of fire on his head. There have been many such misinterpretations of the pañcāgni.

Patañjali says that one who goes through the five fires will be purified; would cross over to the other side. But the scriptures have been wrongly understood. People thought that one who passes through five actual fires would be purified. So, they lit fires all around and started fire-walking and torturing their bodies. This is called *rākṣasī* tapas.

Tapas is of three kinds—sāttvika, rājasika, and tāmasika.

Sāttvika tapas is one in which you are not even aware that you are doing it. You are just part of the phenomenon. The world today is a phenomenon and you are just a part of that phenomenon. Where do you exist? There may be so many waves or ripples in a lake but it is ridiculous if each one of them thinks that it exists as a wave. When wind blows, so many waves arise, and they all subside a little later. Similarly, in the ocean of consciousness, many waves have arisen. One wave calls itself Jyoti, another Rohit, and there would be others, Shivanya, Lucy and Lalita. Those limited waves have been given different names. All these waves will subside in a few years, and new waves will arise. One goes through the fire of life with this awareness. This is sāttvika tapas.

Rājasik tapas are practices that are done with a desire to achieve something. A motive exists even when some service or sevā is being done. This has a mixed effect. This is rājasik tapas—the tapas a person does to show off. One may fast, meditate or do great service and broadcast it as well. So the tapas is done with pomp and show; with much 'I-ness'.

Tāmasik tapas is the demonic tapas, where people torture themselves, because they cannot torture others. If you torture yourself, nobody will question you. People stick nails all over the body and walk on fire.

What does tapas do? Why should we undergo tapas?

It purifies and strengthens our system. That is the purpose of tapas but it can boost the ego in a person. Unfortunately, people think by doing tapas, they will become very great. An out of proportion glorification of tapas leads to ego. That is why the next thing to be done immediately after tapas is *svādhyāya* because tapas without svādhyāya leads to ego.

The second component of kriyā yoga is svādhyāya—introspection, self-study.

Svādhyāya is being alert in self-study, in observing one's breath and emotions. It is wondering where the thoughts and emotions come from and what happens inside you because of them—observing and studying yourself.

Usually people interpret it as the studying of the scriptures. Scriptures are just reflections of the experiences of people of the past. But these experiences are true and alive even today. So looking into yourself, observing the Self itself is svādhyāya. *'Svā'* means self and *'adhyāya'* means study. Study your mind, study your intellect. Study how your intellect works day and night; what type of logic it resorts to and how illogical it can be sometimes. How it justifies, the defence it puts up, the complaints it comes up with, the cravings it has, the fears, the anxieties that come into your mind. Study all this turmoil that goes on within and you will see another layer of existence opening up in front of you. You will see there is a cause, a reason behind every one of your emotions and the turmoil within. Then you move on to the subtle realm of reality from where everything happens. That is when you see that you are just a puppet in the hands of the angels or the Divine.

Svādhyāya is also looking into the motives behind your actions. Often, you do not go for things that you really want. You go for them because others want them. You may even go for something depending on what others would say or think. And many times you are not clear about what you want because you have never really looked into yourself. You are swayed by fleeting thoughts, fleeting emotions and fleeting desires.

Your desire may not even be your own. Maybe, some external factors—food, events, situations or company have raised a storm in you and you start believing that storm as your very Self. That is why often you are not happy even when your desires are fulfilled. You should observe the Self. You should wonder who you are and what you are. You have purified the body but are you the body? You have made your mind light but are you the mind? Are you your thoughts? Are you your emotions? Who are you? This self-study leads you upwards to the universe that is unknown to us. Self-study takes you a step further and eliminates misery and suffering of the mind.

Buddha has said this so beautifully. He said *kāyānupāsanā*—observe the body. That is also tapas. *Vedānupāsanā*—observe the sensations in the body.

Cittānupāsanā—observe the mind, its impressions, thoughts and feelings.

Dhammānupāsanā—you should observe your very nature; observe the *dharma*.

So what comes to you by practising svādhyāya?

Iṣṭadevatāsamprayoga—connection with the subtle aspects of the Divine within. That comes when self-study is done on a regular basis. The question 'Who am I?' is also a part of self-study. Self-enquiry is a part of self-study. Who am I? What is this world all about? How long am I going to live? Is all this permanent? Instead of 'this one says this and that one says that', realizing that all these are just wave functions, and raising yourself to another level of existence. Knowing from where everyone is motivated or functioning. Knowing that the consciousness is putting this thought into this person and that thought into that person. Raising yourself from the material 'who is who' to the how and what of the universe is svādhyāya. And svādhyāya is very important.

Svādhyāya is that which brings out the relation or connection with the subtle realm of existence. Svādhyāya can eliminate all mental and emotional impurities, uncertainties, fears, and anxieties.

And *īśvarapraṇidhāna*—love of God and surrender to the Lord will complete the process. The third component of kriyā yoga is īśvarapraṇidhāna. Without love, self-study becomes another dry topic. Without surrender, self-study is not charming. Without love and devotion the spiritual path becomes dry like styrofoam. It is like a cake or pudding without sugar; bread without salt.

Some things you understand, some things you don't. What you know you surrender and what you don't know, that also you surrender. The deepest rest anyone can ever have is only through surrender.

How can love for the Lord, wanting to surrender to Him, blossom in us? The first step is to see the Lord as different from you—Lord and me. Two are needed for surrender when you feel that He is the Lord of all virtues and you are nobody. In this 'nobody-ness', the union takes place. The realization dawns that all is the Lord and all that is me too. The realization dawns that the universe is the Lord's, your body is His, your mind with all its conflicts and with all its beauty is also His. This offering itself is a technique which brings you back home.

Īśvarapraṇidhāna brings about samādhi, or ecstasy in meditation. Offering candles, incense or flowers is not great. You should offer every part of your body, offer every moment of life, offer every breath, offer every thought—good, bad, pleasant, unpleasant, anything. Offer all those *vāsanas* or those things which you consider are your negative points. Offer all your negativity and offer all your positivity. By offering all the negativity, you become free and by offering all the positive virtues you think you possess, you become free. You will not become arrogant. Your virtues make you arrogant. They make you behave as if you are special. And your drawbacks pull you down and make you feel bad about yourself. And if you start feeling bad about yourself and unconnected to the Divine, there is nothing that can make you feel connected.

It is up to you to feel close to the Divine. It is up to you to feel close to anybody for that matter. Even if somebody does not feel close to you, you should start feeling close. It does not matter if they do not feel that you are close to them. And how do you know this? You cannot know just by their behaviour. It is not the right way to judge. This applies to the Master too. This is because nothing else can convince you that you are close and dear to the Divine other than your own mind and your own self. You should stop comparing. You may feel that somebody is close to the Master because he smiles at and talks more often to them than he does to you. This is your illusion. It does not matter if the Master does not talk to you. You should start feeling you are the only one and that you are the closest to him. Then you will see that what you want will start happening; that it will start blossoming.

Whatever seed you sow, that will grow. If you sow the seed that you are hopeless and no good, then that no-good seed will grow. Often, weeds and other useless things grow without any cultivation. You do not need to cultivate weeds. That is why they are called weeds. They just grow and thrive on their own but a useful plant needs some attention. In your field many weeds are coming up every day—useless, unwanted and unnecessary doubts and thoughts. You don't need to sow them. They just come up by themselves. By svādhyāya, you can weed them out and maintain only that which is essential in life.

tapaḥ svādhyāy-īśvarapraṇidhānāni kriyā-yogaḥ

But that is again a doing. Kriyā means activity. This is the yoga of action. You have to do this. Kriyā yoga means that you have to consciously do tapas, consciously do svādhyāya and consciously do īśvarapraṇidhāna.

But there is another thing which is just happening. Īśvarapraṇidhāna also happens. Suddenly the feeling of surrender comes to you automatically. That feeling is a happening, not a doing. For those who have natural surrender in them, a natural feeling of oneness or devotion in them, they don't need to practise it. It is not a sādhanā; it is a fruit of their action. But for someone who has all the burden on his head, worries, tension, headaches, surrender is an action and that is why it is called kriyā yoga.

The third way of looking at this is even when you are doing something, you should think that you are not doing it. You should be a silent witness. There is a depth in you, a silent corner that does not change. All the activity is taking place in this silent space. Every atom is revolving around the nucleus and all the planets are moving around. Yet, there is silence.

Tapaḥ svādhyāy-īśvarapraṇidhānāni together is kriyā yoga.

What is the purpose of kriyā yoga?

samādhibhāvanārthaḥ kleśatanūkaraṇārthaśca

Kriyā yoga is practised to bring about samādhi and to minimize the miseries or afflictions.

Kleśa is misery. Tapas will help you to lessen the misery. When you're feeling miserable and I say, "This is tapas and you have to do it," suddenly there is relief. "Tapas! OK, I will do it." Suppose there is no salt in the food and you don't want to eat the food. But then you say, "This is tapas for me, so today I will do it." People go for *pañcakarma* treatment, where you are asked to drink ghee and have khichdi without any salt, and they willingly do it. They enjoy it, they want it because they know it is going to do some good for them. So kriyā-yoga is to lead you towards samādhi.

Samādhi-bhāvana-arthaḥ—to lead you towards samādhi and reduce the miseries in life. If anyone is miserable, introduce them to kriyā-yoga. They should do kriyā-yoga. And all these are a part of the Sudarśana Kriyā.

Sudarśana Kriyā is tapas. You have to breathe in, put your effort and breathe; that is tapas. You don't want to attend to the breath but we say—come on breathe, put in your 100%, again and again, so that is tapas. Svādhyāya means letting go of whatever emotion that comes up. There is a feeling of surrender, of letting go.

It is not just some exercise that you do. There is honour and devotion, you do it with sacredness. When you do the Sudarśana Kriyā, you do it with deep reverence. So all the three aspects of kriyā yoga come together in the Sudarśana Kriyā. And does it not bring samādhi to people? To some extent, yes. Does it not reduce the misery of people? It is doing that. We have seen it not just in one place, but in many places around the world.

Types of Miseries

avidyā-asmitā-rāga-dveṣa-abhiniveśāḥ

pañca kleśāḥ || 3||

अविद्यास्मितारागद्वेषाभिनिवेशाः पञ्च क्लेशाः ॥ ३ ॥

The five miseries are ignorance, i-ness, craving, aversion and fear.

Avidyā—ignorance of who you are, who others are, how things are working. Ignorance of the cause of all that happens around you, pleasant or unpleasant, is avidyā.

All your presumptions, your prejudices are ignorance, and most of your ideas are also ignorance. There are hardly any ideas left that are not ignorance. So this is the first cause of misery, the root cause of all suffering. Ignorance is to consider permanent that which is not so; to understand that which is changing to be unchanging; that which is not joy to be joy, and which is not Self to be the Self. It is thinking you are the body when you are not; thinking that you are your thoughts and emotions when you are not. It is considering your body to be unchanging, when it is actually changing continuously. Doctors say that the blood is changed every twenty-four hours and your stomach lining changes in five days. And the skin changes in a month. Every cell in the body changes in a year. In a year all the old cells are dead and you have new ones. Your body is new. Your mind is new. However, you have never considered your body like a river which is undergoing change all the time.

As you awaken to this truth, you will not identify with your old fears and thoughts; with the old you. Your ignorance makes you hold on to them; hold on to your past. You hold on to your idea of who you are. People think it is very complimentary to know who you are; to have an idea about yourself. But if you have an idea of who you are, then you get stuck. The right attitude is to feel that you do not know who you are. This is because you are changing every moment. You understand this process when you do not know your own identity. A fixed idea about who you are destroys you totally. It stops your growth and limits your potential.

Ignorance is considering that which is changing to be non-changing. We try to control others' minds. This is not possible. Someone may have loved you yesterday but they need not love you today or tomorrow. You expect enlightened behaviour from everybody around you and when you do not get it, you become unhappy. You may not be behaving in an enlightened way, but you expect everyone around you to be enlightened and have unconditional love for you. A person who loves you unconditionally is rare—one in a million but you expect it from everybody around you. This expectation makes you unhappy. This is what everybody is doing, consciously or unconsciously. Sometimes, they may not even know what they are expecting. But their expectation is something very big. They are seeking God in everybody. They are seeking God without understanding that God could behave in any manner that He wants. They are looking for a saintly God in everybody around them. Your concept of how things should be makes you miserable.

It is your ideas that bring you misery. It is your ideas that bring you relief also, relief from misery. This is avidyā.

Asmitā—I, my, mine. Asmitā is another cause of misery. Just imagine you are standing next to someone. This someone is speaking rudely to another person next to you. You are just an onlooker and feel pity for the guy who is being rudely spoken to. And in a while that man starts speaking in the same way with you. What happens inside you? Do you feel the same? You were an onlooker when someone else was being rudely spoken to. That did not invoke so much emotion in you, it invoked only your opinions. But what happened the moment he started speaking rudely to you? It hit your heart, it hit your emotions and it rattled you. This is asmitā. You could not watch with the same indifference or the same witness consciousness when it came to you. So asmitā is that sense of I, me, mine.

Asmitā is oneness of our intellect and our Self. Have you noticed that some people stubbornly stick to their opinion despite the facts being contrary to it? They will argue meaninglessly. This happens because they are so stuck in themselves, in their intellect and thoughts, considering them as their own. Asmitā is the inability to see the Self and the buddhi or the intellect, and the power of the organs of perception as separate entities.

During the Vaidika times, when children went to gurukul, the first thing they did was to remove their asmitā. In the āgamas, they initiate a child to study the vedas in a very beautiful ceremony. The child is brought to the Guru and he puts a veil on the child, covers the child with a cloth and makes him stand on an 'Om' written on the floor. He says Om on top of the child's head and tells him, "From head to toe you are just Om. Drop your name, drop the pride of your family, or whatever you have been." In the gurukul, children would come from all over—princely families, from merchant and industrialist families, and from poor families too. If they kept their distinction there, they couldn't have studied together. So the Guru first removes the veil of asmitā—'I am somebody', 'I am something'—that is gotten rid of.

Asmitā is all your achievements. Your qualifications are your asmitā. You are an MBBS or MD. You think you should be respected, "I am a professor, I should be respected, I am so and so, I should be respected. I have been a successful businessman and I should be respected." This 'I am' comes in the way.

Many top officials crib about not having been rewarded as much as they should have been. They feel that they have been under-utilized, for they are highly qualified. And this thought—I am highly qualified and I am not being utilized—this asmitā, makes them miserable. You may have obtained a great degree in business management, business administration, but just a high school dropout might do better business than you. When that happens your asmita simply rattles you, "This man who has not studied anything, is doing so much better than I am. And I have obtained so many degrees". So what? Your masters' degree is only your asmitā and it makes you more miserable. Your achievements can also be your asmitā. That also makes you miserable. Your lack of achievements is also your asmitā. Don't think only those who have achieved have asmitā. Those who have not achieved anything also have asmitā. "I'm a poor guy, I am good for nothing, I wasted my life," such feelings are also asmitā. Asmitā is not only a superiority complex. Inferiority complex is also part of asmitā. Asmitā is the second thing that gives you misery.

Rāga—craving is the third misery. A deep craving in you, craving of the senses. Some people, who are in their 80s, craving for some sensual pleasures, have ended up in jail. An old man who is 80, I don't know if his body is capable of functioning, misbehaved with a girl and landed up in jail. This is rāga. A craving for anything, can cause you misery. You have diabetes and you crave sweets. You gulp down four *rasgullas* and you have to take an extra dose of insulin and suffer.

You crave praise from others. I know a teacher who used to give the volunteers and others around him 10-15 rupees and ask them to praise him in front of Gurudev. So whenever Gurudev would come, those people would start praising him, "Oh! You know, he did such and such sevā, he has such good knowledge." I just winked and asked one of them, "How much did you get?" Of course it is fun, no doubt. But this craving to hear praise about oneself can make people do anything. People will go to any extent for name, for fame or craving for money. All this power, position and money—all these cravings can cause you misery. If someone's face is looking sad and miserable, know that there is rāga behind it, there is a craving in this person's mind. It is obvious. It shines through. You can see through them. It comes out very strongly that they have cravings. You can see that in their faces. Any type of craving will not let you sleep properly. It will make you miserable.

Craving also arises because you have had a pleasant experience and you want that experience to be repeated. The desire for it makes you miserable. This is another type of kleśa.

Dveṣa—aversion is the fourth misery. Aversion brings the same misery as craving. It is the opposite of craving. Some monks, some *sādhus* are averse to ladies and this aversion gets into their heads. They look at ladies, and run away from there. You cannot have so much aversion! I don't know what they might be thinking all night and all day. But they are averse to ladies. Dveṣa is not just aversion, it is one degree higher—it is hatred. Hatred towards anybody for anything in this world—self-hate or hating anyone else is the biggest misery, biggest obstacle on the spiritual path. Hate none.

This is one of the reasons for kleśa. Your asmitā is connected to your hatred and cravings. So if there is no avidyā, none of the other things exist. Avidyā exists, therefore asmitā exists. Because asmitā exists then cravings exist. Since cravings are there, hatred is definitely there.

When all these kleśas are present, eventually, fear grips you. *Abhiniveśa* is fear, fear of the unknown. Though intellectually you may know everything, you will have a bit of abhiniveśa. This fear exists even in scholars.

A little fear should be kept in the body, so that the body can be maintained. It should be less than a pinch of salt. *Vidushaḥ-api*—it is found even in persons who have much knowledge about scriptures.

Actually, it is not fear. It is alertness. There is a difference. Alertness implies being careful. There is a similarity between alertness and fear. That is why Patañjali has used the word abhiniveśa, and not *bhaya* which means fear. There is no equivalent word for abhiniveśa in English. Abhiniveśa in its crude form is fear and in its subtle form is care (or caution). You may be walking at the edge of a lake. You are walking carefully so that you do not fall into the water. If this care (or caution) is not there for the body, then the body could just vanish, disappear. You may feel that when you are not the body, you do not need to attend to it at all. To maintain the body, a certain amount of care is essential. And when this care increases to a little more than what is really needed then there is insecurity. If there is a further increase, then it is fear. If it increases beyond fear it becomes paranoia. It is just like increasing the amount of salt in food. Too much of it and food becomes uneatable. Nature has imposed these fears on everybody. If they become thin, you will evolve and if they remain thick, you will stay unevolved.

You cannot be peaceful if you have hatred towards someone. Fear will creep within you. So for your own sake, you should stop all this. The root is avidyā, ignorance. Even if you can just recognize that you are ignorant, I tell you, the rest of it all will start dissolving.

The recognition of avidyā itself is very difficult. That is what people don't do. They think that they know it, they don't acknowledge they don't know. If you know that you don't know, if you acknowledge, "I don't know", then your asmitā, rāga, dveṣa, abhiniveśa will dissolve. In your mind if you say, "I know this is how things are," but you actually don't know, then it is a problem. This is avidyā solidified. Your staunch concepts can create this type of turmoil and misery in your life. And fear is an obvious byproduct of this.

avidyā kṣetram-uttareṣām

prasupta-tanū-vicchinna-udārāṇām || 4 ||

अविद्या क्षेत्रमुत्तरेषां प्रसुप्ततनूविच्छिन्नोदाराणाम् ॥ ४ ॥

Ignorance is the source of all other miseries. They can be in four stages—dormant, weakened, occasional and very active.

I have already said this. Avidyā is the basis. Your understanding is that you know, but the fact is that you really don't know. You think of misery as joy, that which is impermanent as permanent. This is avidyā. And to what degree is the avidyā inside of you? It is either sleeping or has become active.

prasupta-tanu-vicchinna-udārāṇām

Prasupta—dormant—it is simply lying there and it is weakened. When there is more knowledge, then avidyā is weakened. When you say, "Perhaps, maybe, what I think is not true," that moment the ignorance is already weakened. 'I know it' is ignorance —'I think so', 'Maybe', 'Maybe I am wrong'—indicate that the ignorance has weakened. Whenever people do wrong and say, "Maybe I am wrong," it has already weakened. If I say, "No, this is how it is, I am right," then avidyā is very active; definiteness in hatred, in anger.

So, prasupta is dormant, *tanu* is weakened and then sometimes doubts come, sometimes they go away. They don't stay. Many times people get on to the spiritual path and then they want to run away but they can't. Even if they run away they come back. This happens time and again. Once in a blue moon you get this idea of just dropping everything and running away. But it doesn't last long.

*Udārāṇ*ām—very active. That is doomsday for them, solid negativity, you can feel the negative vibrations in them. They are *ajñānīs*. This is total *ajñāna*.

So, with the passage of time, sādhanā makes these five kleśas, or sources of misery, as thin as possible. You had been getting angry before you were on the spiritual path and after that as well but there is a big difference in the quality of anger. There is a shift. After being on the spiritual path, the anger has become tanu—thinned down. The curtain has become more and more transparent.

anitya-aśuci-duḥkha-anātmasu

nitya-śuci-sukha-ātma-khyātiḥ-avidyā || 5 ||

अनित्याशुचिदुःखानात्मसु नित्यशुचिसुखात्मख्यातिरविद्या ॥ ५ ॥

Ignorance is mistaking the impermanent for the permanent, the impure for the pure, that which brings misery for that which brings happiness and non-Self for the Self.

Avidyā is believing that which is impure to be pure, that which is impermanent to be permanent, that which is misery to be joy and happiness.

You know, some people cannot work with others. They think working alone, independently, is the best way to produce results. They become miserable and do not succeed at all. In business, you have to have the attitude of including everybody. Working with tough people will improve your skill. You will be able to work with anybody and everybody then. You say, "I want to work only with this person and I won't work with that person." What do you know? Do you think that person will be like that all the time? Maybe after six months or a year or two, that person turns around. Maybe the one you wanted to work with will give you more trouble than the others. So do you think our thoughts and opinions are permanent? Are behaviours permanent? No, they can all change. And it is the same with asmitā. Asmitā is the inability to go beyond the intellect and getting stuck in the intellect.

dṛg-darśana-śaktyoḥ-ekātmatā-iva-asmitā || 6 ||

दृग्दर्शनशक्त्योरेकात्मतेवास्मिता ॥ ६ ॥

When the seer is lost in the power of the scenery, a limited sense of 'I' results.

There is the power in the seer and that which is seen. Do you think these two are one?

You have the qualification but qualification is not what you are. You have ability, your ability is not what you are. You have weakness, your weakness is not what you are. You hold onto your weakness, "I am weak, I am poor, I am miserable, I am not worthy." How dare you say that! It is not allowed. At the same time, you cannot brag about yourself, "I am very intelligent, there's nobody like me, nobody is as efficient as I am." What do you mean? When the grace is there even the most incompetent person can do great things. And when the grace is not there the most intelligent person can do nothing. This is all the test of asmitā.

Our first Teachers' Training Programme (TTP) was way back in 1983 or 1984. We went to Kemmangundi, about 200-300 kms away from Bangalore. It is a hill resort. We didn't have this beautiful āśrama at that time. I was travelling, teaching everywhere, and I thought I have to create more teachers. There was so much interest and so much demand for knowledge. People were longing for it everywhere, so I needed to create some teachers. And at that time, I didn't have any plans to go abroad. So in the training, I had three ladies from Italy, a young couple from Delhi and then one gentleman from Solapur, Maharashtra. He was a simpleton, very devoted. His name was Shiva Shankar Madki. There were seven of them. It was quite a rigorous training. I was the only teacher then. There were two courses going on simultaneously—a fifteen day long Advanced Meditation Course with 150 people and the TTP with seven people. So I had to shuttle between these two courses.

When I was conducting the TTP, this man from Solapur, who was about 50-55 years old, would sleep through the whole class. He was not even counted as one of the trainees. So sometimes, the other trainees would say, "It doesn't matter if he is there or not, let us start." But I would say, "Never mind, let him come. Let him at least be seated." Since it was an international TTP, I had to speak most of the time in English, of course I used to use Hindi also. Nobody would even consider him as a teacher. All that he could do well was bhastrikā and a few āsanas. So everyone wondered what he was going to do when he became a teacher.

When he went back to Solapur, he started conducting courses. He could explain all the points and give the intro talks very well. He had the maximum number of participants. He used to draw 100-150 people for his courses. People would not move during and after his sessions. They would sit for 8-10 hours in his class and say that when he spoke it felt as if Gurudev was speaking. He gave great knowledge and could answer any question!

So once I took the other six people with me and went by train, from Bangalore to Solapur. Those days connectivity was not good at all; there were barely any flights from Bangalore. We had only one or two flights to Delhi and Mumbai, that was all. And even if there were flights we could not afford the flight tickets. So all of us went by train. We went there and saw the big programmes he had organized. The others were stunned. Those people who used to wonder why Gurudev is keeping him in the class, like a doll in a showcase, good for nothing, realised that he did the best. He built up the whole centre in Solapur and many people came for advanced courses and the teachers' training courses from there. So we should never underestimate anybody.

sukha-anuśayī rāgaḥ || 7 ||

सुखानुशयी रागः ॥ ७ ॥

Craving is the attraction to pleasure.

duḥkha-anuśayī dveṣaḥ || 8 ||

दुःखानुशयी द्वेषः ॥ ८ ॥

Aversion is the repulsion from sorrow.

How do you get cravings? What is a craving? You experience some pleasure, some joy and you want to repeat it. The desire to repeat that experience of joy is craving. This becomes more intense. Cravings are always based on pleasure. We don't say happiness, but pleasure. You experience some pleasure and that pleasure later on creates the craving to repeat it. The desire to have the repeated experience of pleasure is craving. It can go to the extent of making you violent. You read in newspapers and watch it on television. A boy falls in love with a girl, something happens and he is ready to kill her; ready to kill the person he once wanted to give his life to! It is unbelievable, unimaginable, where the power of craving can take you. All obsessions are reflections of cravings.

Similarly *duḥkha-anuśayī dveṣaḥ*—why do you hate somebody? You feel that a person is the cause of your misery, so you hate them. Hatred is latched on to sorrow. Why don't you want to look at a person? This man is the cause of my misery, my downfall, so I don't want to look at him. This is dveṣaḥ. But it is not true. You go and talk to that person and he will say, "I had no idea that I was the cause."

Hatred is running away from sorrow. One lady came to me saying she was craving to marry somebody, and that man didn't want to marry her because he was already married. He has a child, a happy life and a happy family. But this lady was craving day and night, writing letters to me, wanting to somehow get married to this man. But since this was not possible, the craving for that man turned into hatred and she started hating him. So many such cases come to me every day. A boy is gay and a lady has fallen in love with him. She is miserably craving for him and thinking only about him. When nothing happens, she is hateful towards her family, hateful towards everybody.

And then there are other cases of people who hate themselves. There are many examples, where people slit their wrists. There is hatred inside them for whatever reasons. They hate somebody but that person is not there. That hatred which was for somebody else is turned towards themselves. So they end up slitting their own wrists. I know many such young people, whose parents come to me and say, their daughter or son, bang their heads on the wall, cut themselves because they cannot handle their hatred.

When families break up, this is one of the issues which comes up. The child loves both the parents. When one parent is not there, the comfort that it was getting from that one parent is missing. This creates hatred in them and they start hurting themselves. Fear of misery leads to craving for pleasure and hatred.

sva-rasa-vāhi viduṣaḥ-api tathā-

rūḍhaḥ-abhiniveśaḥ || 9 ||

स्वरसवाही विदुषोऽपि तथारूढोऽभिनिवेशः ॥ ९ ॥

Even in the wise there is an ever flowing, firmly established fear of loss or death.

Someone may be a great scholar, who knows everything, but this fear is kept in the system. It is said even for a highly evolved person, a little bit of fear exists. This fear helps to sustain the body.

When a baby walks, it looks around to see whether it's safe or not, whether it's falling down or not. So a little bit of abhiniveśa keeps one's body intact. What is fear? Fear is that thread which is woven into our being from childhood, from the very beginning, since the body has come into being. Now how much fear is present in us? Ādi Śankarācārya gives a very beautiful example. He says imagine someone has a butterball in his hand and he throws it away. The butter ball is gone, but its mark still remains on the hand. So that bit of avidyā is essential to maintain the body.

Ramakṛṣṇa Paramahansa, a great saint, maintained the avidyā of eating. He maintained *leśa avidyā*. Leśa avidyā means the avidyā is gone but a trace of it is maintained so that the body can be sustained. When avidyā is completely gone the body will also be gone. Then, it is impossible to keep the body alive. So a little bit of avidyā is essential and every enlightened person keeps one or two avidyās. Ramakṛṣṇa Paramahansa made food his vāsanā. One little vāsanā has to be maintained. When someone asked him the reason behind his craving for food he replied, "I need it to keep my body here."

Swami Vivekānanda had the idea of going to America to spread this knowledge. So he went to America, completed his mission and came back. When his wish was fulfilled, his life also got over. According to the *sankalpa* you put, the body sustains itself. So a little bit of avidyā is essential and it is present in the form of abhiniveśa.

You need to keep this sankalpa—we need to spread knowledge everywhere in the world. This too is avidyā, no doubt, but such avidyā keeps you going. We want to bring knowledge to every part of the world. That is one intention—to bring this ancient wisdom to every doorstep. Though this is a part of avidyā because there is nothing to bring, nowhere to go, everywhere it is all Brahman, everywhere it is the same consciousness yet having such a sankalpa gives direction to your life energy and sustains life.

Eliminating the Cause of Misery

te prati-prasava-heyāḥ sūkṣmāḥ || 10 ||

ते प्रतिप्रसवहेयाः सूक्ष्माः ॥ १० ॥

When these (kleśas) are in subtle form, they can be dealt with by resolving them into their source.

First you have to bring those (kleśas) from the gross to the subtle. When you make the sources of misery and the fears more and more subtle, you can eliminate them. Then they let you return to the Self. They let you bring the mind back to the source. When these miseries are very thick, they bother you. They captivate your mind. When they become thinner and thinner, your mind becomes free and gets back to the Self, the source. When you are craving for somebody, you are unable to relax or even be still. However, once that craving is gone, then you are able to relax and meditate. The feverishness is reduced and the mind can get back to the source. This is possible through sādhanā.

dhyāna-heyāḥ-tad-vṛttayaḥ || 11 ||

ध्यानहेयास्तद्वृत्तयः ॥ ११ ॥

Their modifications are destroyed by meditation.

Maharṣi Patañjali emphasized that the five kleśas can be eliminated only through meditation. It helps you become light, hollow and empty. You sing and dance to thin the veil which is on the Self. This is very precious. You may feel bored sometimes but it does not matter. Just be aware that you are burning some old seeds of boredom. If you are averse to boredom, the boredom will never leave you. If you are bored with yourself, just think how boring you would be to somebody else! So even if you are bored, never mind. It will make you more and more sensitive. Know that you are just burning something; think that it is a tapas, a penance. However boring it may seem, just take the step and be determined to do it. You often take up challenges with friends. Similarly, kindle this challenge to get over your boredom. If you do not do it, then what will happen?

Karma

kleśa-mūlaḥ karma-āśayo

dṛṣṭa-adṛṣṭa-janma-vedanīyaḥ || 12 ||

क्लेशमूलः कर्माशयो दृष्टादृष्टजन्मवेदनीयः ॥ १२ ॥

These (five) miseries cause the stockpile of impressions which has to be experienced in the current or future lives.

If you don't cleanse your consciousness of these five miseries or impurities, then you will have to suffer in this life and the next too. All the latent impressions will start manifesting. Some will give fruit today and some in the future.

Some people point out that there is nothing like karma. They agree that every action has its repercussions, which are felt in the current lifetime but they don't come with you to the next life. This is not true. Different seeds have different periods for sprouting.

If you put a mango seed in the soil, it will take at least 5–6 years to become a tree and bear fruit but if you sow cabbage it will be ready in three months. You sow cilantro (coriander), it will be ready to harvest in just a month's time. Similarly, there are certain karmas which you can experience immediately. If you keep your finger in a burning flame it will not say, "I will burn you tomorrow." It will burn you there and then. But if you sow a seed, it will not give you a tree today, it will take time.

Likewise, different karmas will give fruits at different times. Many people ask why bad things happen to good people. Bad things never happen to good people. They may be good at present. But they have done something bad in the past, so they are getting paid for it now. It is as if they had planted neem seeds long ago. So now, they reap the bitter fruits of that neem tree. Currently, they may be sowing mango seeds. They will have sweet mangoes in the future. As you sow, so shall you reap.

So Patañjali says *dṛṣṭa-adṛṣṭa-janma-vedanīyaḥ*—you will have to suffer in this life and in the next life too, because the miseries form *karmāśaya*—a bank of karma. This karma can be washed off and eliminated right away through meditation. You should get rid of the karma and lessen the sheaths of ignorance before your body drops dead. Otherwise, there is no escape for you from these miseries.

sati mūle tad-vipākaḥ-jāti-āyuḥ-bhogāḥ || 13 ||

सति मूले तद्विपाकोजात्यायुर्भोगाः ॥ १३ ॥

As long as those kleśas (miseries) remain as the root, they will keep producing three consequences—birth, span of life and experiences in that life.

As long as this root is there, the fruit of its tree will grow again and again. Karmas are the impressions in our consciousness and cause the following three things.

Jāti means whether you have a human or an animal birth or any other birth.

Āyu is your span of life.

Bhoga is the enjoyment you are going to have in this life. This is also determined by the seed present in the consciousness.

Now the question is, is it all fatalistic? If it is all pre-determined, then is there no way to get over this?

Jāti has no possibility of change because you are already born.

Āyu has a possibility of change.

Bhoga also has a possibility; you can change that. Among the three things—jāti, āyu, bhoga—jāti, meaning to whom and where you are born, is definite. This is determined. If you are destined to be born in Russia, you are born there. If you are destined to be born in Odisha, you are born there. And you are born as a human being, that is also done. The strongest impression in the mind at the time of death persists. There are so many stories in India to emphasize this.

There is a story about Ajāmila. Ajāmila was a king who was an atheist until the time of his death. At the last moment, when he was dying, he thought of his son and called out for him. His son's name was Nārāyaṇa. It seems God thought that He was being called, so Nārāyaṇa came and liberated him. It is an exaggerated but effective way to explain that the last impression carries much weight.

There is a similar story about an enlightened saint. One day, he was meditating on the bank of a river which was in flood. He saw a baby deer being carried away in the flood. So he jumped in and saved it, like any human would. He bandaged its wounds and cared for it but also got very attached to it. It is said that after he died he became a deer in his next birth. It is also said that it is almost impossible for a liberated man to go back into an animal body. But this example is quoted just to indicate that the last impressions are very important.

Āyu, life span, is also fixed most of the time but that can be changed. Your longevity can be increased by meditation, it cannot be reduced by meditation. You can commit suicide out of ignorance, not due to sādhanā. The life of the people who commit suicide is not fixed like that. They are committing suicide on their own will. It is not their āyu. Āyu is not finished for them. That is why till their āyu is over they keep hanging around and cannot move on to their next life. If someone is supposed to live for 60 years and if they commit suicide at 40 or 55 years, their souls keep hanging around here till they have completed the rest of their time on the planet.

Bhoga is the pleasure or discomfort that you are supposed to experiece in this lifetime. What you are to be—engineer, doctor, merchant or whatever, are all part of bhoga. Are you supposed to live a simple life, or a complicated life? Are you to have kids or not, is all bhoga. This also comes with karma.

For no reason at all, people will start blaming you. You wonder why they are doing this. Well, karma! For no reason, you are elevated to a position you are not capable of holding. You are not capable but you suddenly find yourself becoming a Chief Minister or Prime Minister of a country.

Someone here in this state said that he has become an accidental Chief Minister. How did it happen? This man didn't even have minority votes. There weren't even enough members in his own party. He could not even dream of becoming a Chief Minister. He came here (Bangalore āśrama) by accident. He wanted a place to land his helicopter. He landed here and had some snacks, tea and accidentally they went to our Gaṇapati temple. They did pooja and bowed down to the Gaṇapati and one of our swamis said, "You pray to Gaṇapati, you will become the Chief Minister." He must have thought it was a joke, but he did become the Chief Minister of this state, with his opponents supporting him. People who fought against him also supported him. This is bhoga. Grace, sādhanā, and devotion can change it. Jāti, āyu, bhoga—of these three things, one cannot be changed, two can be changed. If you want to be born in a poultry farm, I tell you, it is all possible. The only thing you need to do is think of chicken before you die. You will find yourself there.

te hlāda-paritāpa-phalāḥ puṇya-

apuṇya-hetutvāt || 14 ||

ते ह्लादपरितापफलाः पुण्यापुण्यहेतुत्वात् ॥ १४ ॥

These consequences (birth, lifespan and experiences) give joy or misery based on merit or demerit.

Bhoga does not just mean enjoyment, it also means suffering. The enjoyment and suffering in your life, the happiness you experience and the miseries you experience in your life, all depend on *puṇya* and *pāpa*, the merits and demerits or sins.

If you just look into all the pleasures or joy that you get in life, you will note that they all come with a tax and this tax is sorrow.

pariṇāma-tāpa-samskāra-duḥkhaiḥ-

guṇa-vṛtti-virodhāt-ca duḥkham eva

sarvam vivekinaḥ || 15 ||

परिणामतापसंस्कारदुःखैर्गुणवृत्तिविरोधाच्च दुःखम्

एव सर्वं विवेकिनः ॥ १५ ॥

Since all these experiences lead to more consequences, anxiety and impressions, and the qualities of Nature (guṇas) contradict each other, a wise, discriminating person sees all worldly experiences as painful.

Duḥkham eva sarvam vivekinaḥ—these are very commonly used and remembered words.

For the knowledgeable people, everything is misery. It sounds very depressing. Pain or pleasure, everything is misery. People praise you so you have to be more responsible. This is a misery. If they don't praise you, it is a misery!

Every event causes some pain. An event could be very pleasant and joyful. But it comes with a little pinch, a pain. The pain is that however joyful an event is, it will eventually end and the ending of an event, however pleasurable and joyful, comes with a little pinch. The memories of a pleasurable event also bring pain in proportion to the joy it has given. So before you have something, the feverishness to get it is painful. Then, when you have it, the fear of losing it is painful and, when it is gone the memory of its joy is painful. The whole thing is nothing but pain from the beginning to the end! Pleasure turns into pain and pain turns into pleasure—this is something which we have all seen. Whatever is pleasurable, in the long term, becomes painful, and if it is more than what it should be, it is painful. A responsibility is pleasurable but it could be very painful too.

You say love is so beautiful, but love is also painful. How close can you get to the person you love? Bodies get close but still there is no satisfaction; you get frustrated. Often, in the next life, a male takes up a female body and a female takes up a male body. This is because it is the most prominent craving, or longing in the mind. A male longs for a female and a female longs for a male. This is also the reason why in every male there are female characteristics and likewise in a female, on account of some impressions of the previous birth, there are some male characteristics.

The soul is not satisfied with the physical body coming close. It wants something more. It wants to merge. It wants to vanish and disappear. This is what is called love. In love, there are two expressions—the first is that one wants to merge with the other, and the other is that one wants to consume the other so that s/he disappears. These are the two expressions that lovers say to each other. They do not know why they are saying so. They are not cannibals! Does love make you a cannibal? Really, if that was possible, each one would literally gulp down their boyfriends or girlfriends. Then, there would be no more worry. They would not have to be bothered about who they are looking at and where they are going. Otherwise, the mind is constantly engaged in checking. Lovers become watchdogs after a while. Often when they come to the meditation course, they do not meditate. Their attention is entirely on their boyfriends or girlfriends. They have to be told to meditate without any worries; their boyfriends or girlfriends would be taken care of. Love creates pain; a tremendous amount of pain and so does separation. A wish creates much pain and pressurizes the mind. Trying to please somebody creates pain, and not knowing whether they are pleased or not also creates pain. You want to totally know the mind of the other person. How is this possible? You do not even know your own mind, so how can you know somebody else's mind? And it is impossible to know anybody's mind by just their words. They say the tongue has no bone, so it can move in any way it wants. It has no value; no loyalty. It is not steady. It may say something one day and something totally opposite the next. You cannot trust your tongue even if you can trust every other thing in the world. You feel good and joyful when you do what somebody else wishes. However, suddenly this feeling is not there! Now, doing what had once given you joy becomes painful.

It takes an effort to do spiritual practices and that is painful. If you don't do it, it is even more painful. One day, you may not be feeling good and you attribute it to your not having meditated that day. Or, after you have meditated, you feel you have not done it long enough and that is the reason you are not getting the proper results. You always find something to complain about.

So for the *vivekinaḥ*—the wise person—everything is misery. He sees life, every activity, friendship, and enmity, everything as misery.

But when he thinks everything brings misery, he doesn't become miserable. When you don't know everything is misery then you become miserable. People who are depressed have craving and aversion inside them. When you kick out that aversion or craving, there is no cause or reason to be depressed and when you consider everything as misery, there is neither craving, nor aversion, nor fear, nor I, me, mine.

No intelligent person claims misery as his own. Neither the objects of pleasure nor the cause of pain should be identified with oneself. That is *viveka*. Viveka is not identifying the cause of pain nor the cause of pleasure as one's own. So for a *vivekī*, for the one who is wise, everything is misery. That is why he performs his action but doesn't get attached to them.

guṇa-vṛtti-virodhācca

Different qualities are in conflict with each other. That is how nature is. Fire is in conflict with air, air is in conflict with water, water is in conflict with fire. All the *tattvas* are in conflict with each other, yet they cannot be without each other either. Without air there can be no fire. But too much air and the fire will get extinguished.

It is the same with water. It is the liquid which causes the flame to come up, and it is the liquid which extinguishes the fire. Fire can evaporate water, and if there is no fire there can be no water either. It will become ice. So, conflict is basically embedded in the *guṇas*.

It is the same with *sattva, rajas* and *tamas*. Tamas is in opposition with sattva and rajas. Rajas is in opposition with sattva and tamas. Yet, if any one guṇa is absent neither can exist. As a result there is conflict.

You have held a position and your position is gone. Your position was not permanent. Sometime or the other you would have had to get out of that position. Robert Mugabe occupied the position of Prime Minister and President of Zimbabwe for 37 years. He was 92. A journalist asked him, "When are you going to retire? When are you going to give your position to somebody else?" He slapped him and said, "I am still alive!"

You have become so old, yet you do not want to let go of your position. People move into rented houses but when they are asked to leave, they don't leave the house in a nice condition at all. They just ransack the house. They leave it in a very bad condition. The experience of leaving the house, quitting the office, and letting go of a position is painful. You do not realise it because it is so subtle in the subconscious mind, but you do not behave normally. Even though you think you are normal, others notice that you are not normal.

Once I met an ex-president of some country. He had just retired a couple of days back and invited me to bless his home. When I went he asked the house help to bring some refreshments for everybody. Obviously there will be a little delay to prepare everything. This ex-president took it very personally. He said, "Gurudev, look, when I was president he would bring me anything immediately. But now I see that he is taking time. Even my house help does not respect me". This is all in our own mind. We think people do not respect us if we do not have a position. Your respect should be in your character, in your ability, in your behaviour, not by position. I just smiled and told him, "It is all in your mind. How will someone not respect you just within two or three days of your retirement? That means you have not reflected on your own personality, you have not projected yourself—who you are". Our identification with some joy, pleasure, position, and some status makes us miserable. This is *pariṇāma dukha*.

The impact of happiness, remembering that you had such a nice time, can make you miserable now. You had pleasure, but what is its impact now? All 'ex's', ex-wives, ex-husbands, ex-presidents, ex-prime ministers, this 'ex' makes you really miserable. When you remember the nice time you had with that guy, who is now gone and married to somebody else, something happens in the stomach, you feel like throwing up. This is pariṇāma dukha.

You have become old and cannot play cricket as you used to, you cannot lift weights in the gym like you used to; your body is not allowing it. This makes you sad, this is pariṇāma dukha and *tāpa dukha* is the current situation.

Pariṇāma, tāpa and samskāra are three types of miseries.

Pariṇāma dukha is the memory of the pleasures, glories that you have had, that makes you depressed and unhappy now.

Tāpa dukha is your current situation. You are boiling with anger, hatred, and jealousy now. All these are tāpa dukha. This current moment you are miserable. Or you have a physical ailment which makes you miserable in the current moment. You had a fight with someone close to you, it makes you miserable now, in the current moment. This is tāpa dukha.

Samskāra dukha—the misery has gone but the memory of the misery, the seeds are still there. You ask someone, "Why are you crying?" He says I am not crying, my face is like that. This is samskāra dukha. You made a habit of complaining and even though there is nothing to complain about, you complain. You have made a habit of being miserable, being upset and being sad.

The habit of crying can be found even in children sometimes. They cry for no reason. The more mom and dad pamper them, the more they cry for no reason. This is samskāra dukha. You have made a habit of being sad, being miserable, and even masochism is a part of this. You find a little bit of joy in being sad. You have experienced it in your childhood. When you cried you got all the attention. When you are sad you get attention and that attention makes you feel better. So, somewhere in the subconscious mind, you think, if you are miserable only then will you get attention and you remain like that. Who would like to sit with someone who is miserable all the time, who has a long face, who always wants attention for no apparent reason? Such people are not worthy of even compassion. This is samskāra dukha. This is the impression of misery that you are holding on to. Nobody can relieve you of it until and unless you come out of it yourself. Keeping a long face all the time, finding some or the other excuse to be unhappy, is stupidity.

When pleasant moments are over, they leave an impression and that impression causes misery. Unpleasant events happen and go away, but those impressions again cause misery. Whether a pleasant or an unpleasant event, whether you are in a high post, rich or poor, all those samskāras which are there in your consciousness will only cause misery.

Let's suppose that you are the richest person. How long can you stay the richest? How long can you stay at the top of the list of the richest people in the world? Every six months or every year there is a revision of the list. Someone else is more competent and becomes richer than you. The man who was ranked number one in the list came down to number ten in just two years. And to number thirty in three years, and in five years time, he is not even on the list. This causes misery.

It is the same with fame. You have a talent and little later another talented person comes along and if you hang on to this fame, money, position, company, relationship—all of them can cause you misery. This doesn't mean you should not have them. Just be aware of this fact. *Duḥkham-eva sarvam vivekinaḥ*—an intelligent person recognises that these are all causes of misery.

When you realise that everything is painful, then what do you do? You have to do something to stop this pain. What will you do?

heyam duḥkham anāgatam || 16 ||

हेयं दुःखम् अनागतम् ॥ १६ ॥

The misery which is yet to come is worth avoiding.

It is very clear. The purpose of yoga, the purpose of spirituality is to stop the misery, which is about to come, before it comes.

The root cause of pain needs to be eliminated. That pain and misery which has not yet come in life and that sorrow which has not yet sprouted should be nipped right in the beginning.

How do we do that? How do we avoid it? It must be avoided and that is what the Sādhanā Pāda is about. All these sādhanās should be practised to avoid the miseries that may befall you.

The purpose of yoga is *heyam duḥkham anāgatam*—just remember this one sūtra—that is good enough.

The misery which has not yet come, should be avoided and it can be avoided. The method is given in this one sūtra, which is the hidden message or the purpose of the whole Yoga Sūtra—*heyam duḥkham anāgatam*.

The Scenery and the Seer

draṣṭṛ-dṛśyayoḥ samyogaḥ-heya-hetuḥ || 17 ||

द्रष्टृदृश्ययोः संयोगोहेयहेतुः ॥ १७ ॥

The cause of pain which is to be avoided is forgetting that one's Self is separate from the scenery.

The forgetfulness of 'me' being separate from 'this', is the cause of misery. There was a story in the olden days. The life of a king was in a parrot; if this parrot was killed, the king would die too. He would not die if somebody did anything to him. If the king had to be killed, the assassin would have to go to a remote island which had a fort. It was very difficult to get into it. If the assassin did manage to get in, he had to enter a palace inside the fort. The palace was full of cobras. He had to get past them. Then, he had to go underground where a door would open leading to a cage with the parrot in it. However, the assassin could not touch the cage. If he did, it would burn him down! The parrot had to be killed without touching the cage, only then would the king die. Similarly, people live as if one's life is not in one's Self. Their life is somewhere else—in a bank account. You have not just deposited money in the bank, you have deposited your life too. You will die if the bank shuts down or if something else happens to it. When you give something more importance than to life itself, then that becomes the cause of your suffering.

The main cause of pain is forgetting that one's Self is separate from the scenery. Being a manager is a role. If you think you are the manager then that becomes the cause of your misery. You play the role of a manager and the role may disappear anytime. When you identify yourself with that role, it becomes the cause of misery.

You identify yourself with your qualification—I am a tech guy, I am an MBA, I am a doctor, I am an MD. My dear, being an MD is only a role, it is not you.

This identification, even with your goodness, 'I am very good', causes misery. Many people become miserable thinking they are very good. When you think you are very good, you find that others are not so good. Thinking others are not so good and you are very good, is the formula for anger and hatred to spring up. Self-pity is the worst thing. People who pity themselves are ready to hate others. They have prepared themselves to hate others. This is the formula for hatred. You think you are very good, dedicated, efficient and others are not. Now you have begun the journey towards misery. Nobody is the cause of your misery. Your own identification is the cause of your misery. There is a beautiful proverb in Saṃskṛta:

kaṣṭasya sukhasya nako'pi dātā

There is no giver of misery or happiness. It is of your own making. So, self-pity should be done away with. If you think you are very good, then you fail to recognise your shortcomings. When you fail to see your shortcomings, there is no way for your growth. You have shut yourself. There is a shutdown in your brain, in your evolution. That gives rise to arrogance and you become incommunicable. Self-righteous people are very hard to communicate with. They are not ready to see and they don't even accept that they are not ready to see. They don't even accept that they are incommunicable.

prakāśa-kriyā-sthiti-śīlam bhūta-indriya-ātmakam

bhoga-apavarga-artham dṛśyam || 18 ||

प्रकाशक्रियास्थितिशीलं भूतेन्द्रियात्मकं

भोगापवर्गार्थं दृश्यम् ॥ १८ ॥

The scenery exhibits three characteristics—luminosity, activity and inertia. It is of the nature of the five elements and the senses. The scenery is meant for experience and liberation.

Then what is the purpose? Does it mean that you have to run away from the scenery? No, the scenery has a purpose. This world is here for your enjoyment. Patañjali was very clear about it. The beautiful scenery is there for you to look at. The good food is there for you to eat and enjoy but while enjoying it, don't forget the Self.

Remember that you are separate from the scenery. This is viveka.

What is the scenery? The scenery includes the five elements and our own senses—*bhūtendriya-ātmakam*.

Not only *bhūta*, not only *indriya*. Indriya means our senses and they are included in the scenery. What are they for? They are for both enjoyment and liberation, for experience and liberation. Holding on to any experience becomes the cause of misery and you want to be liberated from it.

And what is the nature of the scenery? It appears.

Prakāśa—it exists, it appears, it appeals to you and it has manifested out of consciousness.

Kriyā—everything in this universe is dynamic not static. Mountains appear to be static but they are not. Every atom in this universe is dynamic.

Sthiti—and it also rests. There is inertia.

Do you see the balance in nature? Even in the North or South Pole, when the daylight is 24 hours during summer, it is the exact opposite in the winter. There is exactly the same amount of time in darkness, 24 hours of night. This is the principle the world over. When the day is longer, the night will also be longer, at a different time. Near the equator, and in the regions in the tropical zones, day and night are equal all the time.

prakāśa-kriyā-sthiti

This is the nature of the scenery. The world which is seen is illuminated. Each thing gives you a message. It gives you an idea of how great the consciousness is. Every aspect in this world is an expression of the consciousness and cvcrything is active.

Your senses are attracted by its objects, but it is only for some time. It can never be forever. The good scenery appears to be good only for a short period of time, it also gets into inertia. There is appeal, activity and inertia, among the senses and the objects of senses. Is it not our experience too? Taste, for example. You look at an apple pie and it is appealing to you. You eat it but how much can you eat? One slice, two slices, three... the fourth slice and you want to throw up. You cannot eat anymore. It is the same with sex. Appealing, but then how much can you have? You move away from it as inertia dawns.

The purpose of the scenery is *bhoga-apavarga*—for experience and liberation. You need to get away from it. Prakṛti does it to you, naturally. You start to despise it after some time. If you don't, then you are not mentally sane. If you are stuck to any of it, it becomes the cause of misery. So the dṛśya, the scenery, the world, has its purpose. It is for your experience and liberation.

viśeṣa-aviśeṣa-liṅga-mātra-āliṅgāni

guṇa-parvāṇi || 19 ||

विशेषाविशेषलिङ्गमात्रालिङ्गानि गुणपर्वाणि ॥ १९ ॥

There are four stages of the qualities—specific, unspecific, with an identity and without a definite identity.

This is very technical, Maharṣi Patañjali is a great scientist.

Even among the guṇas, the nature of things, there are specific qualities and some not specific; some which have a definite identity and some which do not have that identity. If you go deeper, you will find different qualities. *Dravya* and guṇa—a substance and its quality, like sugar and sweetness. Sugar is the substance and sweetness is the quality, guṇa. Can you separate the sweetness from sugar? Which comes first? Sweetness or sugar? Of the salty quality of the salt, which comes first, the salty quality or the salt? There are whole treatises on the guṇa and the dravya. Even in āyurveda there is a section on dravya and guṇa. There are people who have expertise in this. Knowledge about the qualities is a very deep science. What are the different types of qualities? Are they specific or unspecific? For example, take a cup of water. You can say the water is cool or hot. Here the qualities or guṇas are changing. The dravya or the substance that is water is not changing but one of its guṇas is changing, whether it is hot or cold. A drink is sweet but how sweet is it? There could be a difference.

This is what he says—*viśeṣa-aviśeṣa-liṅga-aliṅgāni*. There are certain things, the sweetness of the sugar cannot be changed but the degree of sweetness can be varied.

The temperature of water can be changed. Water has some basic temperature to remain water. Otherwise it will become ice or water vapour. The basic quality of water is that it has the fire element in it. That means it has a specific temperature. It could be cool or any other temperature. Whether it is a cool drink or hot drink, there is a variation. Like that, in all the things there are certain qualities which can be identified and certain things which cannot be identified.

Certain things vary and certain things do not vary at all. For example the quality of sight. What is darkness for you is not darkness for an owl or a cat. If you walk around in the house when everything is dark you will stumble, but a cat will never stumble. It will find its way to where the milk is kept. An owl can see what you cannot. So the range of perception is different as is the quality, this is liṅga-aliṅgāni. One is the same for everybody but the other is different, viśeṣa-aviśeṣa. It is specific and non-specific. So what you can see with your eyes is specific to you. It is not the same for an owl, for a cat or for the microbes. However, the fact that everyone has sight is common to all. Certain qualities cannot be different. It is the same sunlight, but it is experienced differently by different people.

draṣṭā dṛśi-mātraḥ śuddhaḥ-api

pratyay-anupaśyaḥ || 20 |

द्रष्टा दृशिमात्रः शुद्धोऽपि प्रत्ययानुपश्यः ॥ २० ॥

Though the seer is pure consciousness, it imagines the scenery (due to its intellect).

The seer is like a mirror. Like reflections appear in a mirror, the seer experiences the scenery. But what is that which is between the seer and the scenery and which is also a part of the scenery? That is called māyā or illusion.

tad-arthaḥ eva dṛśyasya-ātmā || 21 ||

तदर्थ एव दृश्यस्यात्मा ॥ २१ ॥

That (the seer) alone is the reason for the scenery to exist.

Dṛśyasya-ātmā—the Self is the cause of all existence. It is the soul of existence, the soul of the scenery. For your senses to exist, your soul is the cause. Forget about the other scenery. How can your eyes, nose and ears function if the soul is not there? Like the soul is the cause of the existence of your organs; the bigger mind, the consciousness is the cause of existence of all the scenery, the whole world. Our body is also part of the scenery. This is easy to understand. If I am not there, the body cannot exist. If the soul is not there, if the seer is not there inside the body, can the body exist? No, it will decompose. What keeps the body alive? The spirit, the soul. That is what you are—dṛśyasya-ātmā

kṛta-artham prati naṣṭam-api-anaṣṭam

tad-anya-sādhāraṇatvāt || 22 ||

कृतार्थं प्रति नष्टमप्यनष्टं तदन्यसाधारणत्वात् ॥ २२ ॥

For the realised being, the scenery ceases to be, yet it exists for the others.

You are not the body, you are much above the body. The body is just a small pebble tied to a balloon.

Kṛtārtham is when you realise that you are not the body and that you are the pure consciousness, then you are established and that is enlightenment. When you are established in the idea that 'I am the consciousness', even then the body appears for others to be something which is existing. When you are in meditation, what is the experience that you have? You do not feel the body. You don't know where you are, you don't know anything. You are simply there, as a light, as a cloud, as consciousness, as mind. When you close your eyes and sit you do not know where the face is, your eyes could be at the back or anywhere! So in the state when the being is liberated, the body does not mean anything. Yet it is there for everyone to see and experience.

There is another angle to this also. The dṛśya, the scenery, remains for others as a reality but for the one who has realised the Self, it doesn't exist at all.

There is no more suffering for the one who is awakened in knowledge. The world appears completely different and all of this creation is filled with bliss, or is part of the Self. But for others, it exists as they see it. So, you may not be considering this world separate from the Self, but as a part of the Self. It does not exist for you, but for others it does exist. It is just like leaving a plane or a bus after a journey. For you the journey is over. But the plane or bus keeps going on, to take others onwards. The bus does not stop just because your journey is over.

For a man of classical chemistry, the differences still remain, but for a quantum physicist the whole creation is nothing but a wave function.

Just imagine in those ancient times, they brought together such deep wisdom of two very diverse dimensions of reality and made sense of both. Making sense of two paradoxical realities, two completely different realities; to see them as clearly as Maharṣi Patañjali did—the quantum physics angle and the classical chemistry angle, and bringing them together as an experiential reality of consciousness—is absolutely amazing!

sva-svāmi-śaktyoḥ svarūpa-upalabdhi-

hetuḥ samyogaḥ || 23 ||

स्वस्वामिशक्त्योः स्वरूपोपलब्धिहेतुः संयोगः ॥ २३ ॥

The realisation of the nature of the scenery and the seer is the purpose of their conjunction.

So there is a purpose for everything. If you can open your eyes, only then can you close your eyes also. Someone who doesn't have eyes cannot close them. Silence has meaning for one who can talk. For someone who can't speak, silence has got no meaning. So nature is there for you to realise the power of the Self.

tasya hetuh-avidyā || 24 ||

तस्य हेतुरविद्या ॥ २४ ॥

Ignorance is the cause of it (of the conjunction of the scenery with the seer).

tad-abhāvāt samyoga-abhāvo hānam tad-

dṛśeḥ kaivalyam || 25 ||

तदभावात् संयोगाभावो हानं तद्दृशेः कैवल्यम् ॥२५ ॥

Renunciation is the absence of the conjunction (between the seer and the scenery) resulting from the cessation of ignorance. That is the liberation of the seer.

Whenever the seer is engaged with the scenery, there is avidyā. Without that it is impossible to engage with the scenery. But when the seer retrieves himself from the scenery that is called *kaivalya*. Kaivalya simply means only me and nothing but me. The oneness is called kaivalya.

When the seer sees the scenery as different from the seer, and engages with it, that is avidyā. But when the seer sees the entire scenery as himself or herself, then that is kaivalya. When I engage with you as someone different from me, that is ignorance. But when I see you as part of myself, that is kaivalya. If I consider you as I consider my finger then that is not ignorance. But when I see you as a separate entity other than me, it is ignorance. There are a lot of theological fights on this point.

Ādi Śankarācārya, at some point does not accept yoga. It is a secret, many of you may not know it. Ādi Śankarācārya says, *"Yogastu bheda vādinah tanna grāhya."* Don't accept yoga because it is talking about duality. Here the seer and the scenery have separated. There is separateness but it is all an illusion. It is only your own reflection. So Vedānta contradicts yoga. According to Vedānta, there is no yoga. Meditation is nothing. One has to just wake up. Everything is an illusion, that's it. It just mentions dispassion and asks you to discard everything you see as different from you.

But what do you discard? That which appears to be different from you. If everything is a part of you there will be nothing to discard. It is very complicated. But both of them are speaking the same thing; I see no conflict. It is just the language of classical chemistry and quantum mechanics. Both are the same.

So when you consider the other as separate and engage with that, that is ignorance. When you don't see something as different from you, but as a part of you, it is kaivalya, it is enlightenment. Very simply oneness with everyone.

viveka-khyātiḥ-aviplavā hāna-upāyaḥ || 26 ||

विवेकख्यातिरविप्लवा हानोपायः ॥ २६ ॥

Pure awareness of the distinctness (discrimination) of the seer and the scenery is the means of renouncing (the scenery).

Clarity in mind, sharpness of intellect, sharpness of observation is what brings you to liberation. And that can come when the mind is free from kleśas. If there is rāga, dveṣa, craving, aversion, fear, there is no way you can have clarity of perception. Only when the kleśas are annihilated does the mind become clear. Viveka dawns and that is the path to liberation.

Another way to come out of the ignorance is a definite understanding and knowledge in the mind that the body is undergoing changes all the time; that the world is undergoing changes all the time; that the entire universe is in a state of fluidity—it is undergoing changes and at the same time is going on, on its own, according to its nature.

The definite knowledge that you are not the body, that you are the Self, that you are the space, that you are imperishable, untouched and untamed by prakṛti and the world around you, that the body is all hollow and empty, and every particle in this body is ever changing, and the mind is ever changing is the way to get out of this cycle.

tasya saptadhā prānta-bhūmiḥ prajñā || 27 ||

तस्य सप्तधा प्रान्तभूमिः प्रज्ञा ॥ २७ ॥

This discriminative awareness brings forth seven levels of intelligence.

The seven states of consciousness come from here. There are many schools of thought. Some schools say that there are multiple levels of consciousness. But Maharṣi Patañjali definitely puts the limit at seven. The seven states of consciousness are the waking state, deep sleep, dream state, transcendental state, god consciousness, universal consciousness, and unity consciousness.

The Eight Limbs of Yoga

yoga-aṅga-anuṣṭhānād aśuddhi-kṣaye jñāna-ḍīptiḥ-ā-
viveka-khyāteḥ || 28 ||

योगाङ्गानुष्ठानादशुद्धिक्षये ज्ञानदीप्तिराविवेकख्यातेः ॥ २८ ॥

Practice of the limbs of yoga eliminates impurities, brings the light of knowledge and discriminative awareness (awareness of the distinction between the seer and the scenery).

Human consciousness is like a seed. A seed has the possibility of a tree, of branches, of leaves, flowers, fruits, multiplication, etc. So does the human mind. A seed needs proper soil, sunlight, air, and water to sprout and blossom. It is the same with the human consciousness, the human mind. Either the seed can be dormant for many years, keeping its sprouting and developing possibilities within itself or it can start sprouting and growing right away. The sprouting of this seed of human consciousness is viveka—discrimination and wisdom. Freedom comes with viveka, or discrimination. All other species in this creation are completely governed by nature. They do not need discrimination nor do they have freedom. So they never break the laws of nature.

The human consciousness and the human mind have been given freedom. And they also have been given discrimination. It is through this viveka, wisdom and discrimination, that the human consciousness and human mind can be governed to progress or to remain where they are. Generally, you will not find any animal overeating if it is sick. It may do this only if it is mad. Normally, animals eat on time, rest on time and mate in the stipulated season. They have no choice. But human beings have the freedom to do whatever they want. Along with freedom comes discrimination, wisdom, the consequences of the action and knowledge of the consequences of the action. This is to enable humans to choose and lead a life of wisdom.

The speciality of human life is that it is governed by viveka—wisdom and discrimination. And how can this be enhanced? How can this seed be made to sprout and grow into a sapling? It needs watering again and again, until it grows. A seed has the possibility, but if it is not watered then the possibility remains a possibility and does not manifest.

Here Patañjali steps in and says, *yoga-aṅga-anuṣṭhānād*—the seed may be sprouted and made to grow by practising and observing the limbs of yoga. Through yoga, *aśuddhi-kṣaye*, the impurities are eliminated.

Viveka-khyāteḥ—the viveka, wisdom shines forth. The husk is gone and the sprout comes up.

By practising the limbs of yoga, sharpness of intellect, *jñāna-dīpti*—wisdom dawns in you, clarity, discrimination, and intuitive power dawn in you. Now what are the *yogaṅgas* which have to be practised? *Yama, niyama, āsana, prāṇāyāma, pratyāhāra, dhāraṇā, dhyāna, samādhi*—these are the eight *aṅgas* of yoga. Aṅga means limbs/parts of yoga.

yama-niyama-āsana-prāṇāyāma-pratyāhāra-dhāraṇā-

dhyāna-samādhayoḥ-aṣṭāu-aṅgāni || 29 ||

यमनियमासनप्राणायामप्रत्याहारधारणा

ध्यानसमाधयोऽष्टावङ्गानि ॥ २९ ॥

The eight limbs of yoga are rules of social conduct, rules of personal conduct, body-posture, breath-control, withdrawal of the senses, focus of the mind, meditation and samādhi.

ahimsā-satya-asteya-brahmacarya-

aparigrahā-yamāḥ || 30 ||

अहिंसासत्यास्तेयब्रह्मचर्यापरिग्रहा यमाः ॥ ३० ॥

Non-violence, truth, non-stealing, chastity, non-accumulation are the five yamas or rules of social conduct.

Many times people think that the eight limbs are the eight steps, one has to first practise yama, then niyama, and then prāṇāyāma. In the 1960s and 70s when I used to talk about meditation and prāṇāyāma, people would say, "Prāṇāyāma is not possible. You have to first climb all these steps. We don't know yama, niyama, we don't speak the truth. How can we do all this?"

When I first started the programs in prisons, people objected, asking me how I could teach meditation to prisoners! They know neither yama nor niyama and how could I directly give them mantras, make them meditate and practise prāṇāyāma? "This is wrong," they said. I just smiled at all of them. I said, "Thank you very much, I understand your concern. If I have violated the laws of Patañjali, I am ready to go to hell!"

Unfortunately, people think that yogaṅga means steps, one after the other. Samādhi for common people? It is impossible! You have to master yama, then niyama, practise all the others only then can you reach samādhi.

Around the 1960s samādhi was not thought of as a practice or that someone could experience it. If someone had taken samādhi, it meant that they had either died or gone missing in the Himālayas. Samādhi was not a common thing and definitely not for common people. This is a wrong concept that has been prevailing.

People do not see that Maharṣi Patañjali clearly says that these are limbs of yoga. They are not steps of yoga. When a child is born it is born with all its limbs. It is not as if the legs are formed first and then the hands and then the head. That is not how it happens. If you pull one limb all other limbs must come along with it. So yogaṅga means they are limbs of yoga and have to be practised simultaneously, not one after another.

Of course, there is a sequence, but to the degree you experience these, the others will also come along. Also, there is *anuloma viloma*—one method is going from yama, niyama, āsana, prāṇāyāma and so on and another method is to first experience samādhi and then practise all the others. Many saints of this country, in the flash of a moment, got connected to the Being and then their whole life changed. Maharṣi Vālmiki is one such saint. Just one incident, one moment changed his life. The same happened with Angulimāla, a dacoit who just met Buddha and changed immediately. He had a glimpse of samādhi and that changed his whole life. We have seen this happening in the prisons. The moment the hardcore criminals have the taste of what meditation is, their life changes, their attitude changes, everything in them changes. If I wait for them to practise *ahimsā*, satya and then make them practise meditation, it would never have worked.

What is yama? *Ahimsā, satya, asteya, brahmacarya* and *aparigraha* are the five yamas. They are the major vows to be followed by all. These are universal laws. Maharṣi Patañjali says that they are beyond time and are universal—to be practised by everybody without an exception.

jāti-deśa-kāla-samaya-anavacchinnāḥ

sārvabhaumā mahāvratam || 31 ||

जातिदेशकालसमयानवच्छिन्नाः सार्वभौमा महाव्रतम् ॥ ३१ ॥

These great vows are not restricted by any consideration of the life-state, place, time or situation; they are universal.

These are great vows which make you normal, which keep you normal. Even animals follow ahimsā, lions hunt only when they are hungry. They satisfy their hunger, otherwise they don't kill. Ahimsā, non-violence, is practised by nature, not just human beings. If human beings are not practising ahimsā, they are not normal or being filled with rage and hatred, they are mentally sick.

Humans kill each other in the name of God, in the name of love. In this world, mindless violence is prevalent in the name of one's country, religion, etc.

This is a total lack of viveka—wisdom. A violent man cannot hear anybody. His ears are sealed shut.

Violence is the result of pent up frustration. As the frustration builds up, questions may come up. Those very questions turn into violence, and it catches on in the surroundings creating mob violence. Individually a person may not be able to do a violent act. However, in a crowd, he will join hands with everybody and become violent. Viveka can dawn when a person takes this vow of non-violence—that he will not kill or take any life on this planet consciously. Unconsciously, you may be destroying many creatures when you walk. You may be stepping on and killing ants and many tiny creatures. But you are not killing them consciously. It is happening, but an intention of destroying something or being violent can cut your own roots. Dropping this intention for violence is ahimsā.

Further Maharṣi Patañjali tells what one can expect in their life by practising the yamas.

śauca-santoṣa-tapaḥ svādhyāya-īśvara-

praṇidhānāni niyamaḥ || 32 ||

शौचसंतोषतपः स्वाध्यायेश्वरप्रणिधानानि नियमाः ॥ ३२ ॥

Purity, contentment, penance, self study and surrender to the Divine are the niyamas or rules of personal conduct.

What are the niyamas? Śauca, santoṣa, tapas, svādhyāya and Īśvarapraṇidhāna.

Śauca—purity, cleanliness, inside and outside.

Santoṣa—contentment, being happy. If you're keeping a long face all the time, nobody would like to be with you, nor would you be comfortable with yourself. Santoṣa—contentment, happiness is another rule that needs to be followed.

Tapas—penance. Everybody has to do some amount of tapas. Don't think everybody will always praise you. Someone may insult you too. You have to swallow that, hold on and not explode. This is tapas—forbearance, penance.

Svādhyāya—self study, being aware of oneself.

Īśvarapraṇidhāna—surrendering to divinity, devotion to divinity.

vitarka-bādhane pratipakṣa-bhāvanam || 33 ||

वितर्कबाधने प्रतिप्रक्षभावनम् ॥ ३३ ॥

When negative thoughts obstruct the observance of yamas and niyamas, become aware of the consequences.

When the yamas and niyamas seem difficult to practise, one should cultivate *pratipakṣa*—awareness of the consequences.

Suppose your mind rebels, "I don't want to do any of these," then remind yourself that the consequence of not doing this is going to harm you.

When people were not aware of AIDS and HIV, they used to take pride in being promiscuous. That was the sign of a liberated, forward-thinking person. But when AIDS and HIV awareness came up in society, suddenly we went back to our old values of abstinence and loyalty.

So *vitarka bādhane*— '*Why should I not be promiscuous? What is so wrong with it?*' When you go in that direction, this is vitarka bādhane—opposite logic '*Why should I not be aggressive? The lion is aggressive as are all the animals so I can be aggressive too. Napoleon was aggressive as well*'.

When the naxalites came to our āśrama, they said, "We don't believe in democracy. Did Napoleon ask someone to vote for him? He went ahead on the basis of his own strength. Did Alexander the Great ask people to vote? We will be like Alexander, Mao or Karl Marx. We will not go and ask for votes. We will go with our swords and AK-47 guns. We will capture New Delhi." This was their tone. This is what they were saying, "Why should we follow non-violence?" I just asked them, "Would you like to be harmed? If someone points a gun at your family how will you feel?" Suddenly there was silence. All those who take up guns don't realise this because there is no perception of reality, no clarity. They have only kutarka—I want to finish the other guys.

"Why do you want to finish these guys? Where will you land up after that? What will happen to you? You will have to rot in jail. Did you get it?" There is nobody to create that awareness in people who are engaged in violent activity. This is exactly what happened with the guerillas in Columbia. They said non-violence is all hypocrisy, "Don't tell us about non-violence. We lost so many people. So many of our cadres are dead. If we adopt non-violence, how will we answer their parents?" They had very strong logic.

I just smiled at them, "Do you want to lose more of your cadre?"

It took three days to talk to them about meditation. Finally, they declared in the press conference that they would adopt the Gandhian principle of non-violence. It was a surprise even for me.

This is what *vitarka-bādhane-pratipakṣa-bhāvanam* is.

Think of the consequences of not following any of these principles.

It is the same with śauca. Why should I care for cleanliness? The so-called sādhus just keep themselves dirty—matted hair, no bath, stinking. They think this is vairāgya—dispassion, "I have no interest in my body. I don't care for my body. Nails are uncut, hair is unwashed." Even if you don't care for your body, at least keep it clean for others' sake. People cannot stand near you. A completely wrong understanding of dispassion. They don't look bright or full of bliss. Ajñāna—ignorance, total ignorance.

Why should I have contentment? If you don't want contentment what will you do? Move around in sheer frustration. You will only create frustration all around you and it will come back to you multifold.

Tapas—those who don't want to do any tapas will remain weak. And if you remain weak, there is neither material nor spiritual growth for you. One has to toil; do tapas. That is what all of us have done.

When we went to schools, to colleges, we had to toil a lot. Didn't we? School dropouts run away from tapas. You think they are all happy? Is it not inviting misery? That hard work is a tapas. Similarly, don't think because you have obtained a masters' degree you are done with your tapas. You have obtained a degree, one type of tapas is done, but you have not had any experience being with people, being in society, working with different mindsets. This is again tapas. Working with different mindsets is tapas. Swallowing insults is tapas. Not throwing venom at others is tapas."

vitarkā himsādayaḥ kṛta-kārita-anumoditā

lobha-krodha-moha-pūrvakā-mṛdu-madhya-

adhimātrāduḥkha-ajñāna-ananta-phalā iti

pratipakṣa-bhāvanam || 34 ||

वितर्का हिंसादयः कृतकारितानुमोदिता लोभक्रोधमोहपूर्वका मृदुमध्याधिमात्रा दुःखाज्ञानानन्तफला इति प्रतिपक्षभावनम् ॥ ३४ ॥

Negative thoughts like violence etc. (opposite to the yamas and niyamas) lead to actions performed directly by oneself, caused to be done to others, or approved of when done by others. All these may be preceded by or performed through anger, greed or delusion. They can be mild, moderate or intense in nature. Remind oneself that these negative thoughts and actions are the cause of unending misery and ignorance. This is (meant by) the awareness of the consequences.

There are three levels of action—*kṛta-kārita-anumoditā*.

One is doing it yourself—you are personally doing it, violence by your own action. The second is encouraging others towards violence, you are instigating others to do so. The third is approving those who are engaged in violent activity.

We often find that when one person talks negatively, the other person joins in and you inflict it onto the third person. This is *kārita*. Anyone who has come to you, you have thrown negativity at them. You are negative and you have also made others negative.

Someone with a negative mindset comes to a *sevaka* doing seva here in the āśrama and tells him, "Why are you doing sevā here in the āśrama? Such a waste of your time. You better go and get a job outside. Take care of yourself, don't do all these things. Why do you go to flood prone areas? Enough is enough, as though you can take care of all the miseries of the world. You cannot do anything." This is kārita.

Kṛta-kārita-anumoditā

Anumoditā—agreeing with and accepting a negative mindset. When someone is in a negative mindset, you agree to what he is saying. "People are not good in the world. People are hopeless," you confirm the negativity in others, blame the world and the people around. You think the world is a bad place.

In a sādhaka's life, one has to be very cautious with such people. They will be very friendly with you, very sweet with you. Slowly they will say, you are in an illusion. Why do you do all these prāṇāyāmas? What Gurudev is telling you is good for nothing. They will dissuade you from knowledge, from the path, sowing the seed of negativity inside you—about the world, about the *sangha*. Many such elements creep into the sangha and try to destroy the sangha. This is nothing new. This has been happening since Lord Buddha's time. One has to be cautious about them.

mṛdu-madhya adhimātrā

Some actions could be very mild, some moderate and some very strong. And what does it give? Misery for infinite time. There is *ananta phala*—infinite misery.

Lobha—greed, you want more. That greed can make you think in opposition to the yamas and niyamas.

Krodha—anger. In anger you apply your own logic and resort to kutarka.

Moha—delusion, attachment to something.

These are the ingredients for kutarka, which is the logic that comes from us.

Dukha—sadness. This brings you misery. Has spreading negativity ever brought you any joy? It may appear to have given you some relief. And it confounds you, "Oh! What I am thinking is correct. That guy is bad, this manager is bad, and this man is bad. See, everybody agrees with us. Ten of us agree that that person is bad." It gives you some relief. But it is going to bring you sorrow, ignorance and misery. To avoid this, *vitarka-bādhane pratipakṣa-bhāvanam*

These are the consequences. So I am not going to succumb to such negativity. I am going to keep my focus on the knowledge, on the wisdom. This is the attitude one has to take.

ahimsā-pratiṣṭhāyām tat-sannidhau vairatyāgaḥ || 35 ||

अहिंसाप्रतिष्ठायां तत्सन्निधौ वैरत्यागः ॥ ३५ ॥

Being established in non-violence causes everyone in the vicinity to lose the feeling of hostility.

When non-violence is well established in you, in your presence, people near you, who have aggressive or violent tendencies, calm down. The tendencies get dropped. I think most of us have experienced this.

It has happened twice in the USA. Once in Los Angeles, I was giving a talk. A tall, stout, dark Afro-American man, from the back, shouted at me, "You are Satan!" He was coming towards me aggressively. The guards immediately tried to stop him and send him out. I told them to leave him. I just looked at him. In a few minutes he just bent his head down, said sorry and walked away. In just a few minutes! He didn't even come close to me. Said sorry from a distance, and walked out.

Once in Washington DC, we were about 200–300 people. One tall American guy came towards me saying all sorts of things. He came and stood in front of me, to strangle me. Everybody froze because nobody expected something like this to happen. Nobody could get up and everybody was in shock. I looked at him and said, "Wait." Crying, he suddenly came down on his knees. Later on, he became a volunteer for The Art of Living.

Mahāvīra was a contemporary of Buddha. He was the founder of the Jain religion. He emphasized ahimsā. It is said that people up to several kilometres around Mahāvīra would drop their violence. Even thorns would become soft and flat on the ground to avoid pricking anybody. So what Maharṣi Patañjali says is the timeless truth. It is timeless wisdom. It is the truth that stands out. Even today you can see this around you.

Once I was in *ajñātavāsa* and went in a car with the driver—just the driver and me. We were driving through a forest area and there was a log lying on the road. The sun had already set, there was barely any light around and the log had to be removed, otherwise we would not be able to go ahead. Then we saw that there was a lion sitting near the log. It had its prey near it and the driver froze with fear. He said he wouldn't get down. I told him that nothing would happen. So I got down and as soon as I got down, he also came behind me. We removed the log, sat in the car and drove off. Next morning, we happened to pass by his village and within five minutes he gathered everyone to tell them that when Gurudev was there, the lion just went away. It didn't do anything to us!

So, the fear is within us. When our mind is in a state of equanimity, when we are well established in the seer, well established in ahimsā, in our presence *himsā* (violence) will drop, aggression will reduce.

Now don't try this immediately anywhere. You don't have to take that risk.

In my teenage years, I wanted to try all these adventures. I wanted to find out whether all these sūtras really worked. So I climbed a hill in Rishikesh, near the Neelkanth road, on a dark night with one of my friends. We were going ahead when suddenly we heard a voice, "Stop! Don't go any further." We turned back, and continued walking till five o' clock in the morning, eager to find some wild animals but found nothing. We visited a temple on the way back and reached the place where we had heard the voice. It was a tiny strip where we had been walking and on the other side there was a steep hill. One little slip, just five inches, that is it, we would have gone down several thousand feet! So I am warning you—don't try all that! But know that this happens for sure. In the presence of a person who is well established in ahimsā, others also will lose their animosity.

satya-pratiṣthāyām kriyā-phala-āśrayatvam || 36 ||

सत्यप्रतिष्ठायां क्रियाफलाश्रयत्वम् ॥ ३६ ॥

Being established in Truth causes one's actions to bear fruit.

All your actions will become fruitful if you are established in the truth. The actions of many people do not bring about results because there is no truth-consciousness in them. The fruit of an action will follow immediately when there is truth-consciousness.

Any project that we take up in the Art of Living, is a success. The president of the World Bank once asked, "Gurudev, our success rate in all our projects is less than 10%. How come all your projects are successful?" I told him, "It is not just the money that brings success, there is something else. That is sattva, the satya, the truth."

Many times we confuse the truth. All those who are angry swear by the truth—I am truthful. And that is why they are saying it with anger, but that 'truth' is out of ignorance. Here *satya-pratiṣṭhāyam* is being established in that which is beyond time, which is beyond events.

Kriyā-phala-āśrayatvam—success comes to you. There is success in action. Truth is not just the words but also the quality of straightforwardness of the consciousness.

When you tell a lie, your consciousness is not solid. It is not straightforward, there is no strength in it.

satya-pratiṣṭhāyam kriyā-phala-āśrayatvam

Success comes easily to a person who is committed to the truth; who is committed to 'what is'—the presence of Being. It is not that he will not encounter failures. He may, but he will win. *Satyameva jayate*—the truth alone triumphs. Truth will definitely win, though intermittently, it may appear not to be winning. 'We trust in God' written on the American currency notes, is something similar.

I will tell you a story. Mughal emperor Akbar was ruling India. He had a wise minister called Birbal, who was very humorous. There was no parliament or congressmen to debate and pass laws. The emperor would pass odd laws and rules.

Once he heard a talk on truth and was highly influenced. He ordered that anybody found telling a lie would be hanged. This new law created a big commotion. The lawyers felt that it would ruin their business and their profession would be finished. They had a meeting to decide the course of action. Similarly, all the merchants gathered for a meeting to discuss the new law. They wondered how they would be able to sell their products. It was disastrous. Despite being aware that their products were not the best, they would claim them to be so. They would tell many lies to their potential customers and employ various gimmicks to make their business run. With the new law, they would be ruined. They felt that it was outrageous. They would not be able to carry on with the new law in place. There were similar meetings held by astrologers, priests, doctors, etc.

They approached Birbal, a wise minister in the king's court, who promised to help them. The next day when Birbal was on his way to the king's bedroom, the guards outside stopped him. He told them that he was going to be hanged. It was a lie, so the guards took him to the king. If he would be hanged, then he didn't tell a lie; whatever he said was the truth. Then the king would have punished an innocent man and that would be a big crime. If the king were not to hang him, then the law would become obsolete!

To settle this, Akbar called all the ministers and pundits and there was a big debate. If Birbal was hanged, a law would be violated and if he was not hanged, then, too, a law would be violated. Everybody was in a fix, and the king was in a greater fix. Finally, he asked Birbal himself to suggest what was to be done. Birbal said that truth is not what is spoken. Anything that is spoken becomes a lie. The moment you say something, you are distorting 'what is' and 'what is' is the truth.

Following satya is to be with 'what is'. Are your intentions straightforward and clear? Or are you hiding something? Is there some other hook you are keeping?

Be truthful in your life, your presence, your mind, your heart—not merely in your words but also in your intention.

asteya-pratiṣṭhāyām sarva-ratna-upasthānam || 37 ||

अस्तेयप्रतिष्ठायां सर्वरत्नोपस्थानम् ॥ ३७ ॥

Being established in non-stealing causes all the jewels to present themselves.

Wealth comes to you when you are not hankering for it. When you are not stealing, when you are not trying to take things away from others, you will get what you have to get. Stealing will not bring you wealth.

Third yama is *asteya*, not stealing. You may admire somebody's voice and wish you had a good one. You have already stolen it. You may admire someone's looks and wish you looked like her. You have already stolen her looks. This creates jealousy and a desire to have something that you admire. This is the reason why people steal. Asteya eliminates jealousy and the tendency to steal. People steal many things. Some people steal someone else's plans, others steal techniques. Then, again, someone steals other people's things. These things do not work. People who steal remain poor. If you are committed to be sincere and do not steal, then *sarva ratnopalabdihi*—all the wealth comes to you effortlessly. This is the effect of not stealing. Even a slight intention to steal can keep you poor. Most of the time poverty is self-induced. A person wants to be sneaky and tries to grab as much as he can. That is where his luck goes down the drain. Not stealing brings all the wealth.

brahmacarya-pratiṣṭhāyām vīrya-lābhaḥ || 38 ||

ब्रह्मचर्यप्रतिष्ठायां वीर्यलाभः ॥ ३८ ॥

Being established in chastity gives great strength.

Here brahmacarya means two things, one is abstinence. If someone is having sex every day, they are so tired that there is no energy in them. So when you have abstinence, you get strength. You become stronger.

The other meaning, in fact the real meaning of brahmacarya is walking with a broadened awareness, 'moving in infinity'. '*Brahma*' means infinity and '*carya*' means 'moving in'.

You move like a glow of light when you know your vast nature and consider yourself as not just the body. This is when celibacy naturally happens.

When you are sitting in deep meditation, you do not feel you are the body. You don't feel you are an eighty-pound, a ninety-pound or a hundred pound body. You feel very light, like a feather.

When you walk you do not feel the weight of your body. You feel more space. The more joyful you are, the less you feel the body. The more you are in infinite consciousness, the presence, the less you will feel the tension, or the body weight. That is brahmacarya. Our consciousness expanded to the infinite and moving in infinity is our true nature.

The nature that is space brings a lot of vigour, valour and strength in you. A small-minded person will be looking around to check who is good looking or with whom they can have sex. Such people will have low energy, be very dull and nobody will want to be near them. Persons who are obsessed with sex are very unattractive. They create such thick and dull vibrations around them that there is no strength, vigour or commitment in them. They just go anywhere and after anybody without even knowing where they are going. The mind becomes so crazy that there is no strength in it. It is limited and jealousy, anger, irritation, and frustration raise their heads. When these storms of negativity arise in a mind, it becomes very weak and poor.

All the truth about existence disappears. When your mind is obsessed with such a load of negativity, you cannot even observe the beautiful nature that you are in. *Brahma-carya pratiṣṭhāyāma vīrya-lābhaḥ*—great strength comes when brahmacarya is established in you. When you are walking with broadened awareness, the awareness of infinity, you have more strength. When you are walking in the Brahman, you consider yourself more than just the body; you see yourself as consciousness, as Brahman, then you get the real strength—vīrya-lābhaḥ.

The more your mind is engaged in petty things, the weaker you are. But if your mind is reeling in the highest, you are strong. If you are in this wisdom, then Divinity is all-pervading.

dhiyo yo nah prachodayāt

धियो यो नः प्रचोदयात्

That is what the *Gāyatrī Mantra* says—let my mind be soaked in infinity, in Divinity. Being active with this sense, walking with this realization of what is, I am saying 'what is' because it is so obvious once you know it. That alone is brahmacarya and that gives you immense strength. Small mindedness, small cravings, can only make you feel weak.

aparigraha-sthairye janma-kathaṅtā-

sambodhaḥ || 39 ||

अपरिग्रहस्थैर्ये जन्मकथंतासंबोधः ॥ ३९ ॥

Being established in non-accumulation gives complete knowledge of the underlying causes and reasons of previous lifetimes.

Aparigraha means not taking things. Whatever is coming to you, comes due to your karma. But if you take things, then you are craving for what others are giving you. When you take things from others, whether material or non-material like compliments, insults, anything, they are going to create more karma for you. When a person wants more and more, he just thinks of himself and is obsessed with fear. He does not know the eternal value of life. Life has been there for ages and will continue for ages to come.

Non-accumulation means confidence in one's existence and in one's ability, and having the knowledge of one's Self. If you know how to bake bread, then you will not go on baking and storing it for a year. It will become stale and inedible. You will bake fresh bread whenever you want to.

In China, there is a proverb: what you give, you gain more of. Whatever you scatter, you will have it all. You lose what you hold on to. When you scatter, it all comes back to you. Everything is yours.

A person who is very afraid and has no idea of his strength is very stingy. A stingy person is very selfish and hoards and accumulates.

Parigraha is always taking and wondering what else can be taken. If you do not accept anything from anybody, you will feel different. This is practically not possible in the world. There are people who practise this to the extreme. You do not have to go to the extreme but being aware of t his fact is useful.

When you give things to people, it brings something back to you. There are some good vibrations and this makes you happy. If you are very unhappy one day, then give away something or give some gifts to somebody. Then, your consciousness will change, it will shift. And sometimes when you accept gifts from someone, you feel unhappy.

In the ancient days, they knew this science very well. They used to call wise people home and offer them food and gifts. When they accepted, they would give them one more offering called *dakṣiṇa*. This was to show thankfulness to the wise people for having accepted their offerings.

So, if someone accepts a gift, then the giver should be thankful because the receivers are not just taking the gifts. They are taking away certain impressions or karmas of the past from the donor's mind.

Non-acceptance or non-accumulation of objects, or things from people, is aparigraha.

What happens when you practise aparigraha?

Janma-kathaṅtā sambodhaḥ—when you practise aparigraha and refuse to take anything, whether things, compliments or insults, you acquire the ability to remember your previous lifetimes. The memory of previous lifetimes brings enormous strength in the present moment. It brings clarity, happiness and purposefulness to your actions.

My dear, you are going to depart from this planet very soon. Another 20, 30 or 40 years are not much, the time is not far away. You are going to die and come back again. How clean have you kept your mind? How free have you kept your heart? How sincere have you been in your actions? Reflect on these questions. The memory of your past lives has an important role to play in your life, strengthening you and helping you to not commit the same mistakes that you have made before. How will that knowledge come to you? By not taking in more garbage into yourself. To some extent you all get the idea of being strong and focused but focus can only come with this awareness.

There are two types of focus. When you want to grab something, you are doing something to satisfy your ego, to satisfy your instincts, then you are very focused.

Another focus comes with clarity of mind. The mind is very clear. You know your purpose. The second type of focus is liberating. The first type of focus is binding. It is bondage.

These are the five *māhāvratas*—the great rules, the great vows. You will get results according to the extent of your practice.

śaucāt sva-aṅga-jugupsā paraiḥ-asamsargaḥ || 40 ||

शौचात् स्वाङ्गजुगुप्सा परैरसंसर्गः ॥ ४० ॥

Through cleanliness and purity, one develops an attitude of disinterest towards one's own body, becoming disinclined towards contact with the bodies of others.

Śauca means cleanliness, both inner and outer cleanliness of the body. It is important. In India we say '*Namaste*', we don't shake hands. In many ways it is very good. In the tropical climate, hands are often very sweaty and if you keep shaking hands with many people, you imbibe all those different bacteria from different hands.

All of us have microbes. Even on our forehead, there are three different types of mites. One type lives at the edge of the eyebrows, one in the middle and one at the top of the forehead, near the hairline. Three different types of microbes live in our own body and they do not cross their lines. They have their territories.

Similarly, our nostrils have different microbes. There are bacteria on our skin, in our sweat, in our body. When you keep shaking hands, hugging others, you exchange bacteria. Especially in hot climates like this, it is not advisable; it is not hygienic. Even the Queen of England shakes hands with others with gloves on.

So, namaste is a safe way of greeting and keeping the purity. In the cold climate it is not much of an issue. In cold climates, you are anyway wearing sweaters, gloves and are not sweating so much. In the hot tropical climate when you are sweating so much, it is better not to touch each other. When you are sweating so much, do you feel pure and fresh? No, you want to just take a shower and feel fresh.

So *śaucāt svāṅga-jugupsā parairasamsargaḥ*. What are the benefits of this?

sattva-śuddhi-saumanasya-ekāgrya-indriya-jaya-
ātma-darśana-yogyatvāni ca || 41 ||

सत्त्वशुद्धिसौमनस्यैकाग्र्येन्द्रियजयात्मदर्शनयोग्यत्वानि च ॥ ४१ ॥

And purification of the intellect, pleasantness in the mind, one-pointedness, victory over the senses and the eligibility for self-realisation.

What are the benefits of śauca?

Sattva-śuddhi—clarity in the intellect, purity in the intellect. You can try this. If you don't have contact and don't crave anything, then your mind is more focused.

Saumanasya—the mind is pleasant, happy.

Cittaikāgratā—there is focus in your attention, your awareness increases.

Indriyajaya—you have a say over your senses.

Ātmadarśana yogyatvāni—ability to realise the Self comes with the practising of śauca.

If you don't want any of these benefits, never mind. But if you want purity in the intellect, sharpness in awareness, then you practise śauca to whatever extent you can.

Now, this śauca does not apply to the mother and her children, parents and children, husband and wife. Śauca is beyond these relationships. A baby comes and hugs the mother anytime. This is not *aśauca*. But if you are in a relationship and when you break your relationship, you undergo big time misery. This is called *samsarga doṣa*. You are associated with someone and when you part, misery comes up in you. This is aśauca.

Whenever somebody dies, misery takes over and that period is called aśauca, meaning there is no śauca then. There is no purity because the mind is polluted by sadness. The mind is afflicted by sadness. So in India, the ten days after someone's death are considered as aśauca. Nobody goes and touches the grieving family members and if they do they have to take a bath. The association of miserable persons is to be avoided because those miseries get transferred to you. This doesn't mean that you should not do sevā. Miserable people are those who need sevā the most. When you do sevā, aśauca doesn't happen to you. But when you are associated with the negative mindset or a miserable mindset, you will see that those things also enter your mind.

So śauca, purity, can bring clarity of mind, focus in the mind, happiness in yourself, and the ability to realise the Self—ātmadarśana yogyatvāni.

When you do advanced silence programs and sit for long meditations, your mind is focused and becomes like a laser. At other times, the mind is all over the place, scattered, thinking about this friend and that friend, but when you meditate, there is focus, there is a feeling of purposefulness, clarity, and purity. How many of you have experienced this? This is śauca. This is ātmadarśana yogyatvāni. That is why we put you into a silence program. Get out of everything and for sometime, be by yourself.

But don't tell your husband or wife not to touch you, that aśauca has happened. No. And when your children come and hug you, it is not aśauca. Take it for certain that this rule of śauca aśauca does not apply to children and babies. Is that clear?

But personal hygiene is very important. Along with that, the mind also needs to be kept clean—*antaha śauca bāhya bheetara śauca.*

santoṣād-anuttamaḥ sukha-lābhaḥ || 42 ||

संतोषादनुत्तमः सुखलाभः ॥ ४२ ॥

From contentment comes unparalleled happiness.

We are miserable with what we don't have and we are also miserable with what we have. You have to get out of this vicious cycle.

Ask yourself what makes you unhappy? Losing a lot of money? Could that make you unhappy? So what! Anyway, you are going to lose this body, which is going to enjoy those millions of dollars. It has to happen. So many people had millions of dollars but they too died. What else are you unhappy about? Is your friend leaving you? Your own body is going to desert you!

Why are you so worried about your friend deserting you? The strength of your happiness is measured by your attitude in adverse situations. If everything is smooth then your big smile is worth nothing. You should smile in an adverse situation. You should feel that, even if the world dies and disappears, you are not going to sell your smile and that you are not going to be unhappy. Then santoṣa dawns.

Santoṣa—contentment and happiness. They are attitudes. If you are used to being unhappy, you will grumble and be unhappy even in the best of situations. Nothing can make you happy in the world. What happens when you are happy; when you smile? There is much relaxation on your face, in the muscles of the face, in the head, etc. There is freedom, joy and relaxation. And if you have trained your muscles and your nervous system to be unhappy, then there will be knots and stress on your face. There will be stiffness in your head and in your body, you will remain unhappy irrespective of the situation, surrounding, etc. Santoṣa is a practice. Being happy is a practice. Unconditional happiness is a practice. You have to develop it yourself. Nobody else can do it for you. Nothing else can give it to you. If anybody else or anything else gives it, it will only be temporary.

You need to decide that you are going to smile no matter what happens. You need to feel that everyone and everything is going to die and disappear anyway. So, do not worry. You need to feel that you will be happy, and you will not mind it if somebody is upset or something is wrong. At the least, you can breathe happily. Nobody is going to hold your nose. If you feel like this, then you are free.

Do you know, you sell your happiness for peanuts? You sell your smile for a penny. The entire world is not worth losing your smile. Even if you are made a king or an emperor of the world, it is not worth giving away your smile. This is the second niyama—the rule, the condition for yoga .

If you were to die today, how would you want to die? With a sense of having enjoyed enough, isn't it? But saying 'enough is enough' is a sign of frustration. I am content, I have had enough, I am in abundance—that is contentment. Practise this again and again. If you crave, things are not going to appear. Further, contentment is not in any way in opposition with creativity. Nor does it make you complacent. Contentment at every step brings you unparalleled happiness.

kāya-indriya-siddhiḥ-aśuddhi-kṣayāt-tapasaḥ || 43 ||

कायेन्द्रियसिद्धिरशुद्धिक्षयात्तपसः ॥ ४३ ॥

Penance eliminates impurities from the body and brings perfection to the senses.

In this regard, the Jain saints are to be appreciated a lot. They walk bare feet, in the summer, in the winter. They wear very few clothes. And they walk miles and miles. They are not allowed to sit in a vehicle. What is the impact of this? Not liberation. Do not make the mistake of thinking that anyone taking a lot of strain on their body gets liberated. But one thing surely happens—*kāyendriya siddhi*—their senses and body become very strong. Very few of them fall sick.

Aśuddhi-kṣayāt—the body gets rid of impurities. So tapas is needed, not for liberation, but to bring purity to your body and senses.

svādhyāyād-iṣṭa-devatā-samprayogaḥ || 44 ||

स्वाध्यायादिष्टदेवतासंप्रयोगः ॥ ४४ ॥

From Self-study and reflection, one attains contact with the subtle beings.

By Self-study, svādhyāya, the *devas* or divine presence is felt and experienced. By Self-study, by observing and by being hollow and empty, you become a channel. You become a part of the Divine. You are able to feel the presence of Divinity. The angels and devās, which are different forms of your consciousness, start blossoming.

Iṣṭa-devatā samprayogaḥ means contact with the subtle Divinity that can come to you in any form, or light, or vibration or feeling. See, when you perform *yajña*, meditation, tapas, certain vibrations take over you. Many of you have experienced this. Whenever you sit in big *homās, poojās*, you feel some vibrations. That is iṣṭa-devatā samprayogaḥ. Participating in a yajña is also part of svādhyāya. This is also called *kuhana*. Kuhana has one more meaning—tickling. There is a sūtra, in the *Vijnāna Bhairava*, which says that by kuhana you can get enlightenment. People interpreted it as tickling. Kuhana also means yajña. Participating in a yajña, or listening to the chanting of the mantras, to devotional hymns, uplifts the energy and then you experience or come in contact with the subtle divine beings.

samādhi-siddhiḥ-īśvara-praṇidhānāt || 45 ||

समाधिसिद्धिरीश्वरप्रणिधानात् ॥ ४५ ॥

By surrendering to the Divine, perfection in samādhi is attained.

If you are holding on to anything inside you, samādhi is impossible. You have to let go of everything. Iśvarapraṇidhāna simply means being like a child in the lap of the mother. You let go of everything. When the child is lying in the lap of the mother to sleep, it does not hold on to anything. It lets go of everything.

Letting go, not holding anything back, offering it to the infinite divine Being, samādhi happens to you. *Samādhi-siddhiḥ* means, perfection in samādhi is attained. You may get a tiny glimpse of emptiness, a little quietness but we have to achieve perfection in samādhi.

Iśvarapraṇidhāna is very essential. Even an atheist and an agnostic can attain samādhi but cannot perfect samādhi. To make the mind empty, you don't have to believe in God. You don't have to believe in anything. You don't have to have faith in anything. You can just make your mind blank for some time. That is okay. Having a blank mind is only the beginning of samādhi, not the end of samādhi. But to gain perfection in it, you let go of everything that you have held onto and offer yourself to Divinity. That is essential.

samādhi-siddhiḥ-iśvarapraṇidhānāt

The seer has an impact on the scenery as does the scenery on the seer. This is what we have seen. The subject and object are interdependent—the theory of relativity! The sūtras present here very clearly enunciate that the scenery and the seer, the subject and object are dependent on each other. They're relative to each other's existence. So we read about the yama, niyamas and their benefits. We read why they should be practised and what the consequences are if you don't practise them. If you are ready to bear the consequences, then don't practise them. You have all the right to be miserable if you want to! That's what the Maharṣi has now said. If doubts come to your mind—*vitarka-bādhane pratipakṣa-bhāvanam*—you have to handle your own doubt. Nobody can remove your doubt. The Guru is not here to remove your doubts. The Guru is here, in fact, to plant a few more doubts in you. So that you can be churned as cream.

Pratipakṣa-bhāvanam—you have to take the opposite stand and see that if you don't do what is suggested, what the consequences would be. So Maharṣi Patañjali makes you think about the consequences and when you understand that the consequences are very grave, you naturally adopt or come back to the yamas and niyamas—the rules and regulations.

Then come the āsanas—the cobra pose, the bow pose, the *matsyāsana, markatāsana, tādāsana,* etc—none of these āsanas that we practise is in the *Patañjali Yoga Sūtra*. Even *sūrya namaskāra* is not there. Of course *Hathayoga Pradipīkā* has mentioned them but that doesn't come under the main body of the scripture because it is a subordinate limb.

As it is, yoga is a subordinate limb and Hathayoga Pradipīkā and all other scriptures are tributaries drawn from the Patañjali Yoga Sūtra.

Here Maharṣi Patañjali says:

sthira-sukham-āsanam || 46 ||

स्थिरसुखमासनम् ॥ ४६ ॥

Posture is that which is steady and comfortable.

An āsana is a position in which you feel stable; you are not wobbly. You stand on one foot but it's not an āsana because a little later you start wobbling. It is not comfortable. So anything that is not comfortable is not an āsana. *Sthira sukham āsanam*—that which is stable and is pleasurable is āsana.

prayatna-śaithilya-ananta-samāpattibhyām || 47 ||

प्रयत्नशैथिल्यानन्तसमापत्तिभ्याम् ॥ ४७ ॥

By letting go of the effort, alignment with infinity is attained.

Let go of the effort and align with infinity. Here comes the crux—if you are already comfortable, then there is no effort and unless there is an effort, how can you let go of the effort? It's a very nice way to say just let go of the effort, which means that you have to put in the effort first, in order to let go of it. There are certain questions asked in a similar way, "Come on, tell me, when did you fight with your wife? Yesterday or today? Answer in yes or no." To fight with your wife, you have to have a wife first! Similarly, to let go of the effort, you have to put in the effort first.

Here Maharṣi Patañjali gives you a very simple clue for an āsana. If you stay for a little longer in any āsana, it appears to be an effort. And especially for one who is restless, even simply sitting will not be comfortable.

Now you be sthira, meaning be stable. When you are asked to be just like a statue, it becomes uncomfortable. This is an effort by itself. And then letting go of the effort—here is the clue for all other āsanas. He has not mentioned any āsana. He says you make an effort to go into any posture and then you let go. Relax. Then each āsana aligns you with infinity. Any āsana brings that blankness, emptiness in your mind. It has to happen. Otherwise it is just gymnastics. You go to the gym and lift weights. There is no letting go of effort. There is no alignment with infinity.

In the beginning, you put in an effort to do the āsana and then later on it just flows. You find yourself aligned to infinity in each posture you do.

What is the effect of this? What does it do?

tato dvaṅdva-anabhighātaḥ || 48 ||

ततो द्वन्द्वानभिघातः ॥ ४८ ॥

Through that, one is able to be unperturbed by the opposites.

It strikes at the duality or the conflicts in you. It roots them out—dvaṅdva-anabhighātaḥ

You should do āsanas whenever you are confused and your mind is in conflict. Sit in an āsana and there will be clarity right away. The effect of an āsana is clearing out all conflicts and dualities.

If you have mastered the āsanas, if you have *āsana siddhi* then it helps you to overcome the opposites—heat and cold. When I was young I had to sit like this on the stage for 8–10 hours. We couldn't even get out for a washroom break. It would be painful here and there but you simply watch and just be there, it'll disappear. Once the practice happens, then āsana siddhi happens, enormous patience comes to you. The power to endure the opposite dawns in you.

Then you can sit in the āsana and get into meditation. It could be any āsana. But I don't think *śavāsana* is a good āsana! You'll fall asleep because it is too effortless.

tasmin sati śvāsa-praśvāsayoḥ-gati-

vicchedaḥ prāṇāyāmaḥ || 49 ||

तस्मिन् सति श्वासप्रश्वासयोर्गतिविच्छेदः प्राणायामः ॥ ४९ ॥

Having done that (while in the āsana), interrupting the flow of inhalation and exhalation is called prāṇāyāma.

It is obvious. We have done many types of prāṇāyāma. While breathing normally when you change the rhythm of the breath, it is called prāṇāyāma. Prāṇāyāma is when our inhalation and exhalation are practised consciously.

bāhya-ābhyantara-sthambha-vṛttiḥ deśa-kāla

sankhyābhiḥ paridṛṣṭo-dīrgha-sūkṣmaḥ || 50 ||

बाह्याभ्यन्तरस्तम्भवृत्तिः देशकालसङ्ख्याभिः

परिदृष्टो दीर्घसूक्ष्मः ॥ ५० ॥

The various aspects of prāṇāyāma are exhalation, inhalation and suspension of breath. The other parameters to be looked into are

the space (of the movement of breath), the time and count while the breath is deep and subtle.

It is self-explanatory. You breathe in, hold, breathe out, and hold, with some count. Various people and various schools have adopted different counts. We have adopted 4,4,6,2 and it works very well. It is safe and most effective. Certain times, if prāṇāyāma is not done under proper guidance, it can be harmful. You may lose touch with reality, this reality. Prāṇāyāma has to be done under guidance, under supervision.

We have our own bhastrikā and we have a scientific explanation to back it. Though we spontaneously did this bhastrikā, scientists came and said this is really good and we felt happy about it. Even science has put a stamp of approval on it. When you lift your hands up in bhastrikā, the ribcage expands and you breathe in more air. It also activates those parts of the lungs which normally remain dormant.

Those of you who have done *samyama* have learnt the *bogar prāṇāyāma*. That has a different count. It's a little more strenuous but good for the advanced stages.

bāhya-ābhyantara-viṣaya-ākṣepī caturthaḥ || 51 ||

बाह्याभ्यन्तरविषयाक्षेपी चतुर्थः ॥ ५१ ॥

The fourth type (of prāṇāyāma) happens when the (effort of) exhalation and inhalation is given up.

Sometimes in deep meditation, when all the thoughts and ideas are cleared from the mind there is a spontaneous prāṇāyāma that happens. Either the breath stops or it moves very fast or it goes in its own different, unmanaged, unmanipulated rhythm. This is the fourth type of prāṇāyāma.

Viṣaya-akṣepī—what is happening at that moment? The mind, in those moments, is free from sense objects. When the mind is in a different, serene dimension, beyond the sensory perception, then a fourth type of prāṇāyāma happens.

And what is the effect of this prāṇāyāma?

tataḥ kṣīyate prakāśa-āvaraṇam || 52 ||

ततः क्षीयते प्रकाशावरणम् ॥ ५२ ॥

Thereby, the veil over the inner light is thinned.

What is the benefit of all these prāṇāyāma? The Maharṣi does not tell you anything without enunciating its benefits. He's a very practical person. The benefit of prāṇāyāma is that the cover, the veil around your being begins to thin down. There is a light inside you. In fact, you're light yourself but you do not know this because there is a thick veil around you. The consciousness which is light itself, is surrounded by a veil of ignorance—*āvaraṇa*. This veil comes down or thins down so that the light shines through. It moves from being opaque to translucent and then to transparent. It could be very thick around you. So from a thick veil, it becomes translucent. *Kṣīyate* means it starts reducing. When it is fully reduced, when the āvaraṇa is done with, then the light becomes transparent. Prāṇāyāma thins down that veil, and makes you more transparent so that you are able to see that you are the light.

dhāraṇāsu ca yogyatā manasaḥ || 53 ||

धारणासु च योग्यता मनसः ॥ ५३ ॥

And the ability to focus one's mind follows.

When all the veils around the Being are thinned down, then you gain the ability to practise dhāraṇā—to put your mind wherever you want to without getting distracted.

The mind develops this ability to stay at any one point in the body; to stay on any one thing. It gains the ability to intend. Till now, there was no intention. You were just like a crowd moving. There was no 'you' inside. You had no intention at all. Now with prāṇāyāma, there is clarity and you are able to have an intention and a direction. That is why you will notice, after a good prāṇāyāma, your mind is clearer, steadier and calmer. You are able to meditate better.

sva-viṣaya-asamprayoge cittasya svarūpa-anukāra
iva-indriyāṇām pratyāhāraḥ || 54 ||

स्वविषयासंप्रयोगे चित्तस्य स्वरूपानुकार
इवेन्द्रियाणां प्रत्याहारः ॥ ५४ ॥

Withdrawal of the senses (pratyāhāra) is when as a result of not coming in touch with sense objects, the senses (turn inwards and) follow the nature of the mind.

Our senses are made in a way that they always run outwards. You open your eyes and your mind is running through the eyes. It runs through the ears and listens. Similarly, with smell, taste, and touch. These are the food for our senses and the mind. When the mind turns inwards, it needs an alternative to keep it there.

When the car has to stop on the road, first comes the yellow light and then the red light. When the car has to go, first comes the yellow light and then the green signal, right? How do you prepare the mind to go inwards, when it is running outwards all the time? It needs an alternative food to move inwards. That is pratyāhārā—the fifth limb of yoga.

What does it do? It makes you centred and you gain power over your senses. You have control over your senses. You can use those senses whenever you want to. They listen to you instead of you listening to them. Do your eyes listen to you or do you listen to your eyes? There is a difference. Does the sense of touch rule over you or do you have a say over your sense of touch? Do your taste buds rule over you? Do they compel you to do whatever they say or do you have control over the taste buds? It's not so easy because right from birth or rather from many lifetimes they are used to running outwards. The mind goes outward. Rarely does it settle in. Whenever it does settle in, it goes into inertia, deep sleep. So it is not even aware of settling in. It is not a conscious settling in. Yoga is the conscious retrieving of oneself, conscious retracking to oneself and pratyāhārā is something that helps you to turn within.

When the senses move away from their objects and turn inwards it is pratyāhāra and it is not as difficult as it appears to be.

In fact, every time you experience deep ecstasy, there's a little bit of pratyāhāra in it. Your eyes close and you go inwards when you are eating a tasty sweet or when you breathe in the fragrance of a flower and forget the flower. For a fraction of second your mind goes inwards and if it continues to be there for more time then that is pratyāhāra. The mind looked at the flower, the nose took in the fragrance and the experience of it, at one point, turned you inward. "Wow!" you say. All this pleasure, the pinnacle of pleasure can only and only come from a touch of the Being, touch of the Self. The touch of the Self cannot happen without pratyāhāra.

Pratyāhāra is like the doorway to move in. So obviously in all sense experiences where you have experienced deep pleasure, you have passed through the door of pratyāhārā. But it is so short lived that you don't even recognize it.

You go in, you're happy and you come running out. You think that happiness is experienced because of something that is outside the door. The light has come from inside but it is getting reflected on a piece of mirror or a glass outside and you think that the light is outside. Pratyāhāra is letting go of the reflector and going to the source. We are only holding on to the reflectors all the time. We're not looking, where the reflection is coming from and what it is reflecting. Suppose there is a reflector in front of your home and the light is coming from inside. You are looking at the reflector. You go to hold on to the reflector and the light disappears because the light is behind you. So here Maharṣi Patañjali asks you to look where the light is and to look, you have to turn around. Pratyāhārā is the turning around. In every heightened experience in your life, there is a trace of pratyāhāra which we don't even notice. It just slips away but when you consciously put attention and draw the mind from the five senses, inward, that is pratyāhāra. Just doing pratyāhāra, you gain a say over your senses, mastery over your senses.

Do you know what the difference is between you and a criminal? You get the thought of strangling somebody but you don't act on it. The criminal acts on it and goes to jail. The same thought has come inside both of you. You feel like beating somebody when enraged, don't you? You just don't do it so you are safe. But someone who does it, goes behind bars. What happened? What was the difference? The thought was the same in both places but you had a say over your emotions. You had a say over your thoughts. You had some control over them, so you didn't get into the space that the criminal had gotten into. I have sympathy for these people. Nobody taught them how to control their senses, how to control their mind. They are much more powerful than their tendencies and emotions, yet they are drowned in them. Pratyāhārā helps you to rise above your carnal tendencies and emotions. Maharṣi Patañjali is not saying that the senses and sense objects are bad. No, he never said so. Lord Kṛṣṇa also never says they're bad but if you don't have a say over them, you are doomed. Your mind is the cause for your liberation and your bondage.

Kṛṣṇa has said the same thing in the Gītā but in a different way. When you have mastered pratyāhārā how will it be? When someone attacks a turtle, it withdraws its limbs into its shell. The shell is very hard, even if you place a big stone on it, it doesn't break. So the turtle protects itself by pulling all its limbs inside. A wise man is like a turtle. At will he can retract all his senses and at will he can bring them out. A yogī has that ability. Don't think a yogī cannot get angry. He can get angry. He can get angrier than you can but that anger is in his control. Don't think a yogī is one who is not active, is very laid back, goody-goody with everything going smoothly. No! A yogī can be revolutionary and yogīs are revolutionaries but with awareness. Revolution with evolution. The so-called revolutionaries are simply reactionaries. They react to something that has happened to them or around them. A real revolutionary is one who supports the evolution of the human race, who is a catalyst for evolution, who could change things, and shock people, shake their foundation and that's what yoga is all about. That is what Kṛṣṇa's life is all about. He could play the flute under the trees and have an undying smile all the time. Even in the war field he could smile. But when it was needed he could show more anger than anybody else. Even Bhishma shook at the sight of his anger. So a yogī has this ability to comprehend the extremities of creation. That's what the Maharṣi said in a previous sūtra:

parmaṇu param mahatatva

From the smaller than the smallest to the bigger than the biggest, is in his domain.

Kṛṣṇa said—*tasmāt yogī bhavārjuna*—"Arjuna, you become a yogī before wanting to become a soldier to fight and rule the country. Be a yogī first, get out of this narrow mindset. You're talking as though you are very wise, great, learned, knowledgeable but your actions don't reflect that. Come on, wake up!" He gives the wake-up call. This is the way of the Masters. Sometimes they praise you to wake you up. Sometimes they push you down to wake you up. Pushing down alone will not help, praising alone will not help. Sometimes you have to praise, sometimes you have to put down also. Both the ways are adopted by a Master. He knows when to put down, when to praise and when to uplift somebody. He knows how much they are capable of and what dosage is needed.

tataḥ paramā vaśyatā-indriyāṇām || 55 ||

ततः परमा वश्यतेन्द्रियाणाम् ॥ ५५ ॥

This gives supreme control over the senses.

This brings all our senses, our body and everything else together as one whole. After a good meditation, you feel that you are total. That is why Jesus said that He had come to make man whole; a complete person. That is what you feel when you do Sudarśana Kriyā and when you sing in a *satsaṅga*. Your energy becomes full and you feel total. You become whole.

Tataḥ paramā vaśyatā indriyāṇām—then, all your senses listen to you. You don't have to listen to them. Paramā vaśyate—you will feel contentment, much peace and joy. You will feel real elevation and real completeness. This is the effect of pratyāhārā.

Question and Answers

Question: Gurudev, can we be in samādhi while being awake, even when we are in vṛttis?

Gurudev: Yes, that is *savitarkā samādhi, savicārā samādhi.* That equanimity in your mind is there even when you are acting, when you are doing things. But it comes after long practice. Don't fool yourself, "I am in samādhi yet I am doing all the work." No, it takes some time, some maturity for you to feel meditative while doing something. I can yell at somebody and I can be in a meditative state. That is possible. But for that to happen it will take a long time. We should not fool ourselves.

Question: Do emotions come under some vṛttis of mind? What modulation of mind creates happiness or is happiness?

Gurudev: Happiness and misery are different things. All these five vṛttis are kliṣṭa (miserable) and akliṣṭa (not miserable). They can comfort you or discomfort you. Sleep can bring you comfort. If you don't sleep, it brings discomfort. If you sleep you're happy and if you don't, you're unhappy.

Memories can bring you happiness as well as misery. So smṛti can also be miserable.

Question: Gurudev, why does Patañjali use two different words: samāpatti and samādhi. I know he does not use any words without reason.

Gurudev: Don't be stuck with the words so much, it is the same. *Dhī* is consciousness, dhī is intellect. Same with samāpatti; samāpatti is also the same—equanimous, equanimity.

Question: What is the difference between kleśas and obstacles on the path?

Gurudev: There is a subtle difference. Obstacles come and go but kleśas—deeper impressions—remain longer than that.

Question: Patañjali says about kleśas, *te pratiprasavaheyāḥ sūkṣmāḥ*. What is the process of pratiprasavah or involution?

Gurudev: Patañjali has very clearly said *dhyānaheyāḥ*, meditation is the way. When you do meditation you become self-referral. You get back to the Self. There are some impressions which are active and some which are dormant. So these different types of impressions that we are holding on in our mind, in our consciousness have to be cleansed through meditation.

Question: Gurudev, outside of me, you appear as the scenery and within me, as the seer. I am inspired and joyed by both these forms. Is one of them the truth and the other maya?

Gurudev: That maya is also divine. And it can be crossed over by grace alone. So don't worry! Be integrated both inside and outside.

Question: Gurudev, the yoga sūtras recommend the chanting of Om. Some people say that such a practice is only for the sanyāsīs. Is it true?

Gurudev: It is true. If you practise Om chanting, then very soon you will let go of everything. And then if you are not successful at something you will begin to crib! We have also heard this from our teachers. They would always ask not to chant Om alone on its own. It is OK to chant 'Om Namah Shivay', 'Om Namoh Narayanaya', 'Hari Om' instead. Attach it with Hari or some other mantra then you have success in your work. If you keep chanting just Om, then it will take you to *nirguṇa nirākāra*—attributeless, formless Divinity. Then you won't be able to operate successfully in the *saguṇa sākāra* world—the world of attributes and forms. We have heard this. One may chant Om but should not take it alone by itself as a dhyāna mantra. It is necessary to know this.

Question: Dear Gurudev, how do I develop unshakable faith when you do not look at me but look all around me and keep laughing?

Gurudev: Yes, it is alright! I look at you when you look here and there instead of looking at me. No one can escape my vision, just know this firmly. It might seem that I pay more attention to someone and less to someone else. This is nothing, it is superficial. Rest assured and don't be bothered by this; just forget about it. If

I speak more to someone just think that it must be very important, something must not be alright (Laughter). Know this and be at peace.

Question: Gurudev you had mentioned that valor is a valid means of attaining samādhi. How can this valour be channelized towards samādhi instead of violence?

Gurudev: Valour and violence are different. When you are engulfed in violence there is no valour in you. It shows your weakness. Your anger is your weakness and what you do out of that anger, rage is only a reaction. Valour is something completely different from rage. Never ever confuse rage with valour. A person with valour will never succumb to rage, anger or such weaknesses. Do you get it? A person with valour, you will see, will have all the confidence. He will stand up and face any situation, "Yes I am here, come what may." Anger, rage, hatred are not valour; a person with valour cannot have hatred. Anything you do with hatred weakens you even further. When you act with valour you feel stronger, and even more energetic and powerful but an act you do out of hatred devastates you.

Vibhūti Pāda

Vibhūti

Vibhūti literally means miracle, that which charms, is extraordinary. There is no dearth of miracles on the path of a sādhaka, yoga practitioner.

The extraordinary abilities that exist in you can be invoked by doing samyama. Doing samyama on different aspects will give different results. Discipline for a sādhaka, is different from that of a *siddha*, a perfected being. A sādhaka has to be moderate in sleep, activity, and in just about everything but for a siddha there are no rules. He can do whatever he wants.

An expert cook doesn't have to go through the manuals. Whatever he cooks will always taste good, otherwise he is not an expert cook. A beginner, on the other hand, has to go by the book. He needs to be cautious so as not to burn the food. An expert cook will never burn anything and because of his expertise in the craft he can experiment with any combination. Similarly, a siddha's expertise at his level of consciousness is very different from that of a sādhaka's. So never try to imitate a siddha, a perfected being. "Oh Guruji is doing so and so, why should I not do it?" It is not the right thing to do at all because of the difference in the capacities and the states of consciousness.

The Eight Limbs of Yoga (continued)

deśa-bandhaḥ-cittasya dhāraṇā ||1||

देशबन्धश्चित्तस्य धारणा ॥ १ ॥

Holding the mind in a place is focus (dhāraṇā).

Dhāraṇā is focusing the mind at any one point. Now which point? There are hundreds of dhāraṇās. Even the idols are also dhāraṇās. You keep a śivaliṅga. It is a dhāraṇā as your mind is focused on that. Your mind is fixed on it. You take a candle and stare at it. That is a dhāraṇā too. In Hatha yoga it is called *trāṭaka*. If you look at the Sun for a few minutes, the rising Sun or the setting Sun, it is a dhāraṇā. Similarly, with your eyes closed you do a mantra japa that is dhāraṇā.

tatra pratyaya-ekatānatā dhyānam ||2||

तत्र प्रत्ययैकतानता ध्यानम् ॥ २ ॥

There, an unbroken flow in the content of the mind is meditation (dhyāna).

When the mind is fixed in some place, then it flows like oil. When you drop water, it comes down in droplets, but when you pour oil it comes down as a string, a continuous unbroken flow. Dhyāna is the continuous pouring of the mind.

Your life is full of dhyāna, your worry is also a dhyāna. You have a worry stuck in your mind. When you wake up in the morning, the first thing that comes to your mind is the same worry. You are brushing your teeth and the same thought is flowing through your mind. When you are taking a shower the same thought persists. Whether of worry or anger or righteousness, that thought is making dhyāna happen in you.

Worry is dhyāna, meditation. You are having tea and the same thought is bombarding your head. You are having a conversation with somebody, it is going into your ears, but you are not hearing it. You are sitting in a conversation, but you are in your own world, you are on your own trip. This is dhyāna.

In the Vaidika vocabulary, there is a word called baka dhyāna. The crane stands still in the water as though it is meditating but actually it is keeping an eye on the fish. So if someone is pretending to be meditating they say it is baka dhyāna, meaning the meditation of a crane. You don't know when it will put its beak into the water and come up with a fish. Till then it appears deep in meditation, standing still, very still. So meditation is a part of your life, only that it is misplaced in worries, in tensions and other such things. If you keep thinking, "I'm poor, I don't have, I lack so-and-so thing," then only lack will increase because you are making that type of dhyāna.

tad-eva-artha-mātra-nirbhāsam svarūpa-

śūnyam-iva samādhiḥ ||3||

तदेवार्थमात्रनिर्भासं स्वरूपशून्यमिव समाधिः ॥ ३ ॥

That (meditation) itself becomes samādhi when only pure awareness remains, almost as if there is no self-cognition.

Samādhi is when you are aware and you are there but you feel as though you are not there. It can be described as a boundless feeling. You are centered everywhere but circumferenced nowhere. You don't find you're bound by anything and you are everywhere, but there is no centre. The centre is everywhere. Samādhi is when there is a centre everywhere but circumference nowhere.

Svarūpa-śūnyam-iva—as though it is nothing. This is the beauty of the yoga sūtras.

How are the yoga sūtras different from Buddhism? Buddhism says there is nothing—śūnya—emptiness. The yoga sūtras say as though it is empty. Is it not real emptiness? No, because there is somebody who is experiencing the emptiness. If it is all empty, how can an emptiness say that it is experiencing emptiness? This is such a delicate point.

Lord Buddha said it is all emptiness, there is nothing, there is no Self. Vedānta says, “Then who experienced that it is all empty? There must be someone who experienced this emptiness, someone who cognized that it's all empty. That is the Self!” So here Maharṣi Patañjali says—svarūpaśūnyam iva—as though the Self is not there, as though it is a non-self. That experience is samādhi.

Samyama

trayam ekatra samyamaḥ || 4 ||

त्रयम् एकत्र संयमः ॥ ४ ॥

When all the three—dhāranā, dhyāna and samādhi—come together, it is samyama.

What does samyama do? It brings forth siddhis—powers, in you.

tad-jayāt prajñā-ālokaḥ || 5 ||

तज्जयात् प्रज्ञाऽऽलोकः ॥ ५ ॥

Mastery of that (samyama) brings transcendental awareness.

On perfecting the samyama, you have the access code to another world—the world of lights, the world of heightened and transcendental consciousness.

When do you get the password? When these three things—dhāranā, dhyāna and samādhi—come together and you perfect them.

tasya bhūmiṣu viniyogaḥ || 6 ||

तस्य भूमिषु विनियोगः ॥ ६ ॥

That (transcendental awareness) should be applied in previous planes of awareness.

So when you get this power, it can be utilized. It can be applied. You don't let your money just lie in the bank. You invest it, you use it. Similarly, the power you get, *prajñāloka*, the power of the inner being, inner consciousness, you use it in the world.

trayam antaraṅgam pūrvebhyaḥ || 7 ||

त्रयम् अन्तरङ्गं पूर्वेभ्यः ॥ ७ ॥

These three (dhāranā, dhyāna, samādhi) are subtler (internal) than the previous ones.

'Previous ones', here refers to yama, niyama, āsana, prāṇāyāma, pratyāhāra. Yama and niyama are related to the world. Āsana is again related to the physical body. Prāṇāyāma is related to the breath. Pratyāhāra is also very similar relating the outside to the inside. So compared to these other five limbs, the three—dhāranā, dhyāna and samādhi—are subtler and more internal, *antaraṅgam*. You cannot see someone doing dhyāna but you can see someone doing prāṇāyāma.

tad-api bahiraṅgam nirbījasya || 8 ||

तदपि बहिरङ्गं निर्बीजस्य ॥ ८ ॥

However, they are gross (external) as compared to nirbīja samādhi.

In the higher state of *nirbīja samādhi*, even these are external. *Aṣṭāvakra (*in the later chapter of *Aṣṭāvakra Gītā*) tells Janaka, "You are meditating, that is your problem! You are doing these practices, that is your problem, my dear! Drop all these practices. Drop the meditation. Drop the sādhanā. Drop all these things!" However, that is at a different stage. That is the nirbīja avasthā (seedless state). Here, even these (dhāranā, dhyāna, samādhi) are external. These are not of much use but unfortunately what some people do is they put these two things together and discard everything. Saint Kabir has sung a very beautiful song about it:

काम न छोड़ा, क्रोध न छोड़ा, सत्य वचन क्यों छोड़ दिया ?

नाम जपन क्यों छोड़ दिया, बन्दे नाम जपन क्यों छोड़ दिया ?

You haven't dropped lust or anger but you have given up chanting and meditation. Why did you give up on the truth when you could not leave untruth?

The idea is to leave everything. It is said that even knowledge is like the soap you put on the body. Just because you paid for the soap, you don't keep the soap on your body. If you keep the soap, that itself will become dirt. So you wash it off.

You get into the bus, and when your destination arrives then you get off the bus. You don't ask, "If I have to get out of the bus, why should I get in, in the first place?" If someone argues in such a way, what would you say! You have to get into the bus at some point and you have to get out of the bus at some other point, my dear!

So even these three things are external. With nirbīja samādhi, Patañjali is enunciating the mechanics and science of consciousness. Now let us look at the three *pariṇāmas*.

The Three Outcomes

vyutthāna-nirodha-samskārayoḥ-abhibhava

prādurbhāvau nirodha-kṣaṇa-citta-anvayo

nirodha-pariṇāmaḥ || 9 ||

व्युत्थाननिरोधसंस्कारयोरभिभवप्रादुर्भावौ

निरोधक्षणचित्तान्वयो निरोधपरिणामः ॥ ९ ॥

When the tendency of the mind to express is diminishing and its tendency of restraint is prevailing, then the conjunction of the mind with the restraining tendency is Nirodha Pariṇāma.

It's obvious and very clear. *Nirodha* means to rein in, not express. Nirodha pariṇāma is when the tendency to rein in arises and expressing subsides.

Normally, as soon as you wake up, your mind moves in the field of expression. You want to express it. Nirodha is restraining the expressions of the five vṛttis. The five vṛttis—pramāṇa, viparyaya, vikalpa, nidrā, and smṛti—normally happen to you. Nirodha is you restraining them from being expressed.

tasya praśānta-vāhitā samskārat || 10 ||

तस्य प्रशान्तवाहिता संस्कारात् ॥ १० ॥

A steady flow of such a state results from this impression (due to the practise of Nirodha Pariṇāma).

Restraining is keeping the balance of the mind. When you keep that calmness and pleasantness in your mind, restrain from expression and just be, then the mind flows like a silent river, *praśānta-vāhitā*. There is one river which is flowing through the boulders noisily and another flowing quietly, in an even fashion. Your mind becomes like that calm river without rapids.

The mind is like the rapids all the time but it becomes calm and restrained with nirodha. This is because of the samskāra, culturing the mind. By making a habit of culturing the mind through meditation, it starts flowing in an even and silent fashion.

sarvārthatā-ekāgrātayoḥ kṣaya-udaya cittasya

samādhi-pariṇāmaḥ || 11 ||

सर्वार्थतैकाग्रतयोः क्षयोदयौ चित्तस्य समाधिपरिणामः ॥ ११ ॥

When the tendency of the mind to be scattered diminishes and its tendency to be one-pointed rises, that is samādhi pariṇāma.

The mind is scattered all over the place. You are very confused, looking here and there, doing a hundred things but nothing concrete is coming out of that. You have so many projects, so many things you want to do but the mind is scattered and you are unable to focus on one thing. Your mind which is scattered, as an impact of samādhi, starts becoming like a laser beam—one-pointed, focused. The scattered, scared feeling mind gives way to a steady, sharp, one-pointed, focused mind.

tataḥ punaḥ śānta-uditau tulya-pratyayau

cittasya-ekāgratā-pariṇāmaḥ || 12 ||

ततः पुनः शान्तोदितौ तुल्यप्रत्ययौ चित्तस्यैकाग्रतापरिणामः ॥ १२ ॥

When the one-pointedness of the mind rises and subsides again like any other thought, that is Ekāgratā pariṇāma of the mind.

Often people think concentration is an act. Maharṣi Patañjali says that concentration is an effect—of stillness within, contentment within. When you are content, you are not scattered. When you are content, you are more one-pointed, and it is the effect of samādhi. You have experienced deep stillness and a sense of being everywhere and nowhere. That gives rise to sharpness of observation, perception, experience, and expression. However, when you remain focused all the time, it drains off your energy. He says that you can focus and relax as well. You have mastery over both. Sometimes people are so focused that we say they have a one-track mind. Their focus keeps them stuck. They can see nothing else and are unable to change. People with such mindsets are very difficult to live with. Their families become miserable. That's why the Maharṣi says here—*śāntoditau*—it appears and then it quietens down. Both the ability to enjoy and retire come to you simultaneously. And this consciousness is related to time, elements and senses.

etena bhūta-indriyeṣu dharma-lakṣaṇa-avasthā-

pariṇāmaḥ vyākhyātāḥ || 13 ||

एतेन भूतेन्द्रियेषु धर्मलक्षणावस्थापरिणामा व्याख्याताः ॥ १३ ॥

By this (the three pariṇāmas above) the transformation in the essential nature, the transformation due to time and transformation of characteristics in the senses (indriyas) and the (five) elements is explained.

What to say about this! Do you find anything even close to this wisdom today? How the consciousness, the forms, the matter, and the time are tied together. They impact each other.

śānta-udita-avyapadeśya-dharma-

anupātī dharmī || 14 ||

शान्तोदिताव्यपदेश्यधर्मानुपाती धर्मी ॥ १४ ॥

The dharmī is the unchanging basis common to the latent, manifest and unmanifest characteristics.

That's self-explanatory. *Dharma-anupātī dharmī*—the one who exhibits one's nature, one's characteristics.

krama-anyatvam pariṇāma-anyatve hetuḥ || 15 ||

क्रमान्यत्वं परिणामान्यत्वे हेतुः ॥ १५ ॥

The types of transformations differ due to the differences in the sequence of characteristics.

Forms change, and so do the characteristics. It is time which changes the character and it is time that changes the form. How you were when you were a baby is not how you are today. Every particle, every atom of your body has changed. Time has impacted the change. And the form can impact time also. Not only does time impact the form, the form can change the time.

Do you not impact time? If not for yourself, you do impact it for others; you can definitely make others miserable. Intentionally or unintentionally you have the capacity to do that. At the same time, you have the capacity to impact positivity. When you are happy, time appears very short. When you are miserable, time appears to be very long. When you are in meditation, time stands still. When you are depressed, time doesn't seem to be moving at all. There's a different type of stillness.

Time and characteristics also change. The way you behaved with your parents when you were a child is not the same as when you were an adolescent. And now, when you have become an adult your behavior with your parents has changed. Your character has changed.

If someone pokes your ego, your character changes, your behaviour changes. If someone boosts your ego… wow! The way you behave with them changes immediately.

"Oh! You are the greatest person on the planet. I can do anything for you. I can die for you," so you say when someone boosts your ego.

Form changes, character changes. Don't think a criminal is a criminal forever; he can change. You just talk to the criminals and you'll see there are a lot of positive traits hiding inside them. You look at them through my eyes. I don't see any criminals at all. It is just circumstantial. It is time that has made them criminals.

Many times our people say, "Gurudev, you simply believe everybody. You say a yes to everything!" Well, they're right. But in the practical world things change. On the other hand, if you give too much freedom to somebody, you are spoiling them. They become the worst rogues.

Children need to be really disciplined. If you don't rein them in today, they'll cause misery for you and for others as well. These are all samskāras, not from just one lifetime, from many lifetimes.

You have a deep inferiority complex and you project it as though you are superior, as though you are very correct. Deep inside all the so-called righteous people, resides the seed of an inferiority complex. On the outside, they behave as though they are perfect beings; they are experts, there's nobody like them. You just dig a little, just an inch inside, you'll find there is low self-esteem, fear, and anxiety.

Extraordinary Abilities

pariṇāma-traya-samyamāt-atīta-

anāgata-jñānam || 16 ||

परिणामत्रयसंयमादतीतानागतज्ञानम् ॥ १६ ॥

By samyama on the three-fold transformation (of essential nature, due to time and of characteristics), there comes knowledge of past and future.

These are processes. Samyama on the form, time and character and you get the knowledge of the past and future.

śabda-artha-pratyayānām itaretara-adhyāsāt

saṅkaraḥ-tat-pravibhāga-samyamāt

sarva-bhūta-ruta-jñānam || 17 ||

शब्दार्थप्रत्ययानाम् इतरेतराध्यासात सङ्करः

तत्प्रविभागसंयमात् सर्वभूतरुतज्ञानम् ॥ १७ ॥

The name associated with an object, the meaning of the name and the object itself are commingled with one another. By samyama on the distinction between these three, comes the knowledge of the sounds made by all beings.

Name and form are connected. If name and form are not connected you cannot understand anything. Understanding will disappear from the planet. You say the name and the form appears. I say 'banana' and the form of the banana appears in your head. The name and form also have a sound to them. If I say the word 'waterfall', it is not just an image that is associated with it but a sound as well. When the water falls there is a sound. Waves in the ocean have a sound. When I say 'parrot', the particular sound the bird makes is also connected with its name. The name, form and the sound, its character are all connected. So you just take the name and nature responds.

In muscle testing (kinesiology), you say the words in your mind. You only mention the sound, but the body, muscles, and the cells in you respond to it, act towards it. Have you tested this? OK, let's test this. Bend the middle finger slightly and place it on the index finger. (Gurudev looks at his hand.) Shall I go to Bangalore today? Is it good for me? Not good. Should I eat one mango? Yes. Two? No. Three? Now you can test all parts of the body with this. Is my heart strong? Yes. Are my shoulders strong? Wrong. Is my neck strong? No, a little weak. And is my stomach strong? Yes. So you can place one hand on different parts of the body and do this. Is one *vada* good for me? Two? Three vadas? No. You only mentioned three vadas and the body said no. The sound, the form, name, and characteristics are linked to each other.

And when you do samyama on this—*sarvabhūtarutajñānam*, you understand what the animals are saying, what the birds are saying, what the cows are saying. People who have pets or animals at home, when they just call the animal by name, it comes. At the first seat of Ādi Śankarācārya, Śringerī, there is a river and fishing is not allowed there but you can call the fish by name and the fish will come. Such a thing has happened in some other place also.

Sarvabhūtarutajñānam—you understand the language of not just human beings but all other beings on the planet. You can understand what the horse is feeling, what the elephants are feeling. So this is beyond sound, beyond verbal communication. At four o' clock in the evening, I go to feed my elephants. Before I go, they are here and there. As soon as it is time for me to come, they come to the spot and wait for me. When I come there I tell them to hold their hands. They'll hold their hands. It's not just the training, of course you train them, but beyond training you can understand the feeling of the animals.

samskāra-sākṣāt-karaṇāt pūrva-jāti-jñānam || 18 ||

संस्कारसाक्षात्करणात् पूर्वजातिज्ञानम् ॥ १८ ॥

Through the direct perception of latent impressions, comes the knowledge of previous births.

Your previous incarnation has left some impressions in you and you see that these are your deep impressions. You put your attention on them, do samyama on them, then knowledge of previous lives comes to you.

You can know this by doing our Eternity Process. You lie down and someone guides you through it. You start seeing the past. Only deep impressions from the past will start coming up to the surface in this process. Suppose in your previous life you were only thinking about *Bhāgavatama*, Rādhā and Kṛṣṇa. Suddenly, you find yourself being Rādhā. You may not be the Rādhā but because your mind is in that impression of Rādhā-Rādhā all the time, you find yourself being Rādhā.

Similarly, people in Jerusalem who have grown up with the story of the Bible may suddenly start feeling they are Mary Magdalene. You don't know how many people came to me and said that they are Mary Magdalene, when they saw their past life impressions. So they could be Mary Magdalene or whoever else. Whether they're really that or not is a different question but those impressions in the consciousness come to the surface.

There is a condition called the Jerusalem Syndrome. When people are walking the steps in Jerusalem, they suddenly feel a flash from somewhere in the past and they go crazy. They think they are one of the twelve Apostles of Jesus. Ladies think they are Mary Magdalene. Someone thinks he is Judas. It is a mental condition that people have because of some flash from the past life. They're unable to handle it so they stay in the hospital for a couple of weeks, maybe a couple of months and then become normal. But this is not uncommon.

In this country there was a time when Nehru ji was idolized very much. And in mental hospitals people started saying, "I am Jawaharlal Nehru." I heard of an incident when Nehru ji or some other very famous politician of this country went to the mental hospital for a visit. He found a person there saying, "I am the real Nehru. Who are you?" Nehru ji said, "I am Jawaharlal Nehru, Prime Minister of India. Who are you?"

Once in Mumbai, we had many *māhākriyās,* satsaṅgas, and people had very deep experiences. Some of them even had some past life experiences. Someone said, "You know a secret, don't tell anybody, I was Yashoda Maa." And then someone else said, "I was a Gopi." So they had all the characters of *Bhāgavatam* and Gokul! Finally, they came and asked me about it. I said, "I wonder why all of Gokul landed up in Mumbai. What was the problem? Gokul was such a nice, green place. Why did they all land up in Mumbai, such a crowded place?" They really believed they were these characters. These are the samskāras—past impressions about different characters in the mind and if you hold on too much to them, then you are stuck there. However, if you do samyama on that, the real knowledge comes, not just delusion.

pratyayasya para-citta-jñānam || 19 ||

प्रत्ययस्य परचित्तज्ञानम् ॥ १९ ॥

By samyama on the content of one's mind comes the knowledge of others' minds.

The content of one's mind here means what is happening in your mind. Many times you don't even know what is happening in your mind. That is the biggest problem. You have judgements about everybody else and are stuck with your self-image and judgements. Now you have no chance to know others' minds, but when the mind becomes hollow and empty, like a mirror, you reflect whatever is in others' minds also.

pratyayasya para-citta-jñānam

Just by normal samyama and meditation, your intuitive ability increases to the extent that you are able to know everybody very easily. It doesn't take much time. Knowing everybody doesn't mean knowing their names or where they come from but what is inside them, what they are feeling, what their past and future is. It doesn't take me more than a few seconds to know a person. Have you noticed that when I go in the darśana line, I know everybody? Have you ever seen me without a presence of mind? I attend to every single individual.

pratyayasya para-citta-jñānam

When the mind is clear, hollow and empty, it just reflects others' feelings. I don't put any board saying—Consultations. Ask me your questions! Why does everyone from around the world come to me with questions? What makes them think that I have answers to those questions? Deep inside, the soul recognizes, the Being recognizes the hollow and empty space where you can get the real answer.

na ca tat sā-lambanam tasya-aviṣayī-bhūtatvāt || 20 ||

न च तत् सालम्बनं तस्याविषयीभूतत्वात् ॥ २० ॥

The underlying support of that knowledge (of the other person's mind) remains unperceived because that is not the subject of samyama.

Why would someone bother to dig into somebody else's mind to know them or control them! No yogī does it. No yogī controls others' minds. He only controls his own mind. This is paranoia—"Oh, someone is controlling my mind." Who can control your mind? Nobody can control your mind. So don't be scared. If some yogī, some enlightened person does any such thing, I tell you, his power will immediately vanish in a few weeks. He will not have any power at all. A noble and wise person is not interested in these things. He doesn't do such things at all. So it is just an illusion. Know that your mind is very strong and nobody can poke into it. Got it? Only you can control your mind. You can uplift it or you can bury your mind. You can either make yourself miserable or happy. Nobody else can do it. Got it?

kāya-rūpa-samyamāt-tad-grāhya-śakti-stambhe

cakṣuḥ prakāśa-asamprayoge-antardhānam || 21 ||

कायरूपसंयमात्तद्ग्राह्यशक्तिस्तम्भे चक्षुः

प्रकाशासंप्रयोगेऽन्तर्धानम् ॥ २१ ॥

By samyama on the form of one's own physical body, the perceivability of the body is suspended and it becomes invisible to other people.

These are different siddhis which come over a long period of practice. Your light form, your subtle form can appear in many places or cannot appear in any place. These things are possible. Your presence can be felt far and wide. This is possible because your consciousness is nothing but a wave function. It's energy. You have multiple dimensions and multiple roles to play in that. When you do samyama on the body and the luminosity of the body, then you don't feel that the body is there and at times others can also miss seeing you. It is the disappearing siddhi!

In the same way, as described in relation to sight, one is able to suspend the ability of the body to be heard, touched, tasted or smelt.

There is one more śloka which says that similarly other senses can also be suspended.

These are formulas and Patañjali tells you about the possibilities of human consciousness. He also mentions that while you can practise these siddhis, they may also become an obstacle for further progress in life.

sopakramam nirupakramam ca karma tat-samyamād-

aparānta-jñānam-ariṣṭebhyo vā || 22 ||

सोपक्रमं निरुपक्रमं च कर्म तत्संयमादपरान्तज्ञानमरिष्टेभ्यो वा ॥ २२ ॥

Karma is of two kinds—either fast or slow to manifest. By samyama on these karmas or on the signs of death, comes knowledge of the time of death.

These are all by-products of samādhi. You can foresee, you can even fix the time of your death. A yogī has the capacity to leave the body at will. These are possibilities. They may tell people about it, "At this particular time, this particular moment I'm going to leave the body." It's a very common thing here in India. Many people have done that. Even many simple householders have said, "I'm going to die at this time." All near and dear ones were asked to be there and then they departed. All this is possible.

maitrī-ādiṣu balāni || 23 ||

मैत्र्यादिषु बलानि ॥ २३ ॥

By samyama on friendliness and other attitudes, there comes great strength.

Maitri, karunā, muditā—the qualities of friendliness, compassion and happiness—by doing samyama on these qualities you become strong. It brings you inner strength.

baleṣu hasti-balādīni || 24 ||

बलेषु हस्तिबलादीनि ॥ २४ ॥

By samyama on the strength of an elephant comes a similar strength.

Here is the secret of why Gaṇeśa is worshipped in India. When you feel any obstacles you put your attention on an elephant because it doesn't take anything for an obstacle. It just moves ahead. An elephant doesn't sneak away like a snake; it walks straight and if anything comes in its way, it just throws it aside. Enormous strength, like that of an elephant, needed to overcome the obstacles, comes to you when you pray to Gaṇeśa. So samyama on an elephant brings you the strength of an elephant. And it does happen with this sūtra. I have seen people break iron rods just like that. You do samyama on this, you can do it too—break iron rods. You can jump up and down and nothing happens to you. You become very strong, but for that, you have to spend six months on only food, meditation and total dispassion. When you do all this for six to eight months, all these siddhis can manifest in your life.

pravṛtti-āloka-nyāsāt

sūkṣma-vyavahita-viprakṛṣṭa-jñānam || 25 ||

प्रवृत्त्यालोकन्यासात् सूक्ष्मव्यवहितविप्रकृष्टज्ञानम् ॥ २५ ॥

By shining the inner light, comes the knowledge of subtle, concealed and distant objects.

Pravṛtti-āloka means beyond all the activities in the mind, to see beyond those activities. By doing samyama you can find the hidden or lost articles. Our Intuition Process children also do it. They can tell you where to find lost articles. You can also do it; it is no big deal.

bhuvana-jñānam sūrye samyamāt || 26 ||

भुवनज्ञानं सूर्ये संयमात् ॥ २६ ॥

By samyama on the Sun, comes the knowledge of the physical universe.

The right *nāḍī* is the *sūrya nāḍī.* When you do samyama on the right nāḍī i.e. the sūrya nāḍī, you understand the truth and the non-truth.

Bhuvana-jñānam—you understand the knowledge of the world.

candre tārā-vyūha-jñānam || 27 ||

चन्द्रे ताराव्यूहज्ञानम् ॥ २७ ॥

By samyama on the Moon (the left nāḍī), comes the knowledge of the arrangement of the stars.

In those days without high-powered telescopes or sophisticated instruments people could, with utmost precision, tell about the movement of Saturn, the Sun, the Moon, the planets and the stars in the sky. In those days, they found out that Jupiter had twelve moons. How could they find out? The timing of the eclipses, the calculation of the size of the celestial bodies and the paths of their movement is correct even today, to the fraction of a second. What was calculated millions of years ago stands true even today. What the *śāstras* have said millennia ago has stood the test of time even today.

You think that Galileo found out that the Earth is revolving around the Sun? No, this was stated by the ṛṣis long back. You go to any temple and you'll see the Sun in the middle and all other planets around it. They have said it a long time ago. You take any almanac or *pañcāṅga*—the Indian calendar—you will see the movement of all the stars and planets. They never said the Sun is moving around the planets. They showed that all the planets are moving around the Sun. The Earth was never flat. The Earth was always considered spherical. And the universe is spherical. They called it the golden egg. The Milky Way, the universe, is like a golden egg, with millions of planets, millions of solar systems in it. These were mentioned in our scriptures thousands of years ago. How did they know this? This is through samyama. Through samyama they could say, precisely, that Jupiter has twelve moons.

One is objective knowledge. Another is subjective knowledge—the knowledge that comes to you from within. And that is what the yoga sūtras are all about.

dhruve tad-gati-jñānam || 28 ||

ध्रुवे तद्गतिज्ञानं २७ ॥

By samyama on the Pole Star (Dhruva), comes the knowledge of the movement of the stars.

The Pole Star is that which is not moving. That's why it's called Pole Star. It's a reference star. Doing samyama on the Pole Star, you will know about the movement of the planets. And those days without any equipment, without any sophisticated telescopes, with utmost precision, they could trace the movement of the stars and this is due to their practice of samyama.

Dhruva also means the top of the head. So there are two meanings—one is the Pole Star up there, the other is samyama on the top of the head. Similarly, doing samyama on the sūrya nāḍī, the right knowledge about the world will come to you. Samyama on the left nostril, *candra nāḍī*, will give you the knowledge of the movement of the stars.

nābhi-cakre kāya-vyūha-jñānam || 29 ||

नाभिचक्रे कायव्यूहज्ञानम् ॥ २९ ॥

By samyama on the navel centre, comes the knowledge of the arrangement of the systems of the body.

The navel centre is very important. It is also called the midbrain. By practising samyama on the navel centre, you understand your body better. In Osteopathy, they push the navel to two different sides in order to see to which side it is moving easily and to which it is not. The rise in temperature of the navel also indicates that some part of the body is not okay.

It is the same in āyurveda. When you touch some parts of the body, they are warm. If your liver is cold, it means there's improper circulation in the body. If the pancreas is cold, it indicates a different problem. The temperature, the texture, and the movement, indicate the state of our body. In āyurveda, when *nāḍī parīkṣā* is done, you just place your fingers on the nāḍī and get the sense of what is happening in the body.

Similarly, doing samyama on the navel cakra (*nābhi cakra*) gives the total picture of your body. Those days they never had any ultrasound machines, CT scan etc. All they did was close their eyes and practised samyama on the navel. That gave them the picture of a person's body.

I remember, way back in 1980, I was in Bali for the first time. Bali was a very nice, simple village then; not like what it is today. There was only one tall building that was seven or eight storeys at that time. That was the only five-star or four-star hotel then. The rest of Bali was just villages with very narrow roads. Just like the road near the āśrama kitchen, where only one vehicle can pass at a time. There is tremendous development now and it is nowhere comparable to what it was in 1980. The medicine men there, were amazing. They were like our pundits or priests. The priest would sit in front of you, close his eyes and scan your body like an X-ray and tell you everything about your whole body. He would then prescribe a remedy such as drink the water that comes out of two particular rocks or have natural herbs. Later in the same year, I brought some of the medicine men to India. Unfortunately, they did not speak any language other than Balinese. We introduced them to the āyurvedika doctors of India but because of the language barrier the two groups could not communicate with each other. However, today that whole science has disappeared. We do not find such medicine men in Bali anymore. Bali has become so westernized; its culture has changed. The ancient people had these amazing techniques, all based only on consciousness. It is good, now that we are reviving the Intuition Process for our children, they will be able to do more on these lines. It is a good thing that we are bringing back this lost knowledge.

kaṇṭha-kūpe kṣut-pipāsā-nivṛttiḥ || 30 ||

कण्ठकूपे क्षुत्पिपासानिवृत्तिः ॥ ३० ॥

By samyama on the pit of the throat, thirst and hunger disappear.

This is self-explanatory.

kūrma-nāḍyām sthairyam || 31 ||

कूर्मनाड्यां स्थैर्यम् ॥ ३१ ॥

By samyama on the central channel below the throat, comes stability.

We normally see that when people are upset, they are unstable. What do you do then? You just tap their chest, isn't it? Whenever you feel scared or anxious, where do you place your hands? Naturally, your hands go to the chest. This is *kurmā nāḍī*, the trachea. Bringing your attention and doing samyama there brings stability.

mūrdha-jyotiṣi siddha-darśanam || 32 ||

मूर्धज्योतिषि सिद्धदर्शनम् ॥ ३२ ॥

By doing samyama on the coronal light, visions of the masters can come.

Mūrdha is the top of the head. When you do samyama on the top of the head, you are able to see the siddhas, the ṛṣis and the *munis*. They come to you as a presence or voice or light or just an intuitive message. That is *siddhadarśanam*.

prātibhād vā sarvam || 33 ||

प्रातिभाद् वा सर्वम् ॥ ३३ ॥

Or through intuition, everything could be known.

Prātibha means intuition. Through intuition anything can be known.

hrḍaye citta-samvit || 34 ||

हृदये चित्तसंवित्॥ ३४ ॥

By samyama on the heart, comes the knowledge of the consciousness.

Samvit is infallible knowledge. You may have some knowledge today; tomorrow it may turn out to be ignorance. The knowledge which is well-founded is samvit. The knowledge of consciousness comes into play when you do samyama on the heart.

sattva-puruṣayoḥ-atyanta-asaṅkīrṇayoḥ

pratyaya-aviśeṣaḥ bhogaḥ parārthatvāt svārtha-

samyamāt puruṣa-jñānam || 35 ||

सत्त्वपुरुषयोरत्यन्तासङ्कीर्णयोः प्रत्ययाविशेषो भोगः

परार्थत्वात् स्वार्थसंयमात् पुरुषज्ञानम्॥ ३५ ॥

The subtlest aspect of intellect (sattva) and the Self (puruṣa) are quite different. When they commingle (and one starts identifying with the intellect), it results in experiences which are really for the sake of another (the Self). By samyama on pure consciousness (which is distinct from the subtlest aspect of intellect) comes the knowledge of the Self.

It's a great sūtra. You are so identified with your intellect. That is your basic problem. There is a difference between the intellect and the consciousness, the puruṣā, the Self. And this difference can be noticed only when your mind is very subtle. At a gross level, your intellect appears to be yourself and you act according to your intellect. However, when your mind is very subtle, you see your intellect as separate from you, your feelings as separate from you. The nonsense that goes on within you is separate from you. You have a little glimpse of it in deep meditation, there is something that pulls back. With samyama on that gap, the subtle difference between the intellect and the Self, you get the real knowledge of the Self; who you really are.

When you identify yourself with the intellect, you are called an adamant person. The intellect and puruṣa of all adamant people are in conjunction. They don't see the difference between the two but when the mind of these so-called egoistic, adamant people also becomes very subtle, they see their intellect as separate and the Self as separate. That is wisdom.

sattva-puruṣayoḥ

Sattva here means intellect and puruṣa is the Self. When you see their differences with the subtlest of awareness, then wisdom dawns in you. Real knowledge of the puruṣā, the Self, comes up when you do samyama on this subtlety.

We spoke about this when we talked about asmitā. For example, you are standing next to someone who is blaming someone else and you're just watching. It's does not make your head boil, but if that person starts blaming you, you don't take it the same way as you did for someone else. That is asmitā, oneness or identification with the intellect. The same applies here. When the difference between the intellect and the puruṣa is identified with the subtlest of your consciousness and samyama is done on this subtle difference, you are able to get the true knowledge of the Self.

tataḥ prātibha-srāvāṇa-vedana-ādarśa-āsvāda-

vārtā jāyante || 36 ||

ततः प्रातिभश्रावणवेदनादर्शास्वादवार्ता जायन्ते ॥ ३६ ॥

From that (knowledge of the Self) arises intuitive hearing, touch, vision, taste, and smell.

Only when this identity of the Self and the intellect is distanced or broken, do you get access to another realm within you. Often people who have psychic powers or some extra sensory perceptions are not so intelligent. They are a little bit like blue stars. They're out of touch with reality and flying somewhere else because these subtle perceptions can happen only when you distance yourself from the intellect. Did you get it?

If the intellect comes in and pokes its nose in every experience, even that little experience you have gets spoiled. For example, you are having a good, deep meditation and the intellect says, "Oh! Am I going deeper? Am I getting a good experience?" Finished! The experience is lost. The moment the intellect pokes its nose there, wanting to understand the experience or wanting to repeat that experience, it is finished. Yesterday, you had a deep meditation and today the mind gets stuck on repeating the experience. You become so unstable, agitated and restless. Where is meditation? Where is restlessness? They are poles apart! The intellect can cause restlessness in you and it brings you to the surface, because your intellect is connected with the outer world and outer sensory perceptions.

But when the attention is on the puruṣa or the Self, then inner perceptions pick up, the divine touch, divine taste, divine smell and divine sounds appear. All the saints in India have always sung the glory of *anahata nāda*, the inner sound from the heart. The scriptures say discard everything outside and go in and you hear the sound, the divine music; you taste the nectar, *amṛta*, that's dripping inside you. You find that divine embrace and the touch deep inside. There is a touch from outside the skin and another touch from inside the skin. The touch that comes up from the inside is because of the experiences in the subtle realm. This is possible through the distinction between the puruṣa and the intellect.

Once, I was sitting with Maharṣi ji (Maharṣi Mahesh Yogī ji) and a few other elderly saints. I was the only young one there, twenty or twenty one years old. Everyone was about sixty. Someone came and announced that so-and-so got enlightened. The first question was, "Is his intellect okay?" That is so vivid in my memory. When you get the subtle experience, it is possible that due to a short circuit in your brain, you lose your intellect and go crazy.

You might have heard about Meher Baba, a saint in India. He used to go to the mental hospital and identify those who got those extra sensory experiences, who were considered crazy and put in the hospital. He relieved many people there and gave them back that balance, that understanding and told them what they should do and not do.

You know, there is a lack of understanding on the path of sādhanā. That's why without a Guru, this is dangerous. You could go crazy. You read ten different books and they say ten different things; you do all of them and you could end up in a mental hospital.

Surgery cannot be done without a surgeon; it is not safe at all. Similarly, never do yoga and other spiritual practices without a Master, without a Guru. The Guru's physical presence is immaterial, but just having a Guru, being in that space of consciousness can guide you and keep you on track.

The intellect needs to be strong. Patañjali never asked to destroy the intellect. The intellect must become sharper and active, but the difference between the intellect and the Self gives rise to and attaches another dimension to your life.

In the Bhagavad Gītā, Arjunā says, "I want to see your divine form."

Lord Kṛṣṇa says, "With these eyes you cannot see it. I'm going to give you a special pair of eyes, a special vision to see it." Another pair of eyes, in other words, another way, to look at the truth. Then, Arjunā moved from classical chemistry to quantum mechanics; a shift took place in his understanding. Earlier he was only thinking about the substance, matter, etc. When his thinking shifted to quantum mechanics, he understood that charcoal or diamond are all the same. Gold, earth, mud, metal and a dog; all are the same. Once the vision changed, then the wisdom, that everything is the same, dawned.

You may ask, "What is the practicality of this in my life?" I tell you, life offers many opportunities to change your vision. Many times, you don't. You are stuck with the same vision. You are stuck with an opinion about a person, about things and then any amount of proof or perception or ideas, which are contrary to that idea become unacceptable by your intellect because you are fixed in your mind about it. In some way it is good but in some other way it is not. When you are very stable, connected with positivity, you become resolute. Come what may, if you have fixed your ideas about a goal, about positivity, then it is very good. However, if it is connected to negativity, it completely destroys you. Not just your intellect, but your whole life. It can impact you in a very negative fashion.

You have a sankalpa to do something and you hold on to it. That's okay. But you have an idea about somebody else and you hold on to it, that's not going to help.

te samādhau-upasargā vyutthāne siddhayaḥ || 37 ||

ते समाधावुपसर्गा व्युत्थाने सिद्धयः ॥ ३७ ॥

These (heightened intuitive abilities) are obstacles to samādhi but appear to be attainments or powers to the mind turned outwards.

The subtle visions, subtle messages, connection to the subtle world are called siddhis. They are obstacles for samādhi. When you come out of samādhi these are siddhis but when you want to go deeper into samādhi they become obstacles. Samādhi is getting into the nothingness; to the emptiness.

With your eyes closed, in the subtle world, you will see all these different divine beings. You can have all the fun and might get lost in the Disney World of inner experiences. It is very difficult for you to get out of this external sensory perception but it is ten times more difficult for you to get out of that inner perception. You start having dialogues with yourself and it is another reality, different from this reality. Samādhi is getting out of this sensory perceptual arena to the summum bonum of creation, the core power of the Being. In between you get caught up in another subtle world and have various experiences. It is like another dream. You get the siddhis and you can get carried away by them. Then you're back to zero, to the same point. You have to begin your sādhanā, all over again, to climb up. So siddhis are an obstacle for samādhi, if you hang onto them.

te samādhāvupasargā vyutthāne siddhayaḥ

These experiences resulting from samyama are obstacles to samādhi but appear to be attainments or powers to the outgoing or worldly mind.

When you go outward, they are attainment, powers, but when you want to go inward for samādhi they are obstacles. Then, does it mean you should never have them? You don't need to crave them.

They will manifest automatically, be indifferent to them. That's all. Be indifferent to them. It's okay if they are there. You cannot say that you don't want siddhis. That is again negative. You are blocking your own consciousness from blossoming. When you are centred, siddhis present themselves before you. At the same time you should not say that you want the siddhis. Be very indifferent to them, not boast about them nor crave for or crib about them.

bandha-kāraṇa-śaithilyāt pracāra-samvedanāt-ca

cittasya para-śarīra-āveśaḥ || 38 ||

बन्धकारणशैथिल्यात् प्रचारसंवेदनाच्च चित्तस्य परशरीरावेशः ॥ ३८ ॥

By loosening of the causes of bondage and by the knowledge of the passages of the mind, there comes the ability to enter another body.

There are many such siddhis—entering into other bodies, feeling what is happening in another body in your own body. To some extent everybody has this, even birds. Birds fly in a certain formation. If the leader is tired, that bird will come back and another will lead.

So there is a collective body and an individual body. There is a collective body where you are connected with several other people. If someone very close to you, your family member or your close friend is feeling upset, is hurt, you can feel something in your body. Every mother experiences this when her child is hurt. The mother feels something in her body. Similarly, when a close friend is miserable, somewhere a thousand kilometres away, you feel it in your body.

udāna-jayāt-jala-paṅka-kaṇṭaka-adiṣu-asaṅga

utkrāntiḥ-ca || 39 ||

उदानजयाज्जलपङ्ककण्टकादिष्वसङ्ग उत्क्रान्तिश्च ॥ ३९ ॥

The mastery over udanā, the upward flowing prāṇavāyu, brings the ability to remain untouched by mud, water, thorns and the like, as well as the ability to levitate.

In the same way, there are various other siddhis about the body and connection with the air element. When you do samyama on these you are able to get the corresponding siddhis.

About the flying siddhi—this is also possible. Your body has to be very well prepared for it. I have not seen someone flying and staying like that for long. In *padmāsana* you can lift up your body for a few seconds and then you come down. The moment you lift up, you become aware that you are lifted up, then you come down.

In deep samādhi, you can hop ten feet away. It requires 6–8 weeks of long sādhanā, practise of padmāsādhanā, meditation and samyama. But it is of not much use, you jumping, hopping from here to there. You may feel completely elevated at that time. There is no mind, you are free inside. That state is very adorable. That brings synchronicity between your left and right brain activity. In Transcendental Meditation they have done a lot of experiments by the use of electrodes all over the body and the scientific data is available as to what happens when the body jerks or jumps up.

It is said that when Māhāvīra walked, all the thorns would go down and never prick. That is to say that nature does not hurt you because you are so well in tune with nature.

Even if it is very cold, you can go in the snow without wearing all those big coats. When I used to walk in Davos in Switzerland or in Norway people would wonder how I was walking in these very clothes. The cold would not affect me. It would not touch me. Nothing would happen.

People walk even over fire for a few minutes because their consciousness is so supple and it protects the body in such a way that nature becomes friendlier rather than harsher with you.

We have *pañcaprāṇa, pañcvāyu*—five types of prāṇa in the body—*prāṇa, apana, udāna, samāna* and *vyāna*. Here Patañjali is talking about the udāna vāyu, the upward movement of air. When you are sitting and you get the thought that you want to get up, do you know what that one thought does to you? Your body of 70kg just gets up. How did this 70kg body or a 100kg body rise up? What makes it rise up, what makes it walk? When an 80kg rock is kept somewhere it doesn't rise up like that. Think on these lines.

You keep an 80kg rock somewhere and keep a human being. Here with one thought the human being lifts himself up, there the rock doesn't lift up. What makes you different from the rock? Your vāyu.

The udāna vāyu pushes your energy upward. So the udāna vāyu asks you to move. Your body gets up from the seat and that vāyu, that prāṇa takes you from this point to that point. If the udāna vāyu is not there you cannot get up.

And if you master it, do samyama on it, then the same udāna vāyu which helps you to get up from the chair can also lift you up. It's absolutely scientific. It is common sense. That energy which makes you move can also make you levitate. But it just needs more practise, just like the Intuition Process. How did the children get to use the third eye in three to four days? They could do it immediately. They can read by just touching or putting their hand on any letter. They are able to get it, why could you not get it? Because you have not practised it. You were not taught how to do it.

These are sādhanās and siddhis with which you can experiment and have in your life. But they are not the ultimate. That's what Patañjali says. These siddhis should be taken as a matter of fact. You should not crave to attain some powers. It is not worth it.

Apāna vāyu is the energy in the lower part of the body. If Apāna is too high, then you feel lethargic, sleepy, and dull.

Samāna vāyu is in the stomach region, it aids digestion.

Udāna vāyu is in the upper chest and throat region, it is responsible for emotions. If Udāna vayu is imbalanced, you have no emotions, you become like a stone or you become mushy and weak.

Vyāna is all over the body, it is responsible for movements in the joints, the circulation in the body. If Vyāna prāṇa is disturbed, then the circulatory system is disturbed, your joints are not flexible, there are aches and pains.

Pañcaprāṇa, the five different types of prāṇa are present in everybody, and different prāṇas dominate at different times. The imbalances in the prāṇas are corrected during prāṇayāma and Sudarśana Kriyā.

samāna-jayāt-jvalanam || 40 ||

समानजयाज्ज्वलनम् ॥ ४० ॥

The mastery over samāna, the prāṇa flowing in the navel area, brings radiance or fire.

Samāna vāyu dominates the navel region,

Jvalanam—it can digest anything. It can burn. This is combustion. Phenomena like self combustion have happened several times in the world. Some are recorded, some go unnoticed. Someone is just sitting and he suddenly bursts into flames and turns into ashes. Self combustion! This has happened in several places. In New York or somewhere in the US, they have recorded this phenomenon. Our body is all atoms. It's all just energy and suddenly when this whole energy heats up, the body catches fire.

It is also said that when you do samyama on the samāna energy, you become more radiant. You start glowing, not necessarily burn down. So you can start glowing. This is that aspect of samyama that is called samāna.

The food is transformed into energy, if there is biotin in the body. When there is a lack of biotin, carbohydrates become unusable energy in the body. They just sit as fat and get stored in your body. When biotin is present, the same food that we eat, instead of getting stored as fat, carbohydrates and proteins, transforms into energy that the body can use and it brings radiance in the body.

Focusing on the samāna prāṇa, on the navel area, radiance comes and energy wakes up in the body. All of you might have experienced this in the advanced courses or sometimes when I lead you through the navel meditation or *Padmanābhā* meditation. You feel really light. When we pay attention and meditate on the solar plexus, there is a different quality to it.

śrotra-ākāśayoḥ sambandha-samyamāt-

divyam śrotram || 41 ||

श्रोत्राकाशयोः संबन्धसंयमाद् दिव्यं श्रोत्रम् ॥ ४१ ॥

Samyama on the relationship between space and the sense of hearing brings about a heightened sense of hearing.

Doing samyama on the sense of hearing and space, you can hear divine sounds; sounds which are beyond human frequencies. You are able to hear beyond your stipulated frequencies. Normally, we can only hear within a range of certain frequencies and not something beyond it.

Likewise, we can only see within a certain range. Our brain and senses are just frequency analyzers. When you do samyama on the sense of hearing and space, *ākāśa*, the range of your frequency increases, the bandwidth of your hearing increases. You are able to hear subtle sounds and other sounds in the universe. It's just like taking a microscope and seeing something which cannot be seen through normal vision. The microbes which can be seen only through a microscope and not without it, do exist. What you don't see exists, what you don't hear exists and by doing samyama on this, it expands your range, your scope of hearing.

kāya-ākāśayoḥ sambandha-samyamāt

laghu-tūla-samāpatteḥ-ca ākāśa-gamanam || 42 ||

कायाकाशयोः संबन्धसंयमात् लघुतूलसमापत्तेश्च

आकाशगमनम् ॥ ४२ ॥

By samyama on the relationship between the body and space, the lightness of cotton is attained and with that comes the ability to move through space.

This is the flying sūtra.

Kāyākāśayoḥ sambandha—There is a relationship between space and the body. When you do samyama on the relationship between the body and space, your body becomes *laghu-tūla-samāpatteśca*—like a cotton fibre.

Ākāśa-gamanam—you are able to lift up and fly, when you do samyama on the relationship between space and the body. Again I have not seen people flying like that but we can levitate, that's not a big thing. You can levitate for a few minutes, few seconds, maybe about a minute. Then you jump. But for that you need to follow a strict diet, proper sādhanā, over a period of time and you can do it. It's not something you cannot do. But then from there you have to come back and adjust to this reality. It's also a delicate balance you have to maintain. You don't want to lose your intellect, create a new world and live there. This can also happen when you do too much sādhanā. It's good for some time, but may not be so pleasant for others around you that you live in a separate world. But it is a samyama worth looking into. It's a really good experience that makes your mind get unstuck from the things it gets stuck to.

bahiḥ-akalpitā vṛttiḥ-mahā-videhā tataḥ

prakāśa-āvaraṇa-kṣayaḥ || 43 ||

बहिरकल्पिता वृत्तिर्महाविदेहा ततः प्रकाशावरणक्षयः ॥ ४३ ॥

When the mind can extend beyond the body effortlessly, it is the state of a great disincarnate one. With that, the veil over the light of knowledge is diminished.

You get a glimpse of it even in *yoga nidrā* or *kāyotsarga*. I have created this thing for you to feel the difference between the body and the consciousness. When the thoughtless mind is achieved by your practice, that mind can be projected outside and there are many abilities that come along with that.

sthūla-svarūpa-sūkṣma-anvaya-arthavattva

samyamād bhūta-jayaḥ || 44 ||

स्थूलस्वरूपसूक्ष्मान्वयार्थवत्त्वसंयमाद् भूतजयः ॥ ४४ ॥

By samyama on the aspects of the elements (bhūtās)—gross form, essence, subtle form, interconnectedness and purposefulness, mastery over the elements follows.

That's obvious! The gross element, the subtle element, the name of the element, the idea of it—all these are certain forms of the element. Every form outside, first comes as an idea, then assumes a name, then assumes a subtle form and then the gross form. It's like a seed, a sprout, a sapling and a tree. The entire tree is present in a seed. You can say, "I'm carrying a banyan tree in my bag."

You are right. It's not a lie. But it is in the seed form. That little banyan seed doesn't suddenly become a tree, it has to go through four dimensions—a seed, a sprout, a sapling and then a big tree. In the same way, the five elements have their little reflection or counterpart, their tanmātrās inside you. That is how you are able to experience them.

You know the word 'understanding' is a very scientific and meaningful word. Understanding is standing under the tanmātrā.

You have a certain tanmātrā of sweetness in you. You can experience sweetness only when it is above the level of sweetness that you have.

Your body has a certain temperature. So when you put your hand in the water, you feel either cold or hot. How do you experience it? When the water has either more temperature than you have or less than the temperature you have only then can you experience it. So you are able to understand whatever is below the tanmātrā that you have. Or you can say it the other way around too. Whatever is above the tanmātrā that you have, only that you can understand. You can say it either way. And what is beyond, i.e. if the tanmātrā is missing, you cannot understand it. So all the five elements are present in you. Tanmātrā, a little part of it, the subtle part of it is present in you. Light is present in you, so you can see the light. The light that you can see or understand is below the tanmātrā of what you have.

Now, an owl's tanmātrā of light is different from your tanmātrā of light. It can see more light where you cannot. The elephant's tanmātrā of smell is more than your tanmātrā of smell. You can only smell up to some distance but elephants can smell even from several kilometres away. By doing samyama on these five different aspects of the elements, your arena of experience expands.

tataḥ-aṇimā-ādi-prādurbhāvaḥ kāya-sampad-

tad-dharma-ānabhighātaḥ-ca || 45 ||

ततोऽणिमादिप्रादुर्भावः कायसंपत् तद्धर्मानभिघातश्च ॥ ४५ ॥

Through that (mastery over the elements), come powers such as making the body small. Perfection of the body is attained as well and the elements cause it no harm.

All this takes a lot of time. Have you seen one of the yogīs, Adhunik Bheem, crush glass and then just eat it? People have motorbikes go over their bodies, just by mastering the prāṇa. But they have practised for many years and with those many years of continuous practice, you can acquire any of those skills too. So these different samyamas can bring in different powers over matter and elements.

rūpa-lāvaṇya-bala-vajra-samhananatvāni

kāya-sampat || 46 ||

रूपलावण्यबलवज्रसंहननत्वानि कायसंपत् ॥ ४६ ॥

Perfection of the body includes beauty, gracefulness, strength, and unyielding hardness in receiving blows when struck.

It's self-explanatory. Samyama brings beauty, perfection, strength and the ability to take any blows. In the world you have to take blows. Nature gives you blows. People give you blows all the time. If you run away from it, you are a coward. If you stay and face it; without whining, no matter what anybody may say, you stay strong. This strength comes from the samyama. It makes you beautiful.

You do not need to crush glass and eat it. You do not need to pierce a spear into your tongue and all such things. You only need to know that samyama makes your body very strong. It makes the body perfect, strong, beautiful. It makes you graceful, that is even more important. Are you graceful? Are you smiling? If you are a siddha and you are doing sādhanā, you are a practitioner, you are a yogī but not smiling, you are good for nothing. Your practice is a lie. So with yoga comes your ability to take the blows, an inner strength to endure all difficult, different situations, without grumbling, cribbing and throwing tantrums. Only the weak throw tantrums, not the strong ones. Do you throw tantrums? Better do your samyama. Just tell me who would you like to be with? With those who throw tantrums all the time or those who are very serene?

grahaṇa-svarūpa-asmitā-anvaya-arthavattva

samyamād indriya-jayaḥ || 47 ||

ग्रहणस्वरूपास्मितान्वयार्थवत्त्वसंयमाद् इन्द्रियजयः ॥ ४७ ॥

By samyama on the process of perception by senses, their essence, I-ness, connectedness and purposefulness, comes mastery over the senses.

Samyama on the process and action—what is the process? As you look at a *gulab jamun*, the process is, saliva appears in your mouth. You want to eat it. Are you aware of all the things that are happening? There is a chemical reaction that is happening inside your body. Whether it is a beautiful sight, sound, taste, smell or touch, something is happening. Dopamine, serotonin, and endorphins are getting secreted in you. Are you aware of this process? Are you aware of the action? You're eating the gulab jamun. Are you aware of this very act? Seldom are people aware.

In our Happiness Program, when people do the grape process, they say that in their entire life they have never eaten so consciously. That conscious eating of even one grape brings immense satisfaction. Such satisfaction doesn't happen even if you eat a bunch of grapes or even kilos of them. When you do samyama on the essence of the action, the I-ness inside you—'I am enjoying it', 'I am happy', 'I am miserable', 'I am insulted'—and the purposefulness of the senses and actions, it gives you mastery over the senses. It is obvious. It is a very very beautiful sūtra. I don't think modern day scientists have ever thought about this. They only talk about the experience and the experiencer. The experience, the process of experiencing and how you experience it. The awareness of the I-ness which is experiencing it, is out of the world. You are eating the grapes but are you aware of the shape of the grapes? Then you bite it and you feel the juice coming out of the grapes and mixing with the saliva and getting into the pores of your tongue. My goodness! This process of you being aware of it, gives you mastery over your senses. Even with a little process like the grape process, you get mastery over your taste buds.

Similarly with all other five senses. If you haven't mastered your senses, you are doomed. It is the senses which bring you down, which make you miserable. If you are a master of them, then they are like good servants who help you and you can enjoy life. This is not negating life. Maharṣi Patañjali is not saying don't eat good food. But are you conscious of doing what you do? This is what he says.

tato mano-javitvam vikaraṇa-bhāvaḥ

pradhāna-jayaś-ca || 48 ||

ततो मनोजवित्वं विकरणभावः प्रधानजयश्च ॥ ४८ ॥

By that (mastery over the senses) comes sharpness of mind, perception beyond the senses and supremacy over the Primal Cause (the cause of all existence).

How have all these things manifested? That is the *pradhāna kāraṇa*—primary cause. Knowledge of this comes to you. This knowledge can make you stable and strong. Then you are not caught up in the world of cause and effects. Whenever there is an impact or effect on you, you look for the cause and you believe that, that cause is the ultimate cause. My dear, it is not so! If someone has thrown you out of your position, you think the cause is your boss. My dear, it is not the case. The cause is not the boss. Look beyond the immediate cause. What can you see? There is an unseen cause. That is the primal cause of all happenings. This is the central point of the theory of karma—that the apparent cause is not the cause, but it takes you to the ultimate cause, which is again the ultimate cause for all creation.

sattva-puruṣa-anyatā-khyāti-mātrasya

sarva-bhāva-adhiṣṭhātṛtvam sarva-jñātṛtvam ca || 49 ||

सत्त्वपुरुषान्यताख्यातिमात्रस्य सर्वभावाधिष्ठातृत्वं

सर्वज्ञातृत्वं च ॥ ४९ ॥

Upon being established in the knowledge of the distinction between the intellect and pure consciousness, one attains

mastery over all kinds of feelings and also omniscience.

Sattva is the intellect. When one knows the puruṣa, the Self, as different from the intellect, and does samyama on that, all knowingness comes to you, as a natural phenomenon.

In fact, the seed of all knowingness is present in all of us. Only that it has not sprouted; it has not been activated. What stops it from activation? It is the intellect which has become like a hard nut. However, it sprouts very quicky in children because they are still very pure, the feelings of craving and aversion have not crept in them. Their devotion, connectivity is very pure. As a result, in children it manifests very quickly. So all forms of knowing are well embedded in us.

If you go to a law office, a lawyer has volumes and volumes of books. He knows what is in which book. If you present him a case, he knows which book he has to refer to. If you and I go there we will be lost because we have no idea. But does the lawyer have all those books in his head all the time? No. He pulls out whichever book is required. He does not carry the law in his head all the time. Otherwise he will become crazy.

Sarva-jñātṛtvam means the spontaneous, intuitive ability will be in you. At that moment you will know what is what. This ability to see the difference between sattva and puruṣa, the intellect and the consciousness is embedded in your consciousness.

If someone comes to me, I can, in no time, tell them what they did yesterday or one month ago or what their problem is. I know everything but sometimes I search for my own comb in my black bag. Is it on this side or that side? One would wonder why Gurudev would search for his comb, when he knows secrets which nobody knows about? It could be confusing. The job of a Guru is to confuse, not convince!

This ability of our consciousness to know the subtlest and the deepest is in the process of separation of the sattva—the intellect—from the consciousness. One need not exhibit these abilities all the time. When the time comes, it happens naturally. So even if you gain this ability, it is better you keep it to yourself and use it sparingly. These things come to us very naturally.

Sarva-bhāva-adhiṣṭhātṛtvam—you can establish yourself in all the different types of feelings and have mastery over them. Jesus got angry and threw the priest out of the temple. He threw out those people who were sitting in the temple.

When Lord Kṛṣṇa got angry, he took out the Sudarśana Cakra. So why would Jesus get angry? Why would Kṛṣṇa get angry? On the other hand, Kṛṣṇa had tears when Sudāmā, his old friend, came to see him. He was fully engrossed in that friendship. You might think that He's a yogī so how could He be so friendly with somebody? He went and hugged Sudāmā and brought him in. So why did Kṛṣṇa have tears in His eyes?

He had *sarva-bhāva*—all the feelings, all the *bhāvas*. You should have all the bhāvas present in you but also have mastery over them. If you don't have feelings, there is nothing to get mastery over. If you have no senses, there can be no mastery over the senses. Mastery comes when they exist.

Higher States

tad-vairāgyād-api doṣa-bīja-kṣaye kaivalyam || 50 ||

तद्वैराग्यादपि दोषबीजक्षये कैवल्यम् ॥ ५० ॥

The desirelessness for even that (the attainments in the previous sutra) destroys the seeds of bondage and one attains absolute liberation.

Kaivalya is oneness, a non-dual state achieved that is true liberation. A yogī is much superior to others but he should not get attached to that supremacy. This is very important. This is a lesson for all yogīs. No doubt you have power, you are superior. But you need to behave like an ordinary person. Be friendly, be natural and be connected to everybody. Do not be attached to your supremacy. Then *kaivalyam*, the highest liberation happens. And when it happens naturally, you don't go on tom-tomming about it to everybody. You respect everyone. That is what Lord Kṛṣṇa also did. He was not the king in Dvārkā at all. People simply addressed him as *Dvārkādhīśa*. He was an uncrowned king. Lord Kṛṣṇa, very humbly, would stand up with folded hands and say, "I have an idea. Can I submit it at this august gathering?" So enlightenment brings along with it non-attachment to the powers that come along with it as well.

sthāni-upanimantraṇe saṅga-smaya-akaraṇam

punaḥ-aniṣṭa-prasaṅgāt || 51 ||

स्थान्युपनिमन्त्रणे सङ्गस्मयाकरणं पुनरनिष्टप्रसङ्गात् ॥ ५१ ॥

When invited by the celestial beings, there is no reason to accept the offer or smile with pride as it may again lead to undesirable events.

Angels might invite you, gods might invite you, charm you for something. Don't accept or don't even have the pride of non-acceptance. Here I want to share something with you.

It was in New York, maybe around 2000, millennium time. I was in Vinod's apartment. I was on the upper floor and on the lower floor were Bhanu, John Osborne and others. It was 3 o' clock at night. The angel or *yakṣa* of New York came to me. I never thought the angel of New York would be so pleasant because it was such a stressful city. That was such a beautiful moment. It came and asked me very nicely, "What can I do for you? I want to do something for you."

The natural response in my mind was nothing. If anyone asks me what I want, I say nothing. I have everything. I don't want anything. It looked a little sad and then that entity vanished. Then I felt that maybe I should have asked it to do something. To make it happier, I should have said, "Make a centre for me," or something similar. I just thought it would have made the yakṣa happier; it was my afterthought.

At that point of time, everybody in the house woke up. They had felt its presence. The next morning Bhanu and John asked me if something had happened. They felt a big presence come at that hour. A sort of light shone and everyone woke up. You know what happened the next day?

I was in the United Nations, and I was supposed to address a meeting. I was sitting next to a couple of other dignitaries from the UN and the entire hall was empty, except for 10–15 of our people who had come with me. I thought this had never happened to me before. I come to a program and there is nobody to listen to me. Immediately it struck me, this is the work of that angel, the yakṣa. Something had happened, the doors were closed somewhere.

If you do not know the reality of the subtle world, you will get upset with the organiser or somebody else. The moment I recognised that this happened because he was not happy, the next minute everybody poured in and the hall was full in ten minutes. Why am I sharing this is because the subtle world is much more than what we see in the gross world.

A couple of years ago a gentleman came to the Bangalore āśrama from America, and he measured the energy during the *ṛṣi homa*. He could see a definite pattern when those particular ṛṣis were invoked. In the hall, a different type of energy was coming down and then going back.

The entire universe is filled with many dimensions. It is filled with different types of energies. There are good energies and there are bad energies too. And when you get invitations from these different realms, Maharṣi Patañjali cautions you not to get trapped in them. If you do, you have to go through the whole cycle all over again. Just be cautious about such invitations, and don't get trapped in them.

Many events happened in the 1980s, before we started The Art of Living. Many miracles would happen and people would come only for those miracles. Then I decided this is not the way it should be. They have to listen to knowledge too. Instead of helping people grow, I thought maybe I was making them greedy. Then I decided to let everyone focus on knowledge, rather than on these phenomena. Maharṣi Patañjali here says that when such invitations come then gently and politely you can refuse them.

kṣaṇa-tat-kramayoḥ samyamāt-

vivekajam jñānam || 52 ||

क्षणतत्क्रमयोः संयमाद्विवेकजं ज्ञानम् ॥ ५२ ॥

Samyama on the present moment and its flow results in knowledge that is born from discrimination.

It is obvious. *Kṣaṇa* means this moment. Samyama on the present moment can lift you into another level of knowledge.

jāti-lakṣaṇa-deśaiḥ-anyatā-anavacchedāt-

tulyayoḥ-tataḥ pratipattiḥ || 53 ||

जातिलक्षणदेशैरन्यतानवच्छेदात्तुल्ययोस्ततः प्रतिपत्तिः ॥ ५३ ॥

This knowledge (born from discrimination) brings awareness of the difference between two similar objects, which are not distinguishable by type (or category), qualities or location.

What you cannot distinguish from a normal level of understanding, can be discriminated by heightened awareness, with a special knowledge, when you practise samyama on this.

tārakam sarva-viṣayam sarvathā-viṣayam akramam

ca-iti vivekajam jñānam || 54 ||

तारकं सर्वविषयं सर्वथाविषयम् अक्रमं चेति

विवेकजं ज्ञानम् ॥ ५४ ॥

This knowledge born of discrimination is intuitive and applies to everything, by all means, and arises spontaneously (unlike knowledge born of logic which follows a sequence of inferences).

This higher knowledge is beyond logic. Sometimes when Gurus and Masters speak, it appears to be illogical because it is beyond logic. Not all those who speak illogically are Masters!(Laughter) It transcends normal logic because the knowledge of discrimination which is coming up is from a higher or a subtle plane, not the gross intellect.

sattva-puruṣayoḥ śuddhi-sāmye kaivalyam-iti || 55 ||

सत्त्वपुरुषयोः शुद्धिसाम्ये कैवल्यमिति ॥ ५५ ॥

When the intellect and the consciousness become equally pure, that is absolute liberation.

Now, the puruṣa is pure anyway but if the intellect is not pure, kaivalya will not happen. When the intellect attains its purity then the difference between sattva and puruṣa is well established.

Puruṣa is impure when it becomes one with sattva, the intellect. When that gap between the puruṣa and the intellect is attained, then buddhi, the intellect becomes pure. With this purity, liberation is attained and that is kaivalya.

These are all the stages. Siddhi is only a stage. It is like a lounge. When you have to board a flight, you have to first go to the lounge. When you de-plane, you go to the baggage area and collect your bags. You don't stay in the baggage area. Like this, siddhi is the transient stage that comes in your life. Do not get attached to that. The first siddhi that comes to you is that you curse someone, and it becomes true. Then you get the ability to bless. We have many blessers here. You bless somebody and good things happen. But when you curse somebody, the curse is going to come back to you. When you bless somebody, the blessing will come back to you, manifold.

Lord Buddhā said three things—first, śīla is your character. Your character should be so solid, so strong. You should be well established in ethics, in morality—you don't do what you don't want others to do to you. Even if others do something which you don't like, you don't repeat it. Tit for tat is not at all śīla. Śīla is being well-founded in ethics.

Second, samādhi. Samādhi becomes natural to you, becomes easy for you to experience when you have śīla.

Third, prajñā. This gives rise to discrimination, awareness and heightened consciouness. That is prajñā.

Samādhi is a tool to kaivalya, to rise to the oneness of consciousness. And oneness of consciousness happens, when the analysis happens. Kaivalya is synthesis. When *sattva-puruṣa* analysis is done, when the distinction is done, synthesis of the whole consciousness happens. The oneness of existence comes up. Isn't this amazing?

Oneness does not happen by pulling things together and synthesizing them. Oneness or synthesis happens when analysis happens. When you find the distinction between the puruṣa and the buddhi, the intellect, then puruṣa and buddhi disappear immediately. What remains is kaivalya, the oneness of the Being. So analysis leads to synthesis.

Opposite values are complementary. Synthesis and analysis appear to be different but they're complementary. In fact, they are one. Perfect analysis leads you to perfect synthesis, which is kaivalya. That is the goal of human existence. The purpose in life is oneness. Liberation, freedom—all these are just different names.

When the 'two' is there, then there is fear. When the merger happens, when the oneness is there, there is no fear. So before that oneness happens, one has to be shaken up to remove all the fears. That is what sādhanā is about. Taking out, shaking all the fear out of you and making you realise the distinction between the puruṣa and the intellect.

Questions and Answers

Question: Gurudev, you said that nirvicāra samādhi happens through grace. One can have control or certainty over one's effort but one has no control over grace, it's a happening. Patañjali says *nirvicāra-vaiśāradye-adhyātma-prasādaḥ*. He seems to indicate that one can become an expert in nirvicāra. How does one develop certainty or expertise where a happening is involved?

Gurudev: Lord Kṛṣṇa also says in Bhagavad Gītā *tatsvayam yogasansiddhaḥ kālenātmani vindati*—for one who perfects yoga with self-effort, knowledge of Self comes in due course. You do your preparation, what you need to do but the fruit of that action comes only when it should come. That comes from a very different realm, of very different laws, rather than the law of cause and effect. There is a law which is beyond the cause and effect, that is what grace is and it is called *ahaituki kripa*—it has no cause, no roots, no condition, it can happen anywhere anytime.

Question: This is more of a wonder than a question. I do not speak of those who mistake the rope for a snake but you, someone who knows that there never was a snake or that this life is a dream, a mere shadow. Once awake, doesn't it seem meaningless to return to the dream? I really wish to know your point of view on this.

Gurudev: You think that one does something only for some selfish reason, else it is all meaningless. Had that been the case, there won't be any path of knowledge, path of bhakti, the Bhagavad Gītā would have never come into being! Lord Kṛṣṇa would have said to Arjuna that all that is happening is maya, let what is going on be—Arjuna, you wish to go to the forest? Go ahead! Why fight? I will also rest peacefully in Vrindavan, you also rest.

Arjuna was anyway saying that he wished to leave the battlefield–I want nothing. I do not want the throne. I will go to Rishikesh, Badrinath. I will sit in the snow. What do I want? This is all sin, this world is ignorance, why do I have to live here? Why am I being forced to live here–this is what Arjuna said in the beginning, isn't it?

Why are you dragging me into this sinful act, this maya? Then Kṛṣṇa says, "You speak like a wise person but are a fool." Then He rattles him—"Aren't you ashamed?" Now what is there to be ashamed of once you know it is all maya? What is honour-dishonour when it's all maya!

Kṛṣṇa guides Arjuna step by step. First He pinches his ego, "What will people say about you?" At that time He did not say, "Don't be a football of others opinions." Instead He made him a football. There is no scripture like Gītā in the world because it contradicts itself and thus depicts the truth. It is not merely a story; it is a way of hand holding a student step by step.

At one point, Arjuna says to Kṛṣṇa, "I was already deluded and you have confused me more! When I sit with you for ten minutes, I get more confused. You say, "This is alright, that is alright, do this if you wish to, else do that if you so wish." I have come to ask you once and for all what to do and you are bringing more confusion to me—do this or if you want to, do that or such and such is better or such and such will be left behind. What is all this?" Arjuna asks for definite clarity, "Tell me what is to be done and I will do that." Kṛṣṇa confused him again and again, and then raised the crying, shivering Arjuna up, gave him a few slaps, called him a fool, gave him knowledge slowly, told him that he was a very pious soul and had come to the earth for the greater good.

kim punar brāhmaṇāḥ puṇyā bhaktā rājarṣhayas

He says this in the ninth chapter—You are a Rajarṣi, a king, a great person. Kṛṣṇa pacifies and praises him. When they are praised, immature people start doing some work. The wise do not require praise to do their job. A fool needs a pat on the back. This is what Lord Kṛṣṇa did to Arjuna, and in the end, left the choice to him, "I said what I had to. Now, do what you wish to do, but know that what I want alone will happen."

After saying all this, He said, "Leave all the dharma aside. *Sarvadharmān parityajya*—give up all the dharma. *Mām ekam śaraṇam vraja*—take refuge in Me alone." When a devotee says to the Divine, "I will do it, You also help me a little," then God doesn't work. When you raise both your arms completely, "I have no way out," then help arrives.

Ego has doership in it, "I am the doer, I will look after myself, I do not want anything from you, I will work on my own," this attitude strengthens doership.

There is an incident in Mahabharata. Sri Kṛṣṇa gets up in the middle of His meal, goes out of the room, returns, goes out again and then returns again. This happens quite a few times. Someone inquired what was going on. At that time, Draupadi was calling out for help (when she was being disrobed). However, she was alternating between trying to protect herself, holding on to her robes with one hand and calling Kṛṣṇa. When she let go, raising both her arms up in surrender, leaving everything to God, that is when Kṛṣṇa reached there.

Kṛṣṇa says, "My devotee calls out to Me but he is holding on to some other support. That is why I am unable to go and have to return. If a devotee does not listen to Me, then let him do as he wishes."

Until there is complete surrender, even God cannot come to help us. When Draupadi raised both her arms up in utter helplessness and called out to Hari, her robe became endless. This is the glory of surrender; this has come to people's experience but it should not be misused.

There is a couplet—*ajgar kare na chakri, panchhi kare na kaam, Das Maluka keh gaye sabke data Ram*—the python does not serve anyone; the bird does not work for anyone. Das Maluka pronounces that all creatures are provided for by the Divine. But this is not to be misused—since the Divine feeds and takes care of everyone, let me also keep lying here!

The knowledge of advaita (non-duality) has been misused so much in our country that people went into laziness. Though such lofty knowledge is available, it is not ingrained in life. We claim to have surrendered it all, but it is laziness. Just poke the so-called surrendered ones a little, touch them slightly. They will explode with anger! There is so much ego, I-ness, craving, aversion, anger and then you say you are fully surrendered! This won't work. Those who are really surrendered, do not have all this within them. They can show anger if needed, but do not get angry and become tense. This is what Kṛṣṇa says to Arjuna. In the end, He says, "*Yathechchhasi tathā kuru*o—do whatever you want to do, but know for sure that what I wish alone will happen." Finally, Arjuna says, "Now I remember my friend, who you are, who I am, now I remember. *Kariṣhye vacanam tava*—I will do as you say."

Question: Gurudev, all these years, I have depended on my intellect to solve things. I found out today that it is an obstacle on the path of yoga. How do I learn not to depend on the intellect because the tendency is many years old. Are there any techniques for this?

Gurudev: It is wrong to say that we should not have intellect. We must! Intellect needs to be sharp, alert, awake but there is an aspect in you which is beyond the intellect, which you need to nurture. Yoga nurtures both your intellect and the heart, your feelings, your emotions and something beyond the emotions. If someone is stuck in their emotions, then their perception is flawed. They cannot hear, they cannot act properly. When someone is in rage or crying non-stop, you cannot communicate with them. They become sort of incommunicable. In the same way, someone who is stuck in the intellect cannot see beyond the intellect. Intellect is essential but don't get stuck in it.

It is necessary to wear your *chappals* and shoes but if they stick to your sole and don't come off it's a problem. Correct? It's necessary to wear clothes but if the clothes get stuck to your skin and don't come off, you have to go to a doctor.

Question: Gurudev, you mentioned that nirbija means the seed has burnt and the impression cannot come again. If the seed is burnt how does one return to the normal state?

Gurudev: There are other seeds. Some seeds are burnt, some are not burnt, that's it! See, these are examples. You should not stretch the example too much, then it loses its charm, its value and its significance. Suppose you have some stress and the stress is burnt, that goes out of you, and when you work more, if you are not aware, you accumulate more stress.

Kaivalya Pāda

The Big Mind

janma-auṣadhi-mantra-tapaḥ samādhi-

jāḥ siddhayaḥ ||1||

जन्मौषधिमन्त्रतपः समाधिजाः सिद्धयः ॥ १ ॥

The different kinds of perfection come with birth or are attained through herbs, mantra, penance or samādhi.

Siddhi means perfection. Perfecting the consciousness, its attributes and its abilities is siddhi. Perfecting the body is also a siddhi. It is called *kāya siddhi,* then there is *vāka siddhi*. There are numerous such siddhis. Kāya siddhi means mastery over the body. Gymnastics, six- pack abs—all these are kāya siddhi. Ability of the body to resist diseases, to stand up to heat and cold, and come up with its extraordinary abilities is kāya siddhi.

When there is vāka siddhi, whatever you say will happen.

When there is *citta śuddhi*, purity of mind, then it is called *ātma siddhi*, that is mastery over the Self. And how are these siddhis and perfection attained in life?

1. Some are born with it. For example, I have not done any tapas; what I have is with me naturally.

2. Some attain it by chanting mantras. These mantras should be initiated properly. You shouldn't just open a book, take a mantra and start chanting. That will not work. Only properly initiated mantras will work.

3. Others gain it through herbs. There are a lot of different descriptions that ṛṣis have given on this. There is one herb called soma that aligns itself with the moon; for fifteen days of the waxing moon, it grows leaves and for fifteen days of the new moon, the leaves start withering away. Some of the herbs are only mentioned in the scriptures; they are not found anywhere. We don't know where they are. Some may be in the Himālayas, some in other

places. Āyurveda is a part of this siddhi. Āyurveda uses these herbs to make the body strong. If any part of your body becomes weak, then āyurveda can make it strong through herbs .

4. Some others achieve perfection through samādhi.

5. There are some who get it by practising penance, tapas. Through tapas you can get perfection. The chanting of mantras gives *mantra siddhi*. Through chanting mantras regularly, incessantly you can get perfection. From mantra siddhi comes vāka siddhi. Your words fructify. So, all different siddhis come through tapas.

jāti-antara-pariṇāmaḥ prakṛti-āpūrāt || 2 ||

जात्यन्तरपरिणामः प्रकृत्यापूरात् ॥ २ ॥

Transition into another life-state or form (in the next birth) comes as a result of what is filled in one's nature (forms natural tendencies).

The birth you wish to take in your next life depends on what you fill in your citta in this life.

Jāti-antara refers to how you want to be born and where you want to be born. For a non-sādhaka, one who is not on the path, it is bound by his karma. A sādhaka can choose where he wants to be born, with whom he should be born, etc. These choices exist for him.

nimittam-aprayojakam prakṛtīnām

varaṇa-bhedaḥ-tu tataḥ kṣetrikavat || 3 ||

निमित्तमप्रयोजकं प्रकृतीनां वरणभेदस्तु ततः क्षेत्रिकवत् ॥ ३ ॥

Incidental cause or action does not fill up one's nature (which happens on its own) but it does remove the obstacles to the process, like a farmer (removes the barrier to the field and water fills it up on its own).

The attainment is not based so much on action, but on the being and the attitude. It doesn't depend on the action. Action is very gross but the attitude is what causes the impression. The attitude with which you do an action determines your karma and your next life also.

Take for example, a doctor, who cuts open the belly of a person. His intention is to heal and make the person live longer. But if the same act is done by a dacoit, his intention is to kill. The action is the same, both are ripping open the stomach, but one wants to heal the person and make him live longer; the other wants to kill him. The action may be the same, but the intentions of these two people are very different. Even with the doctor opening someone's stomach, the patient may die. And even after some dacoit stabs somebody, he may still be alive. The action is not what counts here; it is the intention behind the action which counts. That is what makes karma. That is why, Lord Kṛṣṇa tells Arjunā, "You go fight; leave everything to me. You are doing my work. Don't worry about the consequences of the action. You are only executing an order. You do what I say. That sin will not come to you because your mind is clear. Your mind has one attitude that you are just doing what you are supposed to do."

So, the affliction of the action does not happen then.

nirmāṇa-cittāni-asmitā-mātrāt || 4 ||

निर्माणचित्तान्यस्मितामात्रात् ॥ ४ ॥

Doership comes solely from a sense of I-ness.

Nirmāṇa citta refers to the desire to do something. Doership comes from asmitā, the sense of 'I' within you. When he says doership comes from asmitā, you don't have to think, "I should not have doership." Here Maharṣi Patañjali is not telling you whether it is good or bad. But, he wants you to recognize this nirmāṇa citta, the doership, that is coming out of asmitā.

pravṛtti-bhede prayojakam cittam-

ekam-anekeṣām || 5 ||

प्रवृत्तिभेदे प्रयोजकं चित्तमेकमनेकेषाम् ॥ ५ ॥

It is the one mind that is the director of different activities (or tendencies).

In our body, there are billions of cells. They all have their own lifetime. There are many that are born every day and there are many that die every day. You scrub off and let go of all dead cells. In your body there is birth every day and death every day.

In the same way, people are all engaged in doing different activities, different things. They are not aware of that one consciousness while performing those activities. Like you are not aware of so many cells functioning in your body even though you are the centre of it all.

Similarly, there is a big mind that is the central point of this entire existence, of which all these different activities, the small minds are only a part. Does that make sense? Many people may be born, many people die, but the big mind remains forever.

tatra dhyānajam-anāśayam || 6 ||

तत्र ध्यानजमनाशयम् ॥ ६ ॥

There, the tendency or activity born of meditation is free from latent impressions.

When you are meditating on this big mind, you are free from all impressions.

Nuances of Karma

karma-aśukla-akṛṣṇam yoginaḥ-

trividham-itareṣām || 7 ||

कर्माशुक्लाकृष्णं योगिनस्त्रिविधमितरेषाम् ॥ ७ ॥

The actions of a yogī are neither white nor black. They are three-fold for others.

Here is the difference between a siddha and a sādhaka. A siddha, a perfected being, has neither good nor bad karma. There is no white or black; no good or bad karma. But for non-perfected sādhakas, they are of three types. What are they? Good karma, bad karma and mixed karma (mixture of good and bad)—white, black and grey. Now this has nothing to do with racism. It is not that white is good, black is bad or black is good, white is bad. We are simply saying, 'Kṛṣṇa, śukla' which can be interpreted as Kṛṣṇa meaning growing and śukla meaning reducing. It can be interpreted in different ways.

tataḥ-tad-vipāka-anuguṇānām-eva-

abhivyaktiḥ-vāsanānām || 8 ||

ततस्तद्विपाकानुगुणानामेवाभिव्यक्तिर्वासनानाम् ॥ ८ ॥

As they (the three-fold actions) lead up to fruition, they manifest corresponding latent impressions.

Whatever karma you have inside; the good karma, the mixed karma or bad karma, you are accordingly drawn in those directions.

When good karma is active, you start doing good things.

When bad karma appears, then you do all sorts of wrong things and start justifying.

When it is mixed, there is a little guilt, but there is a little justification as well. You think, "Oh I shouldn't be doing this."

But then you may also think, "That is okay. I should do this." The yoyo effect is a result of mixed karma. As is the type of karma, so is the type of impression we accumulate. This is how patterns develop in us. You have come to the planet with some patterns, you develop on those patterns and then those patterns rule your life. It also attracts similar patterns towards you.

jāti-deśa-kāla-vyavahitānām-api-ānantaryām

smṛti-samskārayoḥ eka-rūpatvāt || 9 ||

जातिदेशकालव्यवहितानामप्यानन्तर्यं

स्मृतिसंस्कारयोः एकरूपत्वात् || ९ ||

Even if there is interruption in life-state, time and space, karma unfolds with unbroken continuity because memory and latent impressions are of the same nature.

Time and space have an impact on karma. Though you may have some karmas, when you come to where a siddha or a sādhaka is, they change.

You have certain negative tendencies. Those tendencies get fueled even more when you go to those areas, where there is more negativity. But when you come to a positive place, those impressions change. Even if some of those impressions are there, they become dormant, if you don't act on them. Similarly, at certain times, your patterns are more proactive. At certain other times, those patterns remain dormant.

tāsām-anāditvam ca-āśiṣo nityatvāt || 10 ||

तासामनादित्वं चाशिषो नित्यत्वात् ॥ १० ॥

Those (patterns of impressions) are beginningless because the desire to live is eternal.

As long as there is a will to live, some or other patterns keep happening in you, and you get into those patterns.

hetu-phala-āśraya-ālambanaiḥ saṅgṛhītatvād eṣām-

abhāve tad-abhāvaḥ || 11 ||

हेतुफलाश्रयालम्बनैः संगृहीतत्वादेषामभावे तदभावः ॥ ११ ॥

Impressions are held together by cause, motive, basis and support. Disappearance of these four factors causes the impressions to disappear as well.

Any impression is held by a cause. You attribute a cause to it, there is a motive behind it and these two form a substratum. And it is always attached to some object. Suppose you remove all the objects from your consciousness, all impressions are gone. If you don't keep the cause and effect, only the impression is what is left. If you hook it on to a cause, then it is all the more reason for the impression to stay. When you remove the cause, then the karma vanishes.

For example, you have been accused by somebody, rightly or wrongly. Now you hold on to it in your mind. You hold that person responsible for the pain that is inflicted on you. What has happened? When someone accuses you of something that you have not done, you feel pain, right? Or if you have done something and they point a finger at you, then it is guilt. In fact, even guilt is a sort of pain. So, who is the cause for the pain or guilt which you experience for something which you did or didn't do? That guy or that lady. You hook on to the cause. Now the karma has become stronger.

The karma has become strong because you connected your pain to a cause. And when there is a cause, then you have a motive to give it back to them. Correct? You cannot keep quiet. When someone is the cause, you react. That reaction again results in another cause. Thinking someone else is the cause creates one karma. The motive to do something in vengeance is another karma. And when you react, it is yet another karma.

So how to cut the cycle of karma? Do not react and do not see the other person as a cause. Know that, the man or woman was only a postman. In simple terms, as we have always been saying, take responsibility for all your experiences. What happens when you take responsibility for your experiences? You stop building karma. You become powerful. You become solid, strong. Isn't this amazing?

It is the mechanics in the mind. Even if you think someone is the cause, it should be only on the surface. In life you cannot do this on a day to day basis. But what you can do is when you find someone is the reason for your hurt, go into why they hurt you. They must be hurt themselves. You push the cause a little back. Find out what is the real cause of the behavior of the person.

You must go beyond the cause of the apparent cause. Even looking for the motive behind an action is short-sightedness. In simple words, don't see intentions behind others' actions. Even if it was intentionally done, then the doer was not in his proper mind; he was ignorant, that is why he did it. He was sick, so he did it. You don't hold sick people responsible for something which they do, do you? If someone is crazy, even courts don't hold him responsible for his actions. In fact, they will send him for treatment to a mental hospital, not to jail. When you see motives, your ignorance becomes solid; stronger.

I usually tell a story about a saint, who went to Narendra Nagar palace. Narendra Nagar was a kingdom situated above Rishikesh. In the palace, they used to welcome saints and serve them food. The food in the palace was served in silver and gold utensils. The saints would come, eat and go back. All that they needed was food. Once it so happened that a saint took one golden cup, put it in his bag and left. This news reached the king. He was surprised and thought, "How could a saint do this? If he had asked me, I would have given him four golden cups. Then why did he take the cup away quietly?" He was confused. But three days later, he came for his meal and placed the cup back. That confused the king even more. So, he called all the vaidika scholars and started discussing why such a thing happened. The scholars and the other saints who were there asked him, "What is it that you fed him that day?" They said, "Analyse not the behavior of the saint, but the source of food that he was served that day." This is how you find the cause. You go to the cause behind the cause. Now instead of you getting angry and agitated about an incident or a person, you look at the cause of the incident; cause of the apparent cause. This is the way you annihilate karma. This is jñāna—knowledge. This is wisdom.

Wisdom is not to take the apparent cause as the absolute cause. Then your karma is already getting finished.

Now on with the story. The security had captured dacoits and confiscated some foodgrains from them. Food prepared from that lot was fed to the saint. But how come others didn't get affected? How come it was just that saint who was affected? Probably because he was much more sensitive to everything.

Jaisa ann vaisa mann—yathā annam tathā buddhi—you are what you eat. How the food is, determines how the mind works. The impact or effect of that food, the vibration of the food, stayed only for three days. Usually, the effect of food on the body stays only for a short period of time; maximum three days. So, when the impact of the food was gone, the saint came and put the cup back. That is why, when food is prepared, you pray, "Let this food give me the right thoughts. Let this food make me go towards Divinity." This is the prayer everybody has to say before eating and even before cooking.

Whenever grains and pulses were brought home in ancient days, even up to the recent 50–60 years, people used to receive it with great reverence. They used to store them in barrels and worship them by applying kumkum and chandan. They would even put sandalwood paste and flowers on the barrels and bow down in reverence. A special barrel (marattāl in Tamil), open from the top and with a small hole at the bottom, was used to store the grains for a whole year. As kids we used to go and just open the hole at the bottom of the barrel and watch the paddy gush out like water. It used to be a great joy for us. Our grandmother used to come chasing after us for the mischief we had done or for climbing on top of the huge marattāl made of wood.

So, knowing the cause of the cause clears you of karma and ensures that karma is not accumulated.

Perceiving Power of the Mind

atīta-anāgatam svarūpataḥ-asti-adhva-

bhedāt dharmāṇām || 12 ||

अतीतानागतं स्वरूपतोऽस्त्यध्वभेदाद् धर्माणाम् ॥ १२ ॥

The past and the future exist in reality, owing to differences in characteristics.

Past and future exist here at this moment. Your future exists here as a seed. Your past exists now as a memory. Both are impressions. Your craving is an impression; your aversion is an impression; your wants are an impression; your fears are an impression; memories of the past are impressions; hopes and desires of the future are an impression. All these are just impressions on your consciousness. And your consciousness is beyond time.

te vyakta-sūkṣmāḥ guṇa-ātmānaḥ || 13 ||

ते व्यक्तसूक्ष्मा गुणात्मानः ॥ १३ ॥

Manifest (when in the present) or subtle (not manifested when in the past or the future), they (characteristics) are of the nature of the (three) guṇas (sattva, rajas and tamas).

Everything happens through the three guṇas. Your form is made of three guṇas. If even one guṇa is taken away, your form will disappear. For anything to exist and be continuous, you need three.

When one of the most accomplished nuclear scientists, Dr. Hans Peter Dürr, came to the āśrama, he brought a model of the Chaos Pendulum—three metallic balls attached to a string. If one ball goes up, the other two come down. They move in cycles.

The universe is a continuum, because it has three components. Without the power of three, the universe cannot exist. Nothing can destroy the power of three. The universe will go on forever. How was this knowledge perceived or conceived during vaidika times?

Triguṇatmikā—all the forms, shapes and substances you see in the world are made up of three guṇas and you will see that only because of these guṇas things happen.

pariṇāma-ekatvāt vastu-tattvam || 14 ||

परिणामैकत्वाद् वस्तुतत्त्वम् ॥ १४ ॥

The reality of an object comes from the uniformity in change (of the guṇas).

This explains why mango seeds produce only mango fruit, human beings give birth to only human beings. If human beings start giving birth to dogs, there will be no continuity after that. Though all the forms are made up of one thing, the guṇas help sustain a particular pattern in every form. The whole thing is made up of one consciousness. Yet the forms are continuing because the impact or effect of consciousness is very particular.

The characteristic of an object appears to be a single unit. Though there are changes happening, the change is the same. There is continuity in the change. This is very subtle, very technical.

All objects come from space. Space is the summum bonum of creation and it keeps changing. Even though everything is changing, the change is also constant. Change is uniform. Do you think either things are uniform or they're changing? No. Change is also uniform. Your DNA gets transferred to your children and this continues to their children. You can go back up to 40, 50, 60 generations, the DNA has been continuous since then. Though it is changing; you are not your grandfather, but your grandfather's DNA is continuing in you. The same change is continuing in you. If you have a more scientific background, scientific temper, you can understand this better.

vastu-sāmye citta-bhedāt-tayoḥ-

vibhaktaḥ panthāḥ ||15 ||

वस्तुसाम्ये चित्तभेदात्तयोर्विभक्तः पन्थाः ॥ १५ ॥

Same objects may be perceived differently by different minds because of the difference in paths of perception.

An incident, an event, even an object can be perceived by different people in different ways, because the mind is different. See, in a group, one person is seen as a villain by some people; the others see him as a hero. You will be looked at by some people as a good person and perceived as bad by somebody else. You are perceived as a nasty lady by somebody while some others say you are the kindest. Perceptions are different, because the minds are different. But all that is not reality.

na ca-eka-citta-tantram vastu tad-apramāṇakam

tadā kim syāt || 16 ||

न चैकचित्ततन्त्रं वस्तु तदप्रमाणकं तदा किं स्यात् ॥ १६ ॥

The (existence of the) object does not depend on any one mind. If it does, what happens to the object when it is not perceived by that mind?

Though the subject has an influence on the object, the object has certain independence from the subject. That's what it means. The theory of relativity is true, no doubt. But still, the object has its own nature independent from that of the subject.

tad-uparāga-apekṣitvāt cittasya vastu

jñāta-ajñātām ||17 ||

तदुपरागापेक्षित्वात् चित्तस्य वस्तु ज्ञाताज्ञातम् ॥ १७ ॥

The object needs to influence or colour the mind and accordingly it is known or unknown (by the mind).

You are able to see certain things, which other animals are unable to see. And you are unable to see certain things which other animals are able to see. Similarly, different people see different things; different characteristics. So whatever colour falls on your mind that is what you perceive.

Beyond the Mind

sadā jñātāḥ-citta-vṛttayaḥ-tat-prabhoḥ

puruṣasya-apariṇāmitvāt || 18 ||

सदा ज्ञाताश्चित्तवृत्तयस्तत्प्रभोः पुरुषस्यापरिणामित्वात् ॥ १८ ॥

The modifications of the mind are always known by its lord (the puruṣa) as the puruṣa is changeless.

Wisdom is latching on to that non-changing aspect in you. From there, you get stability. Your perception changes or improves. Your expression improves. Your attitudes don't get stuck. A whole lot of change happens the moment you latch on to that non-changing aspect of your consciousness.

na tat svābhāsam dṛśyatvāt || 19 ||

न तत् स्वाभासं दृश्यत्वात् ॥ १९ ॥

That (mind) is not self-illuminating as it is an object of perception (by the puruṣa).

These are all experiential sūtras. Even your mind is innate. It is an inert object. Even the mind is considered an object here, because the mind also depends on the chemicals in your body. If you are injected with certain chemicals, your perception will be different. When you are given anesthesia, your mind goes to sleep. If you have been on an operation table, when they give you anesthesia, you might have experienced a little glimpse of samādhi. When you are under anesthesia, you have a sense of 'being there', but you don't feel your body. You just feel that something is happening. So, the mind is also an object. This is higher knowledge.

A meditator cannot be hypnotized. A sādhaka cannot be hypnotized. But someone who has not started the journey; not meditating or not regular in meditation or not done enough of it, can be easily hypnotized. What is hypnotism? Seeing the mind as an object and manipulating it. But for a meditator, for a jñāni, it doesn't work. Why? It is because you have experienced the 'no -mind' state. You may have experienced a little bit, just one percent of 'no-mind', a few moments of samādhi during the sahaj samādhi meditation! That is good enough for you to rise above the web of the mind as an object, which can be hypnotized.

eka-samaye ca-ubhaya-anavadhāraṇam || 20 ||

एकसमये चोभयानवधारणम् ॥ २० ॥

And both (the mind and the puruṣa) cannot be cognized simultaneously.

When there is a mind, the self-illuminating consciousness is obscured. When you go into meditation, deep samādhi, the mind is not there. This is what Buddhā calls the 'no-mind'. You simply feel the illumination. In Buddhism and Taoism, it is commonly known as the state of 'no-mind'. Lord Kṛṣṇa says in the Bhagavad Gītā:

śanaiḥ śanairuparamēd buddhyā dhṛtigṛhītayā

ātmasaṅstham manaḥ kṛtvā na kiñcidapi cintayēt

|| Bhagavad Gītā 6.25 ||

शनैः शनैरुपरमेद् बुद्ध्या धृतिगृहीतया ।

आत्मसंस्थं मनः कृत्वा न किञ्चिदपि चिन्तयेत् ॥ ६·२५ ॥

Having established your mind in the ātman, don't think about anything else.

Ātmasaṅstham manaḥ kṛtvā—when the intellect and mind are embedded in the Self, it is a way of samādhi. Either the illuminating Self is there, or the mind is there. This is *paramārtha satya*, the ultimate truth. And then there is what is called, *vyavahāra satya*—in dealing, in vyavahāra; in activity, the mind will be there.

cittāntara-dṛśye buddhi-buddheḥ-atiprasaṅgaḥ

smṛti-saṅkaraḥ-ca || 21 ||

चित्तान्तरदृश्ये बुद्धिबुद्धेरतिप्रसङ्गः स्मृतिसङ्करश्च ॥ २१ ॥

If one mind is known by another, which is known by another and so on, there would be an endless progression and a mixture of memories.

One mind cannot illuminate another mind. Mind does not have a life of its own. Mind gets life from the Self. Mind is like the Moon. The Moon has no light of its own; no energy of its own. The Moon gets the light from the Sun. When the Sun is up in the sky, you can't see the Moon. When the Moon is shining, can you see the Sun? No! Likewise, the mind and the Self cannot shine at the same time. Also, similar to how one Moon cannot reflect another Moon, one mind cannot make the other mind shine.

citeḥ-apratisaṅkramāyāḥ-tad-ākārāpattau

sva-buddhi-samvedanam || 22 ||

चितेरप्रतिसंङ्क्रमायास्तदाकारापत्तौ स्वबुद्धिसंवेदनम् ॥ २२ ॥

Consciousness is unchanging and when the intellect assumes its form, self-cognition is possible.

It's obvious. Next.

draṣṭṛ-dṛśya-uparaktam cittam sarvārtham || 23 ||

द्रष्टृदृश्योपरक्तं चित्तं सर्वार्थम् ॥ २३ ॥

The mind which is coloured by the knower and the knowable can know all objects.

When you realise this unchanging mind of yours, itself is taking the form or shape of the changing mind, there is a realization, "Oh! This is only me." It is not just internal. When it can be externalized, you will see this mind, that mind, every mind is part of my mind only; my big mind; my Self playing this role, that role, all these roles. This is a siddha's state; the state of a perfected being.

All these different bubbles that are arising on the surface of water, the water knows that they are mine only. It is all a game. It is all a dream.

Different figures appear in a laser show—the hero and the villain, weapons and vehicles. But are those figures real? No! It is just one beam that is creating all these different figures. When this realization comes that all consciousness is just that laser beam and I am that laser beam, not the show that is on the screen, that is kaivalya; that is liberation!

The mind is totally liberated then.

tad-asaṅkhyeya-vāsanābhiḥ-citram-api parārtham

samhatya-kāritvāt || 24 ||

तदसङ्ख्येयवासनाभिश्चित्रमपि परार्थं संहत्यकारित्वात् ॥ २४ ॥

Though the mindfield is full of innumerable impressions, it can act only in combination (with the senses, sense objects, ego etc). Therefore, its objective is for another (not for its own sake; here, 'another' is the puruṣa, the witnessing consciousness).

Don't think the vāsanās and eṣaṇās, impressions, are just present only in your mind. It is present in the whole atmosphere; in the mindfield as such. If you go to Wall Street in New York or to Dalal Street in Mumbai, your mind can catch all those thoughts related to money; creating greed. Those eṣaṇās can catch you.

Similarly, if you go to a red light area, the feverishness of lust can catch you.

When you go to a place of worship, even though you did not have any interest in praying, some vibrations change your mind at that time. Haven't you experienced this?

If you go to a street which has only bars and nightclubs, you feel that the energy is very different. How many of you have experienced that, even while just driving through those areas? While driving through a stock exchange, vibrations are different.

So, impressions are not only in one's consciousness, it is in the mindfield. That is why, here it is called the mindfield, the mind is not just an object. It is not a cap you are putting on. It is a field. That is why satsaṅga is very important. The type of company you keep is very, very, very important. Yogīs and siddhas always say—

your company should be of satsaṅga, of Truth; of people who are positive. If you sit with people who are depressed, you are sure to get depressed.

I was told, many psychiatrists, at some point of time become patients themselves. Once our teacher Michael Fischman was taking a course in New York. There were about fifty participants; half of them doctors and the others were patients. They came with their patients to experience Sudarśana Kriyā. Mikey called me and said, "Gurudev, I didn't know who among them were the doctors and who were the patients! They all looked the same and spoke similarly." Later, someone in the AAPI conference also said that most psychiatrists need medical intervention, because they are in that sort of atmosphere all day long. If you don't take care of your mind, disassociate with your work and rest in the depth of your Self, if you don't experience the deep rest of meditation, those impressions will get to you.

Yogīs sometimes don't care about compassion too much. Do you know why? People who are too compassionate put those impressions in their own mind. You do what you need to do, but don't get attached to that situation or circumstance or get those impressions inside you too much. This is the skill in doing sevā. Do sevā but save your mind. Don't take pride in your sevā. Never! That will kill you. Similarly, attachment to the sevā will also kill you. If you get mentally attached to poor or sick people, you are taking all those impressions into your mind and it will bother you. It will take the sheen out of you. This is a PhD lesson, don't go and tell this to everybody out there. This is for the most sensitive people. This is for the yogīs or sādhakas who are very sensitive. Not everybody is so sensitive. So, the world is safe; you don't have to worry about it. But if you become more and more sensitive, more and more of these impressions will get on to you. You safeguard your mind then.

Maharṣi Patañjali is not asking you to be selfish. No! He just says, "You must do sevā. You must serve others, not viewing them as others."

Suppose you have no impressions in your mind, you are totally free but still others see you differently than what you are.

They impose their own mind on you. They cannot see who you are. Only when you know yourself, can you know others thoroughly.

viśeṣa-darśina ātma-bhāva-bhāvanā-vinivṛttiḥ || 25 ||

विशेषदर्शिन आत्मभावभावनाविनिवृत्तिः ॥ २५ ॥

For one who distinctly experiences the Self (distinct from the intellect), the curiosity about the nature of one's own Self vanishes.

For the one who has experienced the distinction between the seer and the scenery, the false identities simply fall away all by themselves. Then you don't even have the curiosity about your own nature—"Who am I? What is my nature?" You no longer remain a seeker.

If you are a seeker, you cannot be a siddha. But you have to be a seeker till that point where the distinction between the seer and the scenery is very well understood. Once that is done, the false identities fall off. Then the curiosity and longing for enlightenment will also go. It should be dropped! But only after the false identity drops off. If the curiosity to know the Self drops much before, then you remain stuck with your false identity. This is very important!

There are people who say, you don't need a Guru; you don't need techniques, you can directly cognize yourself. They are saying so because their false identity has not fallen off. They have no guidance. Once all this is done, then why do you have to meditate or do Kriyā? You don't need to do prāṇāyāma. You don't need to do anything. You just rest. That is good enough for you. Simple resting becomes samādhi. But till the false identities fall off, you must do these practices. That is why, all siddhas, enlightened beings, continue to do their practices only to set an example for others. They caution you. You might slip otherwise. Even for yogīs, there is a fear of slipping if they don't adhere to the rules. Though there are no rules, the fear of slipping can still be there. That is why all these methods are to be followed unless and until you become a perfect siddha and become very strong. A sādhaka needs to be cautious.

tadā viveka-nimnam kaivalya-prāgbhāram

cittam || 26 ||

तदा विवेकनिम्नं कैवल्यप्राग्भारं चित्तम् ॥ २६ ॥

Then, the mind starts inclining towards discrimination and gravitates towards absolute liberation.

When the mind is inclined to the highest knowledge, viveka (discrimination), it naturally gravitates towards liberation. It then becomes your second nature. Actually, it is your first nature, but colloquially, we say that it has become your second nature. That means it has just become a part of you. Then liberation is right there.

tat-chidreṣu pratyaya-antarāṇi samskārebhyaḥ || 27 ||

तच्छिद्रेषु प्रत्ययान्तराणि संस्कारेभ्यः ॥ २७ ॥

When there are gaps or breaks in that discrimination, other thoughts and ideas come up in the mind due to earlier impressions.

hānam-eṣām kleśavat-uktam || 28 ||

हानमेषां क्लेशवदुक्तम् ॥ २८ ॥

These can be removed with the means of getting rid of misery explained earlier.

Sometimes, from an unconscious mind, some impressions may arise. At that time, you can do the same that we have spoken of before, to get rid of those impressions.

Absolute Liberation

prasaṅkhyāne-api-akusīdasya sarvathā

viveka-khyāteḥ-dharma-meghaḥ samādhiḥ || 29 ||

प्रसंङ्ख्यानेऽप्यकुसीदस्य सर्वथा विवेकख्यातेर्धर्ममेघः समाधिः ॥ २९ ॥

When there is no interest even in the fruits of being established in that discriminative awareness, there comes the samādhi which brings a cloud of virtues.

Dharma megha—megha means cloud. When you are in samādhi, your state of being is full of that positive energy of dharmā. Then anyone who comes near you feels uplifted. Anyone who comes near you mentally, not physically. Anyone can be close to you but covered in his own māyā. When anyone connects with you mentally, they experience all the virtues right there. So in the state of dharma megha samādhi—a samādhi or state of mind which is full of virtues—others can feel it too.

tataḥ kleśa-karma-nivṛttiḥ || 30 ||

ततः क्लेशकर्मनिवृत्तिः ॥ ३० ॥

Thereafter, all afflictions and impressions are removed.

Kleśa means pain; karma means impressions. All kinds of kleśas and karma get removed. This happens here in the āśrama every day. People come with so many kleśas; they go back smiling.

tadā sarva-āvaraṇa-mala-apetasya

jñānasya-ānantyāt-jñeyam-alpam || 31||

तदा सर्वावरणमलापेतस्य ज्ञानस्यानन्त्याज्ज्ञेयमल्पम् ॥ ३१ ॥

Then, free from all the veils of impurities, with knowledge that is infinite, there is almost nothing to be known.

Nothing to be known...

Every being is divine, but has three veils—*mala, āvaraṇa, vikṣepa*. Mala means impurities; āvaraṇa is the veil of wrong understanding, ignorance, and vikṣepa means restlessness. These three have to go in order for you to shine forth as yourself. They keep you shrouded, limited and obscure self-knowledge. When the three things are done away with, self-knowledge shines through you.

Āyurveda, yoga and vedanta respectively are the three remedies to eliminate mala, vikṣepa and āvaraṇa. While āyurveda helps people to calm their thoughts, prāṇāyāma and meditation help one become happy from the core of their Being.

Satsang can also help you come out of vikṣepa and wrong indoctrination that gets into your head. Satsaṅga brings positivity. Then, when someone comes and tells you that so-and-so is a hopeless guy, you say, "Ok, so what!" You don't get affected by that. Otherwise, if someone says this guy is a hopeless guy, you say, "Oh yes, he is a hopeless guy. I believed in this guy and I went to tea with him and gave him money…" and this way the mind goes on. So, satsaṅga takes you out of this cycle and gives you a positive attitude.

tataḥ kṛtārthānām

pariṇāma-krama-samāptirguṇānām || 32 ||

ततः कृतार्थानां परिणामक्रमसमाप्तिर्गुणानाम् ॥ ३२ ॥

Thereafter, the purpose of the (three) guṇas is fulfilled and their sequence of transformation comes to an end.

Kṛtārthānam—when you have done everything, automatically the guṇas go back to their source. The guṇas then no longer impact you so much. And at some point, the body, on its own, decomposes or doesn't decompose at all but gets back to its original elements.

kṣaṇa-pratiyogī pariṇām-aparānta-nirgrāhyaḥ

kramaḥ || 33 ||

क्षणप्रतियोगी परिणामापरान्तनिर्ग्राह्यः क्रमः ॥ ३३ ॥

Sequence (in the above sutra) means that which is perceivable at the end of a transformation that happens through moments of time.

Kṣaṇa-pratiyogī—here we are talking about time. Every moment is movement or dynamism in the consciousness. The consciousness is beyond time, but it prevails every moment, pratikṣaṇam; kshana pratiyogī. It is very subtle to grasp that.

The present moment is not flat; it is not just one point, it is very deep and high. Every moment is deep and the depth of the moment, of the seconds, can be perceived only by a yogī. In that, there is the seed of past, present and future. It opens you to another dimension all together. From there you can cognize many other levels of creation.

puruṣārtha-śūnyānām guṇānām-pratiprasavaḥ

kaivalyam svarūpa-pratiṣṭhā vā citi-śaktiḥ-iti || 34 ||

पुरुषार्थशून्यानां गुणानां प्रतिप्रसवः

कैवल्यं स्वरूपप्रतिष्ठा वा चितिशक्तिरेति ॥ ३४ ॥

Absolute liberation is when the guṇas, now devoid of the puruṣa's purpose (having attained it already), resolve back to their source or when the consciousness is established in its nature.

It is very obvious. Kaivalya—all the primary elements resolve back to their origin. What is the purpose of human life? Human life is a cyclic journey to get back to the source. From where the spirit became matter and in its different manifestations moves around to get back to its true nature. That is the human cycle; the universal cycle of life.

From stone, you become plants; then insects, animals and all different bodies, you finally come to a human birth; and in the human birth you have an interest in spiritual knowledge and find the right path. Then you do your practice and come to the original source from where we have come, in one word—Self-realization. Because that word is used so much, and we don't know what the Self is, what realization is, it is all a big confusion. We simply say, get back to the source. That is kaivalya. Then there are no two; only one! Kaivalya simply means, being the ONE.

The Art of Living
&
The International Association for Human Values

Transforming Lives

The Founder
Gurudev Sri Sri Ravi Shankar

Gurudev Sri Sri Ravi Shankar is a universally revered spiritual and humanitarian leader. His vision of a violence-free, stress-free society through the reawakening of human values has inspired millions to broaden their spheres of responsibility and work towards the betterment of the world. Born in 1956 in southern India, Gurudev was often found deep in meditation as a child. At the age of four, he astonished his teachers by reciting the Bhagwad Gita, an ancient Sanskrit scripture. He has always had the unique gift of presenting the deepest truths in the simplest of words.

Gurudev established The Art of Living, an educational and humanitarian Non-Governmental Organisation that works in special consultative status with the Economic and Social Council (ECOSOC) of the United Nations in 1981. Present in over 156 countries, it formulates and implements lasting solutions to conflicts and issues faced by individuals, communities and nations. In 1997, he founded the International Association for Human Values (IAHV) to foster human values and lead sustainable development projects. Gurudev has reached out to more than 450 million people worldwide through personal interactions, public events, teachings, The Art of Living workshops and humanitarian initiatives. He has brought to the masses ancient practices which were traditionally kept exclusive, and has designed many self development techniques which can easily be integrated into daily life to calm the mind and instill confidence and enthusiasm. One of Gurudev's most unique offerings to the world is the Sudarshan Kriya, a powerful breathing technique that facilitates physical, mental, emotional and social well-being.

Numerous awards have been bestowed upon Gurudev Sri Sri Ravi Shankar which includes Padma Vibhushan (India's second highest civilian award) and the highest civilian awards from Paraguay, Mongolia and Colombia. Gurudev has addressed several international forums, including the United Nations Millennium World Peace Summit (2000), World Economic Forum (2001, 2003), World Summit On Ethics In Sports at FIFA Headquarters,

Zurich (2014, 2016), UNESCO (2015), Parliaments of France, Britain, Norway (2016) and others.

Gurudev has played a key role in conflict resolution across the world including Colombia, Kashmir, Iraq, Ivory Coast, Naxal inhabited regions of India, and many other places.

Follow Gurudev on:

Twitter - @srisri

Facebook - www.facebook.com/Gurudev

Website - www.srisriravishankar.org

YouTube - www.youtube.com/srisri

Instagram - www.instagram.com/srisriravishankar

LinkedIn - www.linkedin.com/in/srisriravishankar

The Art of Living
In Service Around The World

Founded in 1981 by Gurudev Sri Sri Ravi Shankar, The Art of Living is engaged in stress-elimination programs and service initiatives. The organization operates globally in 156 countries with one of the largest volunteer bases in the world and has touched the lives of over 450 million people.

The organisation works in special consultative status with the Economic and Social Council (ECOSOC) of the United Nations, participating in a variety of committees and activities related to health and conflict resolution.

In 1997, Gurudev Sri Sri Ravi Shankar also founded the International Association for Human Values (IAHV) to coordinate sustainable development projects, nurture human values and coordinate conflict resolution in association with The Art of Living. In India, Africa and South America, the two sister organizations' volunteers are spearheading sustainable growth in rural communities, and have already reached out to 40,212 villages.

The Art of Living movement has spread peace and transformation across communities through diverse humanitarian projects.

- Conflict Resolution
- Alleviating pain in War Zones
- Relieving trauma in Post Terror Attacks
- Disaster Relief
- Environment
- Education
- Empowerment of Women
- Prisoner Rehabilitation
- Rural Transformation

The Art of Living Programs

The Art of Living programs are guided by Gurudev Sri Sri Ravi Shankar's philosophy of peace: "Unless we have a stress-free mind and a violence-free society, we cannot achieve world peace." To help individuals get rid of stress and experience inner peace, The Art of Living offers stress-elimination programs which include breathing techniques, meditation and yoga. They cater to every age group - children, youth, adults and every section of society – rural communities, governments, corporate houses, etc. These programs have helped millions around the world to overcome stress, depression and violent tendencies. Emphasizing holistic living and personal self-development, the programs facilitate the complete blossoming of an individual's full potential. The cornerstone of all our workshops is the Sudarshan Kriya, a unique and potent breathing practice.

Introductory Programs:

- **The Happiness Program (Age 18+):**
  The 3-day program equips participants with practical knowledge and techniques to unlock their deepest potential and bring fullness to life.

- **Sahaj Samādhi Meditation (Age 18+):**
  Meditation technique that deeply relaxes the mind and rejuvenates the system.

- **Utkarsh Yoga (Age 8-13):**
  Introduce your children to spirituality, nurture human values, inculcate self-discipline, and develop their personality to be healthy and well-rounded.

- **Medha Yoga (Age 14-18):**
  Dynamic and innovative educational program for both high school and college students.

- **Prajñā Yoga (Age 5-18):**
  Helps children tap into the inherent intuitive abilities of the mind.

For more information please visit: www.artofliving.org

International Centres

INDIA
21st km, Kanakapura Road, Udayapura,
Bangalore - 560 082, Karnataka
Telephone: 0091 - 80-67262626 / 27 / 28
Email: info@srisripublications.com

GERMANY
Bad Antogast 1, 77728 Oppenau,
Baden-Württemberg
Telephone: 0049 - 7804-973-90
Email: info@artofliving.de

CANADA
13 Infinity Road, St. Mathieu du Parc,
Quebec G0X 1N0
Telephone: 001 - 819-532-3328
Email: artdevivre@artofliving.org

USA
639 Whispering Hills Rd,
Boone, NC 28607
Telephone: 001 - 828-263-4910
Email: info@artoflivingretreatcenter.org

www.srisriravishankar.org
www.artofliving.org
www.iahv.org